The Development of American Strategic Thought 1945–1969

A six-volume facsimile series reproducing government documents with previously limited distribution, RAND Corporation studies not widely available, and important articles from the period.

Edited by MARC TRACHTENBERG
University of Pennsylvania

A Garland Series

Contents of the Set

THE DEVELOPMENT OF
AMERICAN STRATEGIC THOUGHT:

Writings
on Strategy
1945–1951

Edited with an Introduction by
MARC TRACHTENBERG

Garland Publishing, Inc.
New York & London 1987

These facsimiles have been made from copies
in the Yale University Library, with the
exceptions of the following:

Bernard Brodie, "New Techniques of War and
National Policies," from a copy in the Library
of Congress, and Bernard Brodie, "Must We
Shoot from the Hip?" from a copy provided
by the RAND Corporation.

Library of Congress Cataloging-in-Publication Data

The Development of American strategic thought 1945–1969 / edited by
  Marc Trachtenberg.
      p.   cm.
    Contents: — 2. Writings on Strategy, 1945–1951.
    ISBN 0-8240-9718-1 (v. 2)
      1. United States—Military policy.   2. Strategy—History—20th
century.   3. Nuclear warfare.   4. Bombing, Aerial.
I. Trachtenberg, Marc, 1946–
UA23.D49   1988
355'.0385'73—dc19   88-4168

All volumes in this series are printed on
acid-free, 250-year-life paper.

Printed in the United States of America

Introduction

During the period from 1945 to 1951, air strategy came into its own. With the atomic bomb, there could no longer be any doubt about the effectiveness of strategic bombing. But the new arsenal was not so destructive that a full-scale air war would be tantamount to mutual suicide. A war with the kinds of atomic weapons that existed at the time was actually fightable, and an air war would therefore be the dominant form of warfare.

In other words, the basic insight gradually reached during this period—and reflected in the articles in this volume—was that the atomic bomb, although tremendously important, was not an absolute weapon. The central goal of strategy was therefore to consider how an air war might be, and in fact should be, fought.

Marc Trachtenberg

Contents

THE IMPLICATIONS OF THE ATOMIC BOMB FOR INTERNATIONAL RELATIONS

JACOB VINER

Professor of Economics, University of Chicago

(*Read November 16, 1945, in the Symposium on Atomic Energy and its Implications*)

In his Message to Congress of October 3, 1945, President Truman stated that: "In international relations as in domestic affairs, the release of atomic energy constitutes a new force too revolutionary to consider in the framework of old ideas." Beyond a few facts and a few surmises about the military effectiveness and the cost of atomic bombs, however, I unfortunately have no materials to work with except a framework of old ideas, some of them centuries old, with respect to the inherent character of international relations. I suspect that practically every non-scientist is in substantially the same predicament, except that many are unfamiliar even with the old ideas about the character of international relations.

I am fully aware that I cannot tell this audience anything about the nature of the atomic bomb as a military weapon which it does not know more fully and more accurately than I do. But I want to disclose the atomic-bomb premises upon which my argument is based so that if my information is incorrect in any vital respect you will be in a position to discount appropriately the argument I base upon it.

A single atomic bomb can reduce a city and its population to dust. A single airplane can carry the bomb. A single person can carry the explosive ingredients of the bomb, and it can be deposited at an appropriate spot and detonated at an appropriate time by pressing a button or setting a time-clock. The bomb has a minimum size, and in this size it is, and will remain, too expensive—or too scarce, whether expensive or not—to be used against minor targets. Its targets, therefore, must be primarily cities, and its military effectiveness must reside primarily in its capacity to destroy urban population and productive facilities. Under atomic bomb warfare, the soldier in the army would be safer than his wife and children in their urban home.

Secrecy as to the fundamental scientific principles underlying the atomic bomb is already non-existent. Secrecy as to manufacturing know-how is probably already less than perfect and can at the most delay the manufacture of such bombs for other countries by only a few years. The atomic bomb is susceptible of further improvement. But, even if our superior supply of scientists, of industrial resources, and of industrial technique could be relied upon to keep us always ahead of other countries in the quality of the national brand of bombs, this would probably have little strategic significance. The atomic bomb, unlike battleships, artillery, airplanes, and soldiers, is not an effective weapon against its own kind. A superior bomb cannot neutralize the inferior bomb of an enemy. It does not much matter strategically how much more efficient the atomic bomb can become provided superiority in efficiency affects chiefly the fineness of the dust to which it reduces the city upon which it is dropped.

There are differences between countries in their military vulnerability to atomic-bomb attack. Since the bomb can have destructive effect which will justify its own cost only if directed against major targets, a country is more vulnerable: (*a*) the greater the proportion of its population which lives in large cities; (*b*) the greater the average size and density of these cities; (*c*) the greater the urbanization or other regional concentration of its major industries of military significance; (*d*) the smaller its total and per capita resources of capacity for production (and stockpiling); therefore, other things equal, the smaller the margin of expendable resources which needs to be consumed before the military and civilian economies are brought to their physical or psychological breaking-points.

There seems to be universal agreement that under atomic-bomb warfare there would be a new and tremendous advantage in being first to attack and that the atomic bomb therefore gives a greater advantage than ever to the aggressor. I nevertheless remain unconvinced. No country possessing atomic bombs will be foolish enough to concentrate either its bomb-production and bomb-throwing facilities or its bomb-stockpiles at a small number of spots vulnerable to atomic bomb or other modes of attack. Let us suppose that a country has been subjected to a surprise attack by atomic bombs, and that all its large cities have been wiped out. If it has made the obvious preparations for such an eventuality, why can it not nevertheless retaliate within a few fours with as effective an atomic-bomb counter attack as if it had made the first move? What difference will it then make whether it was country A which had its cities destroyed at 9 A.M. and country B which had its cities destroyed at 12 A.M., or the other way round? It may be objected that the country first to attack can evacuate its cities beforehand so that when the counter attack comes it will lose only its cities, but not their inhabitants. But mass evacuation of a great city is a process which is both time-consuming and impossible to conceal. Such evacuation would to any country feeling itself at all in danger be an advance signal that an attack was in the offing. It may be argued that the existence of atomic bombs would make a surprise attack by paratroopers directed at the production facilities for atomic bombs and at the stockpiles good strategy, and that therefore, while there may be no particular advantage in a surprise attack *with* atomic bombs, there will be a great inducement for a surprise attack with other weapons *on* atomic-bomb facilities and stockpiles. But these facilities and stockpiles can readily be maintained at relatively inaccessible locations and can be strongly guarded.

There seems to be no prospect of an effective specific defense against the atomic bombs. In theory their military effectiveness can be somewhat reduced, however, by planned decentralization of industry and deurbanization of population. Carried on on only a modest scale, this would have negligible military significance unless it was directed primarily at setting up a miniature war-economy and military organization, insulated from the economy as a whole and always ready to act on short notice in pursuit of military objectives even when the economy as a whole was engulfed in a disaster situation. Carried on on a grand scale, it would be painfully expensive; there would always be the risk, moreover, that before mass-decentralization had been carried far some new development of lethal weapons would have made it waste effort. In any case, I leave it to you to judge whether the decentralization of New York, Philadelphia, Chicago, Detroit, San Francisco, can be regarded as physically, economically, politically, practicable. But our military planners, in

deciding upon the location of new facilities of military significance, should of course give careful consideration to the bearing of the atomic bomb upon the logic of strategic location. This logic calls for as wide a dispersal of facilities, as complete an avoidance of metropolitan areas as possible and as little dependence as possible of military communications and transportation, military stockpiles, and military staff personnel on urban-centered facilities.

The atomic bomb does not, *per se*, render armies, navies, airfleet, artillery, and TNT obsolete. But speculation on the nature of military strategy in an atomic-bomb world, if at this stage it can be sensibly pursued at all, must proceed from alternative hypotheses as to the phase in war at which atomic bombs would be used.

Let us first assume that the atomic-bomb phase would come early in a war. Each side having laid waste the other's cities, the hostilities would continue with weapons of less lethal power until a decision or a stalemate was reached. The major changes that the discovery of the atomic bomb would then seem to call for in the technical character of future warfare would be: first, that atomic bombs would supersede other weapons for attack on large cities and their inhabitants, and, second, that the drain of economic and manpower resources caused by the destruction, disorganization, and demoralization brought about by the enemy's use of the atomic bombs would force a drastically reduced scale of use of other weapons. It seems to me, indeed, that a war which opened with atomic-bomb attacks on both sides could then proceed only on a supply-from-stockpiles basis for a limited period and thereafter only on a token warfare scale, with defense in both stages at an advantage and large-scale offense, for logistic reasons, next to impossible.

A much more plausible hypothesis is that in a war between two fairly-equally-matched states possessed of atomic bombs each side would refrain from using the bombs at the start; each side would decide that it had nothing to gain and a great deal to lose from reciprocal use of the bombs, and that unilateral use was not attainable. The bombs would then either never be used or would be used only when one of the countries, in the face of imminent defeat, falls back upon their use in a last desperate effort to escape a dictated peace. In such a war the first stages at least would be fought with all the standard apparatus of war.

A third hypothesis is deserving of consideration.

The universal recognition that if war does break out there can be no assurance that the atomic bombs will not be resorted to may make statesmen and people determined to avoid war even where in the absence of the atomic bomb they would regard it as the only possible procedure under the circumstances for resolving a dispute or a clash of interests.

The atomic bomb does not change the ancient rule that victory in war will go to the strong. The atomic bomb does, however, create a new pattern of distribution of military power in one sense. More accurately, it restores an ancient pattern which was destroyed by the development in the nineteenth century of massive weapons of war and of great mobility of armies and navies, and by the development in the twentieth century of the airplane. The small country will again be more than a cipher or a mere pawn in power-politics, provided it is big enough to produce atomic bombs. The small country will still not have prospects of successful defense against an aggressor great country, but even the strongest country will no longer have any reasonable prospects of a costless victory over even the smallest country with a stock of atomic bombs. Even complete victory over a small country will involve the probable loss on the part of the victor of its major cities and their population. Such relatively costless victories as those of Prussia over Denmark, Austria, France in the nineteenth century, and of Nazi Germany over Poland, France, Norway, Holland, Belgium, and Denmark in World War II, will no longer be possible—or at least safe for an aggressive-minded country to count upon.

The atomic bomb makes war a prospect horrible to contemplate. Moreover, even without the atomic bomb other new military weapons of unprecedented capacity to destroy life and property already perfected or soon to be perfected threaten us with horrors not much less awesome than those of Hiroshima and Nagasaki. Every person of sane mind and sound morals is anxious that mankind be protected against these horrors by whatever political means are available. The physical scientists, presumably because they are better aware than we laymen are of the death-dealing potentialities of these new weapons, and because they have had more time to consider what dread fate is in store for us if these potentialities should ever become actualities, have been particularly active in calling for action, and rightly so. I gather, however, that they, like many others,

think there *must* be an effective remedy, that such a remedy is in fact known and available, and that it consists in the establishment of "World Government." I gather also that many of them think that all that stands in the way of adoption of this remedy is the stupidity of politicians and ordinary citizens, or their failure to understand how terrible the atomic bomb is or how impossible it is for any country to retain a monopoly of it. I fear that the problem is not so simple; that complacency and ignorance are not the only barriers to world government.

Norman Cousins, in an editorial in the *Saturday Review of Literature* of August 18, 1945, which has received wide distribution, gives us the following advice:

There is no need to discuss the historical reasons pointing to and arguing for world government. There is no need to talk of the difficulties in the way of world government. There is need only to ask whether we can afford to do without it. All other considerations become either secondary or inconsequential.

I do not think we can afford to take this advice to disregard whatever experience has to teach us, to substitute hysteria for history. We are told that when some danger menaces the ostrich he buries his head in the sand. Here we are advised to meet the menace of the atomic bomb by hiding our heads in the clouds. Neither appeals to me as wise procedure.

In theory the world can be effectively organized for peace through universal pacifism, through universal monarchy, or through world government, world government in this connection meaning a world state which in military matters at least can give the law to national governments or peoples. We do not know how to get universal pacifism. We do not want universal monarchy, or the rule of the world by a single nation-state; even if we did want it—presumably, for ourselves—we probably would not be willing to pay the price at which it would be obtainable, if at all. World government has been possible in the fairly recent past. It may again be possible in the somewhat distant future if, as a result of the wide distribution of atom bombs, or of other conceivable developments, military power is once more widely distributed. But I do not believe it is possible now or even that it is possible now definitely to begin planning it for the future.

The successful establishment of the United States of America out of separate colonies is often cited in support of the practicability of a United States of the World. The American precedent has little bearing on the present problem as long as the United States and Soviet Russia have a near monopoly between them of military power. Let us suppose that the New York and the Pennsylvania of 1789 were of approximately equal importance, that one of them at least was at some distance from the center of government, and that between them they had, say, 80 or 90 per cent of the total military resources of the Union. Under these circumstances, neither of them could have been relied upon, at times of crisis and of strong emotions of fear or anger, to have accepted without resistance a ruling from the central government which seemed to it to threaten its vital interests, nor could the ability of the central government to overcome that resistance by force or otherwise have been relied upon. That is substantially the situation we are in now. The United States and Soviet Russia are each too strong, relative to the total power potential of the world, to be proper members of a world government, even if their governments and their peoples were genuinely willing to enter such a government. In a narrow legal sense sovereignty can easily be formally surrendered, but actual power is more difficult to surrender and can be effectively surrendered only to an agency still more powerful. In the present state of the world such an agency with superior power not only does not exist but cannot be manufactured out of existing ingredients, even if the genuine will to do so existed, *unless that will goes to the extent of preparedness on the part of the United States and of Soviet Russia to dismember themselves.* Splitting the United States and splitting Soviet Russia seem to present a more difficult problem than splitting the atom proved to be. Setting up a facade of world government where the power-basis for its successful functioning was not present would be worse than useless. No government would be fooled thereby into a false sense of security, but every government would be impelled to pretend that it was, and all diplomacy would be carried out in an atmosphere of superficially-concealed insincerity.

I am forced to the conclusion that the only conceivable ways in which the world even in theory could be effectively organized so as to assure peace are not available now. We may regret this or we may rejoice in it. I for one deeply regret it. But our regret and our joy are equally irrelevant. That

does not mean, however, that there is nothing that can be and should be done to make war less probable. On the contrary. Let us consider the possibilities of action in this direction.

The balance-of-power system is discredited today. References to it, even by professional historians and international lawyers, commonly imply either that it was a system for preventing war which repeatedly failed or that it was a system for making war which often succeeded in its purpose. The balance-of-power system had, in fact, neither peace nor war as its primary objective. Its primary objective was the maintenance of the independence of the states in the system by associating states in alliances too strong to be overwhelmed by any single state or combination of states outside such alliance. The principle of the balance-of-power called for defensive wars and even for preventive wars to stop any power from growing so strong that it could upset the balance. The system often was abused. During the period of its dominance as a European system, say, 1648 to 1918, its record in preventing war was certainly not striking. Indeed, it probably was itself responsible for starting more wars than it prevented. As human institutions go, however, it did have extraordinary success in attaining its primary objective, that of maintaining national independence. To the best of my knowledge, only one major European state, Poland, and only a few minor German states permanently lost their independence through external aggression in the entire period 1648 to 1918, and in even these instances the failure of England to play its customary and, I am willing to avow, its useful role in the balance-of-power system was probably a significant contributory factor. The balance-of-power system also deserves some of the credit for the receptiveness of belligerents during that period, including definitely aggressor nations, to limited warfare when actual hostilities were under way, to early termination of hostilities, and to moderate peace terms.

Whether we like or detest its record, however, the balance-of-power system is probably now only of historical interest. In the first place, the same factors which have created new barriers to world government have probably destroyed the availability of the balance-of-power system. To have any chance of effective operation in maintaining international equilibrium, the system requires that military power be fairly widely distributed so that there are no overwhelmingly strong concentrations of power, even regional ones, in single states, and so that there is always some hope, or fear, that timely negotiations of new alliances will restore a balance temporarily destroyed. Abstracting from the atomic bomb, the world was emerging from World War II as a two-power world, with Britain deprived of the necessary economic base for sustained military effort, with Germany, Japan, and Italy reduced to military ciphers, and with France's underlying weakness finally exposed to view.

The development of the atomic bomb promises to restore some military significance to the weaker countries; it gives a strong weapon to *any* country able to use it. It thus tends to make all countries strong, or to make all countries weak, as you prefer. It seems doubtful, however, whether it goes, or will go, far enough in that direction, whether it will scatter military power widely enough to make it possible to create a single world agency strong enough to exact obedience from any single country. Should it do so, however, then not only an effective balance-of-power system but even world government will again be possible, and to the discovery of the atomic bomb will belong the credit. On the other hand, the atomic bomb removes the physical and administrative restrictions on warfare which helped to make "limited-warfare" attractive even to aggressors and therefore tends to deprive the balance-of-power system of its only merit with respect to the issue of peace or war, namely, that it reduces the damage done by war when war does occur.

This leaves a Concert or League of Great Powers, committed by solemn covenant to the maintenance of peace, as the only immediately available type of political institution for preserving peace. The League of Nations, as it actually operated, was, I believe, essentially a Concert of Great Powers. The United Nations Charter, with its single-veto privilege for the Great Powers, provides more frankly and honestly for such a Concert. The essence of Concerts of Powers is that they aim to include all the major powers; that they start with good intentions; that they have the means and have agreed or can agree upon the procedures by which to enforce peace upon the small and weak countries; but that they have neither the means nor the serious intention to enforce peace upon each other. They should not be despised as useless or evil. Earlier Concerts of Powers did serve to maintain peace for a time. The League of Nations never had adequate membership and never was given a fair chance. The United Nations Organization will start with at least two advantages over the League of Nations: essentially complete membership and an ambitious program of beneficent economic and social activities which may succeed in fostering a feeling of community between the governments and the peoples of the world strong enough to withstand the strains of the clashes of interest and of emotions which will inevitably arise. But Concerts of Powers are essentially self-denying ordinances, embodiments of good resolutions terminable at will and unilaterally. They cannot have within themselves effective means for *enforcing* their own survival. They may promote peace; they cannot assure it. As an English poet, Blackmore, said in 1700 of an older Concert of Powers:

To Leagues of Peace the neighbours did agree
And to maintain them, God was guarantee. . . .

There is one more thing, in my opinion by far the most important, that can be done although it is unfortunately not in the least spectacular, revolutionary, soul-stirring, or exciting. That is the conscientious and unrelenting practice by the statesmen of the Great Powers, day after day, year after year, of mutually conciliatory diplomacy. Wilful disturbers of the peace do arise from time to time: Louis XIV, Frederick the Great, Napoleon, Bismarck, Hitler. But for the most part wars arise out of mutual fear of peace, out of fear of loss of national independence or of other nationally treasured objectives unless war is resorted to, more than out of love of war or than out of lust for war booty. Countries most often go to war because they fear the consequences of remaining at peace. If rulers act as statesmen, and if their peoples permit—and still better, demand—that they so act, if rulers so behave as not to arouse or sustain fear in other countries, lasting peace will still not be guaranteed, but it will be probable. By making the peace a mutually more satisfactory one, we will further lessen the risk that some day some country may fear continuance of the peace more than it fears war. By adding to the horror of war and therefore to the attractiveness of peace, the discovery of the atomic bomb will aid instead of hinder the diplomacy of peace. In any case, it is on the quality of postwar diplomacy and of postwar diplomats, and on the texts of charters only as they are incidental to, facilitate, and are supported by the exercise of good diplomacy, that we must rest our main hopes for the maintenance of peace.

It would be wonderful if it were possible to *enforce* peace. It would be wonderful if a workable scheme could be devised whereby the atomic bomb itself could either be used as the equivalent for the world of the policeman's baton or could make the baton unnecessary. For the reasons given, however, I believe that this is under existing circumstances not within the realm of the possible and that at the best it can be regarded only as a distant goal. And if it is not, or even probably not, possible in the near future, I believe

it is unwise to pretend that it is possible, and thus to divert attention from those things that *are* possible and that are possible *now:* full support of the United Nations Organization so that it may realize its fullest potentialities for promoting mutual trust and collaboration in good causes; public insistence that diplomats gather with the determination to reach agreement on vital issues rather than with irresponsible readiness to quarrel on secondary issues. In both cases, this means a call to action, immediately, and right here in our own country as well as elsewhere.

I. WAR IN THE ATOMIC AGE

By BERNARD BRODIE

Most of those who have held the public ear on the subject of
the atomic bomb have been content to assume that war and
obliteration are now completely synonymous, and that modern man must therefore be either obsolete or fully ripe for
the millennium. No doubt the state of obliteration—if that
should indeed be the future fate of nations which cannot
resolve their disputes—provides little scope for analysis. A
few degrees difference in nearness to totality is of relatively
small account. But in view of man's historically-tested resistance to drastic changes in behavior, especially in a benign
direction, one may be pardoned for wishing to examine the
various possibilities inherent in the situation before taking
any one of them for granted.

It is already known to us all that a war with atomic bombs
would be immeasurably more destructive and horrible than
any the world has yet known. That fact is indeed portentous,
and to many it is overwhelming. But as a datum for the
formulation of policy it is in itself of strictly limited utility.
It underlines the urgency of our reaching correct decisions,
but it does not help us to discover which decisions are in fact
correct.

Men have in fact been converted to religion at the point of
the sword, but the process generally required actual use of
the sword against recalcitrant individuals. The atomic bomb
does not lend itself to that kind of discriminate use. The

21

wholesale conversion of mankind away from those parochial attitudes bound up in nationalism is a consummation devoutly to be wished and, where possible, to be actively promoted. But the mere existence of the bomb does not promise to accomplish it at an early enough time to be of any use. The careful handling required to assure long and fruitful life to the Age of Atomic Energy will in the first instance be a function of distinct national governments, not all of which, incidentally, reflect in their behavior the will of the popular majority.

Governments are of course ruled by considerations not wholly different from those which affect even enlightened individuals. That the atomic bomb is a weapon of incalculable horror will no doubt impress most of them deeply. But they have never yet responded to the horrific implications of war in a uniform way. Even those governments which feel impelled to the most drastic self-denying proposals will have to grapple not merely with the suspicions of other governments but with the indisputable fact that great nations have very recently been ruled by men who were supremely indifferent to horror, especially horror inflicted by them on people other than their own.

Statesmen have hitherto felt themselves obliged to base their policies on the assumption that the situation might again arise where to one or more great powers war looked less dangerous or less undesirable than the prevailing conditions of peace. They will want to know how the atomic bomb affects that assumption. They must realize at the outset that a weapon so terrible cannot but influence the degree of probability of war for any given period in the future. But the degree of that influence or the direction in which it operates is by no means obvious. It has, for example, been stated over and over again that the atomic bomb is *par excellence* the weapon of aggression, that it weights the scales overwhelmingly in favor of surprise attack. That if true would indicate that world peace is even more precarious than it was before, despite the greater horrors of war. But is it inevitably true? If not, then the effort to make the reverse true would deserve a high priority among the measures to be pursued.

Thus, a series of questions present themselves. Is war more or less likely in a world which contains atomic bombs? If the latter, is it *sufficiently* unlikely—sufficiently, that is, to give society the opportunity it desperately needs to adjust its politics to its physics? What are the procedures for effecting that adjustment within the limits of our opportunities? And how can we enlarge our opportunities? Can we transmute what appears to be an immediate crisis into a long-term problem, which presumably would permit the application of more varied and better considered correctives than the pitifully few and inadequate measures which seem available at the moment?

It is precisely in order to answer such questions that we turn our attention to the effect of the bomb on the character of war. We know in advance that war, if it occurs, will be very different from what it was in the past, but what we want to know is: How different, and in what ways? A study of those questions should help us to discover the conditions which will govern the pursuit of security in the future and the feasibility of proposed measures for furthering that pursuit. At any rate, we know that it is not the mere existence of the weapon but rather its effects on the traditional pattern of war which will govern the adjustments which states will make in their relations with each other.

The Truman-Attlee-King statement of November 15, 1945, epitomized in its first paragraph a few specific conclusions concerning the bomb which had evolved as of that date: "We recognize that the application of recent scientific discoveries to the methods and practice of war has placed at the disposal of mankind means of destruction hitherto unknown, against which there can be no adequate military defense, and in the employment of which no single nation can in fact have a monopoly."

This observation, it would seem, is one upon which all reasonable people would now be agreed. But it should be noted that of the three propositions presented in it the first is either a gross understatement or meaningless, the second has in fact been challenged by persons in high military authority, and the third, while generally admitted to be true, has nevertheless been the subject of violently clashing interpretations. In any case, the statement does not furnish a sufficient array of postulates for the kind of analysis we wish to pursue.

It is therefore necessary to start out afresh and examine the various features of the bomb, its production, and its use which are of military importance. Presented below are a number of conclusions concerning the character of the bomb which seem to this writer to be inescapable. Some of the eight points listed already enjoy fairly universal acceptance; most do not. After offering with each one an explanation of why he believes it to be true, the writer will attempt to deduce from these several conclusions or postulates the effect of the bomb on the character of war.

I. *The power of the present bomb is such that any city in the world can be effectively destroyed by one to ten bombs.*

While this proposition is not likely to evoke much dissent,* its immediate implications have been resisted or ignored by

* Always excepting Major Alexander P. de Seversky, who has reiterated in magazine articles and elsewhere the notion that the atomic

important public officials. These implications are twofold. First, it is now physically possible for air forces no greater than those existing in the recent war to wipe out all the cities of a great nation in a single day—and it will be shown subsequently that what is physically possible must be regarded as tactically feasible. Secondly, with our present industrial organization the elimination of our cities would mean the elimination for military purposes of practically the whole of our industrial structure. But before testing these extraordinary implications, let us examine and verify the original proposition.

The bomb dropped on Hiroshima completely pulverized an area of which the radius from the point of detonation was about one and one-quarter miles. However, everything to a radius of two miles was blasted with some burning and between two and three miles the buildings were about half destroyed. Thus the area of total destruction covered about four square miles, and the area of destruction and substantial damage extended over some twenty-seven square miles. The bomb dropped on Nagasaki, while causing less damage than the Hiroshima bomb because of the physical characteristics of the city, was nevertheless considerably more powerful. We

bomb exploded over Hiroshima would not have damaged the New York financial district any more than a 10-ton bomb of TNT exploding on contact. Major de Seversky did in fact inspect the ruins of Hiroshima; but a great many others also did so, and those others seem well-nigh unanimous in regarding the Major's views as preposterous. Brig. Gen. Thomas F. Farrell rebutted Major de Seversky's testimony before the Senate Atomic Energy Committee by observing that it would have taken 730 B-29's to inflict the same damage on Hiroshima with TNT bombs that was done by the single Superfortress with the atomic bomb. He added that according to careful calculations, eight atomic bombs of the Nagasaki type would suffice to destroy New York and that three of them could destroy Washington, D. C. New York *Times*, February 16, 1946, p. 17. See also below, p. 101.

have it on Dr. J. Robert Oppenheimer's authority that the
Nagasaki bomb "would have taken out ten square miles, or
a bit more, if there had been ten square miles to take out." *
From the context in which that statement appears it is apparent that Dr. Oppenheimer is speaking of an area of total
destruction.

The city of New York is listed in the *World Almanac* as
having an area of 365 square miles. But it obviously would
not require the pulverization of every block of it to make the
whole area one of complete chaos and horror. Ten well-placed
bombs of the Nagasaki type would eliminate that city as a
contributor to the national economy, whether for peace or
war, and convert it instead into a catastrophe area in dire
need of relief from outside. If the figure of ten bombs be challenged, it need only be said that it would make very little
difference militarily if twice that number of bombs were
required. Similarly, it would be a matter of relative indifference if the power of the bomb were so increased as to
require only five to do the job. Increase of power in the individual bomb is of especially little moment to cities of small
or medium size, which would be wiped out by one bomb each
whether that bomb were of the Nagasaki type or of fifty times
as much power. No conceivable variation in the power of the
atomic bomb could compare in importance with the disparity
in power between atomic and previous types of explosives.

The condition at this writing of numerous cities in Europe
and Japan sufficiently underlines the fact that it does not require atomic bombs to enable man to destroy great cities.
TNT and incendiary bombs when dropped in sufficient quantities are able to do a quite thorough job of it. For that matter,

* "Atomic Weapons and the Crisis in Science," *Saturday Review of
Literature*, November 24, 1945, p. 10.

it should be pointed out that a single bomb which contains in itself the concentrated energy of 20,000 tons of TNT is by no means equal in destructive effect to that number of tons of TNT distributed among bombs of one or two tons each. The destructive radius of individual bombs of any one type increases only with the cube root of the explosive energy released, and thus the very concentration of power in the atomic bomb prevents the full utilization of its tremendous energy. The bomb must be detonated from an altitude of at least 1,000 feet if the full spread of its destructive radius is to be realized, and much of the blast energy is absorbed by the air above the target. But the sum of initial energy is quite enough to afford such losses.

It should be obvious that there is much more than a logistic difference involved between a situation where a single plane sortie can cause the destruction of a city like Hiroshima and one in which at least 500 bomber sorties are required to do the same job. Nevertheless, certain officers of the United States Army Air Forces, in an effort to "deflate" the atomic bomb, have observed publicly enough to have their comments reported in the press that the destruction wrought at Hiroshima could have been effected by two days of routine bombing with ordinary bombs. Undoubtedly so, but the 500 or more bombers needed to do the job under those circumstances would if they were loaded with atomic bombs be physically capable of destroying 500 or more Hiroshimas in the same interval of time. That observation discounts certain tactical considerations. These will be taken up in due course, but for the moment it is sufficient to point out that circumstances do arise in war when it is the physical carrying capacity of the bombing vehicles rather than tactical considerations which will determine the amount of damage done.

II. *No adequate defense against the bomb exists, and the possibilities of its existence in the future are exceedingly remote.*

This proposition requires little supporting argument in so far as it is a statement of existing fact. But that part of it which involves a prediction for the future conflicts with the views of most of the high-ranking military officers who have ventured opinions on the implications of the atomic bomb. No layman can with equanimity differ from the military in their own field, and the present writer has never entertained the once-fashionable view that the military do not know their business. But, apart from the question of objectivity concerning professional interests—in which respect the record of the military profession is neither worse nor better than that of other professions—the fact is that the military experts have based their arguments mainly on presumptions gleaned from a field in which they are generally not expert, namely, military *history*. History is at best an imperfect guide to the future, but when imperfectly understood and interpreted it is a menace to sound judgment.

The defense against hostile missiles in all forms of warfare, whether on land, sea, or in the air, has thus far depended basically on a combination of, first, measures to reduce the number of missiles thrown or to interfere with their aim (i.e., defense by offensive measures) and, secondly, ability to absorb those which strike. To take an obvious example, the large warship contains in itself and in its escorting air or surface craft a volume of fire power which usually reduces and may even eliminate the blows of the adversary. Unlike most targets ashore, it also enjoys a mobility which enables it to maneuver evasively under attack (which will be of little value under atomic bombs). But unless the enemy is grotesquely inferior in strength, the ship's ability to survive must ultimately depend upon its compartmentation and armor, that is, on its ability to absorb punishment.

The same is true of a large city. London was defended against the German V-1, or "buzz-bomb," first by concerted bombing attacks upon the German experimental stations, industrial plants, and launching sites, all of which delayed the V-1 attack and undoubtedly greatly reduced the number of missiles ultimately launched. Those which were nevertheless launched were met by a combination of fighter planes, anti-aircraft guns, and barrage balloons. Towards the end of the eighty-day period which covered the main brunt of the attack, some 75 per cent of the bombs launched were being brought down, and, since many of the remainder were inaccurate in their flight, only 9 per cent were reaching London.* These London was able to "absorb"; that is, there were casualties and damage but no serious impairment of the vital services on which depended the city's life and its ability to serve the war effort.

It is precisely this ability to absorb punishment, whether one is speaking of a warship or a city, which seems to vanish in the face of atomic attack. For almost any kind of target selected, the so-called "static defenses" are defenses no longer. For the same reason too, mere reduction in the number of missiles which strike home is not sufficient to save the target, though it may have some effect on the enemy's selection of targets. The defense of London against V-1 was considered effective, and yet in eighty days some 2,300 of those missiles hit the city. The record bag was that of August 28, 1944, when out of 101 bombs which approached England 97 were shot down and only four reached London. But if those four had been atomic bombs, London survivors would not

* Duncan Sandys, *Report on the Flying Bomb*, pamphlet issued by the British Information Services, September, 1944, p. 9.

have considered the record good. Before we can speak of a defense against atomic bombs being effective, *the frustration of the attack for any given target area must be complete.* Neither military history nor an analysis of present trends in military technology leaves appreciable room for hope that means of completely frustrating attack by aerial missiles will be developed.

In his speech before the Washington Monument on October 5, 1945, Fleet Admiral Chester W. Nimitz correctly cautioned the American people against leaping to the conclusion that the atomic bomb had made armies and navies obsolete. But he could have based his cautionary note on better grounds than he in fact adopted. "Before risking our future by accepting these ideas at face value," he said, "let us examine the historical truth that, at least up to this time, there has never yet been a weapon against which man has been unable to devise a counterweapon or a defense." *

Apart from the possible irrelevancy for the future of this observation—against which the phrase "at least up to this time" provides only formal protection—the fact is that it is not historically accurate. A casual reading of the history of military technology does, to be sure, encourage such a doctrine. The naval shell gun of 1837, for example, was eventually met with iron armor, and the iron armor in turn provoked the development of the "built-up" gun with greater penetrating power; the submarine was countered with the hydrophone and supersonic detector and with depth charges of various types; the bombing airplane accounted for the development of the specialized fighter aircraft, the highly perfected anti-

* For the text of the speech see the New York *Times*, October 6, 1945, p. 6. See also the speech of President Truman before Congress on October 23, 1945, in which he said: "Every new weapon will eventually bring some counterdefense against it."

aircraft gun, and numerous ancillary devices. So it has always been, and the tendency is to argue that so it always will be.

In so far as this doctrine becomes dogma and is applied to the atomic bomb, it becomes the most dangerous kind of illusion. We have already seen that the defense against the V-1 was only *relatively* effective, and something approaching much closer to perfect effectiveness would have been necessary for V-1 missiles carrying atomic bombs. As a matter of fact, the defenses against the V-2 rocket were of practically zero effectiveness, and those who know most about it admit that thus far there has been no noteworthy progress in defenses against the V-2.*

These, to be sure, were new weapons. But what is the story of the older weapons? After five centuries of the use of hand arms with fire-propelled missiles, the large numbers of men killed by comparable arms in the recent war indicates that no adequate answer has yet been found for the bullet.† Ordinary TNT, whether in shell, bomb, or torpedo, can be "countered" to a degree by the dispersion of targets or by various kinds of armor, but the enormous destruction wrought by this and comparable explosives on land, sea, and in the air in World War II is an eloquent commentary on the limitations of the defenses. The British following the first World War thought they had in their "Asdic" and depth charges the complete answer to the U-boat, but an only slightly improved U-boat

* See Ivan A. Getting, "Facts About Defense," *Nation*, Special Supplement, December 22, 1945, p. 704. Professor Getting played a key part in radar development for antiaircraft work and was especially active in measures taken to defend London against V-1 and V-2. See also General H. H. Arnold's *Third Report to the Secretary of War*, November 12, 1945, printed edition, p. 68.

† The new glass-fiber body armor, "doron," the development of which was recently announced by the United States Navy, will no doubt prove useful but is not expected to be of more than marginal effectiveness.

succeeded in the recent war in sinking over 23 million gross tons of shipping. So the story might go on endlessly. It has simply become customary to consider an "answer" satisfactory when it merely diminishes or qualifies the effectiveness of the weapon against which it is devised, and that kind of custom will not do for the atomic bomb.

Despite such statements as that of Canadian General A. G. L. McNaughton that means with which to counter the atomic bomb are already "clearly in sight," * it seems pretty well established that there is no *specific* reply to the bomb. The physicists and chemists who produced the atomic bomb are apparently unanimous on this point: that while there was a scientific consensus long before the atomic bomb existed that it could be produced, no comparable opinion is entertained among scientists concerning their chances of devising effective countermeasures. The bomb itself is as free from direct interference of any kind as is the ordinary bomb. When the House Naval Affairs Committee circulated a statement that electronic means were already available for exploding atomic bombs "far short of their objective without the necessity of locating their position," † scientists qualified to speak denied the truth of the assertion, ‡ and it was indeed subsequently disowned by its originators.

Any active defense at all must be along the lines of affecting the carrier, and we have already noted that even when used with the relatively vulnerable airplane or V-1 the atomic bomb poses wholly new problems for the defense. A nation which had developed strong defenses against invading aircraft, which had found reliable means of interfering with radio-controlled rockets, which had developed highly efficient

* New York *Herald Tribune*, October 6, 1945, p. 7.
† New York *Times*, October 12, 1945, p. 1.
‡ See New York *Times*, October 19, 1945, p. 2.

countersmuggling and countersabotage agencies, and which had dispersed through the surrounding countryside substantial portions of the industries and populations normally gathered in urban communities would obviously be better prepared to resist atomic attack than a nation which had either neglected or found itself unable to do these things. But it would have only a relative advantage over the latter; it would still be exposed to fearful destruction.

In any case, technological progress is not likely to be confined to measures of defense. The use of more perfect vehicles and of more destructive bombs in greater quantity might very well offset any gains in defense. And the bomb already has a fearful lead in the race.

Random and romantic reflections on the miracles which science has already wrought are of small assistance in our speculations on future trends. World War II saw the evolution of numerous instruments of war of truly startling ingenuity. But with the qualified exception of the atomic bomb itself (the basic principle of which was discovered prior to but in the same year as the outbreak of war in Europe), all were simply mechanical adaptations of scientific principles which were well known long before the war. It was no doubt a long step from the discovery in 1922 of the phenomenon upon which radar is based to the use of the principle in an antiaircraft projectile fuse, but here too realization that it might be so used considerably antedated the fuse itself.

The advent of a "means of destruction hitherto unknown" —to quote the Truman-Attlee-King statement—is certainly not new. The steady improvement of weapons of war is an old story, and the trend in that direction has in recent years been accelerated. But thus far each new implement has, at least initially, been limited enough in the scope of its use or in its strategic consequences to permit some timely measure of adaptation both on the battlefield and in the minds of strategists and statesmen. Even the most "revolutionary" developments of the past seem by contrast with the atomic bomb to have been minor steps in a many-sided evolutionary process. This process never permitted any one invention in itself to subvert or even to threaten for long the previously existing equilibrium of military force. Any startling innovation either of offense or defense provoked some kind of answer in good time, but the answer was rarely more than a qualified one and the end result was usually a profound and sometimes a politically significant change in the methods of waging war.*

With the introduction, however, of an explosive agent which is several million times more potent on a pound-for-pound basis than the most powerful explosives previously known, we have a change of quite another character. The factor of increase of destructive efficiency is so great that there arises at once the strong presumption that the experience of the past concerning eventual adjustment might just as well be thrown out the window. Far from being something which merely "adds to the complexities of field commanders," as one American military authority put it, the atomic bomb seems so far to overshadow any military invention of the past as to render comparisons ridiculous.

III. *The atomic bomb not only places an extraordinary military premium upon the development of new types of carriers but also greatly extends the destructive range of existing carriers.*

World War II saw the development and use by the Germans of rockets capable of 220 miles' range and carrying approxi-

* For a discussion of developing naval technology over the last hundred years and its political significance see Bernard Brodie, *Sea Power in the Machine Age*, 2nd ed., Princeton, Princeton University Press, 1943.

mately one ton each of TNT. Used against London, these rockets completely baffled the defense. But for single-blow weapons which were generally inaccurate at long distances even with radio control,* they were extremely expensive. It is doubtful whether the sum of economic damage done by these missiles equaled the expenditure which the Germans put into their development, production, and use. At any rate, the side enjoying command of the air had in the airplane a much more economical and longer-range instrument for inflicting damage on enemy industry than was available in the rocket. The capacity of the rocket-type projectile to strike without warning in all kinds of weather with complete immunity from all known types of defenses guaranteed to it a supplementary though subordinate role to bomber-type aircraft. But its inherent limitations, so long as it carried only chemical explosives, were sufficient to warrant considerable reserve in predictions of its future development.

However, the power of the new bomb completely alters the considerations which previously governed the choice of vehicles and the manner of using them. A rocket far more elaborate and expensive than the V-2 used by the Germans is still an exceptionally cheap means of bombarding a country if it can carry in its nose an atomic bomb. The relative inaccuracy of aim—which continued research will no doubt reduce—is of much diminished consequence when the radius of destruction is measured in miles rather than yards. And even with existing fuels such as were used in the German V-2,

* Accuracy is of course a matter of definition. Lieut. Col. John A. O'Mara of the United States Army considers the V-2 an accurate missile because at 200 miles' range some 1,230 out of the 4,300 launched against England were able to hit the target, "which was the London area." New York *Times*, March 8, 1946, p. 7. In the text above the writer is merely using a different base of comparison from the one Lieut. Col. O'Mara has in mind, namely, the capabilities of the bombing aircraft at any distance within its flying radius.

it is theoretically feasible to produce rockets capable of several thousands of miles of range, though the problem of controlling the flight of rockets over such distances is greater than is generally assumed.

Of more immediate concern than the possibilities of rocket development, however, is the enormous increase in effective bombing range which the atomic bomb gives to *existing types of aircraft*. That it has this effect becomes evident when one examines the various factors which determine under ordinary —that is, non-atomic bomb—conditions whether a bombing campaign is returning military dividends. First, the campaign shows profit only if a large proportion of the planes, roughly 90 per cent or more, are returning from individual strikes.* Otherwise one's air force may diminish in magnitude more rapidly than the enemy's capacity to fight. Each plane load of fuel must therefore cover a two-way trip, allowing also a fuel reserve for such contingencies as adverse winds and combat action, thereby diminishing range by at least one-half from the theoretical maximum, except in the case of shuttle bombing, which in World War II was relatively rare.

But the plane cannot be entirely loaded with fuel. It must also carry besides its crew a heavy load of defensive armor and armament. Above all, it must carry a sufficient load of bombs to make the entire sortie worth while—a sufficient load, that is, to warrant attendant expenditures in fuel, engine maintenance, and crew fatigue. The longer the distance covered, the smaller the bomb load per sortie and the longer the interval between sorties. To load a plane with thirty tons of

* The actual figure of loss tolerance depends on a number of variables, including replacement rate of planes and crews, morale factors, the military value of the damage being inflicted on the enemy, and the general strategic position at the moment. The 10 per cent figure used for illustration in the text above was favored by the war correspondents and press analysts during the recent war, but it must not be taken too literally.

fuel and only two tons of bombs, as we did in our first B-29 raid on Japan, will not do for a systematic campaign of strategic bombing. One must get closer to the target and thus transfer a greater proportion of the carrying capacity from fuel to bombs.* What we then come out with is an effective bombing range less than one-fourth the straight-line cruising radius of the plane under optimum conditions. In other words a plane capable, without too much stripping of its equipment, of a 6,000-mile non-stop flight would probably have an effective bombing range of substantially less than 1,500 miles.

With atomic bombs, however, the considerations described above which so severely limit bombing range tend to vanish. There is no question of increasing the number of bombs in order to make the sortie profitable. One per plane is quite enough. The gross weight of the atomic bomb is secret, but even if it weighed four to six tons it would still be a light load for a B-29. It would certainly be a sufficient pay load to warrant any conceivable military expenditure on a single sortie. The next step then becomes apparent. Under the callously utilitarian standards of military bookkeeping, a plane and its crew can very well be sacrificed in order to deliver an atomic bomb to an extreme distance. We have, after all, the

* It should be noticed that in the example of the B-29 raid of June 15, 1944, cited above, a reduction of only one-fourth in the distance and therefore in the fuel load could make possible (unless the plane was originally overloaded) a tripling or quadrupling of the bomb load. Something on that order was accomplished by our seizure of bases in the Marianas, some 300 miles closer to the target than the original Chinese bases and of course much easier supplied. The utility of the Marianas bases was subsequently enhanced by our capture of Iwo Jima and Okinawa, which served as emergency landing fields for returning B-29's and also as bases for escorting fighters and rescue craft. Towards the end of the campaign we were dropping as much as 6,000 tons of bombs in a single 600-plane raid on Tokyo, thereby assuring ourselves high military dividends per sortie investment.

recent and unforgettable experience of the Japanese *Kami-kaze*.* Thus, the plane can make its entire flight in one direction, and, depending on the weight of the bomb and the ultimate carrying capacity of the plane, its range might be almost as great with a single atomic bomb as it would be with no bomb load whatever. The non-stop flight during November, 1945, of a B-29 from Guam to Washington, D. C., almost 8,200 statute miles, was in this respect more than a stunt.†

If it be true, as has been hinted, ‡ that the B-29 is the only existing bomber which can carry the atomic bomb, the fact might argue an even greater gross weight for the bomb than that surmised above. It might of course be that a bomb having a lighter container would still be highly effective though less efficient, but in any case we know that there is no need for the bomb to be *heavier* than either the Hiroshima or the Nagasaki bomb. The plane which carried the Hiroshima bomb

* On several occasions the United States Army Air Forces also demonstrated a willingness to sacrifice availability of planes and crews—though not the lives of the latter—in order to carry out specific missions. Thus in the Doolittle raid against Japan of April, 1942, in which sixteen Mitchell bombers took off from the carrier *Hornet*, it was known beforehand that none of the planes would be recovered even if they succeeded in reaching China (which several failed to do for lack of fuel) and that the members of the crews were exposing themselves to uncommon hazard. And the cost of the entire expedition was accepted mainly for the sake of dropping sixteen tons of ordinary bombs! Similarly, several of the Liberators which bombed the Ploesti oil fields in August, 1943, had insufficient fuel to return to their bases in North Africa and, as was foreseen, had to land in neutral Turkey where planes and crews were interned.

† See New York *Times*, November 21, 1945, p. 1. It should be noticed that the plane had left about 300 gallons, or more than one ton, of gasoline upon landing in Washington. It was of course stripped of all combat equipment (e.g., armor, guns, ammunition, gun-directors, and bombsights) in order to allow for a greater gasoline load. Planes bent on a bombing mission would probably have to carry some of this equipment, even if their own survival were not an issue, in order to give greater assurance of their reaching the target.

‡ See below, p. 49.

apparently flew a distance of 3,000 miles, and bombers of considerably greater carrying capacity are definitely beyond the blueprint stage. With the bomb weight remaining fixed, the greater capacity can be given over entirely to fuel load and thus to added range. The great-circle-route distance between New York and Moscow is only 4,800 miles. With planes following the great-circle routes even across the Arctic wastes, as will undoubtedly prove feasible, it appears that no major city in either the Soviet Union or the United States is much beyond 6,000 miles from the territories of the other. And if American forces are able to utilize bases in northern Canada, the cities of the Soviet Union are brought considerably closer.

Under the conditions just described, any world power is able from bases within its own territories to destroy most of the cities of any other power. It is not *necessary*, despite the assertions to the contrary of various naval and political leaders including President Truman, to seize advanced bases close to enemy territory as a prerequisite to effective use of the bomb.* The lessons of the recent Pacific war in that respect are not merely irrelevant but misleading, and the effort to inflate their significance for the future is only one example of the pre-atomic thinking prevalent today even among people who understand fully the power of the bomb. To recognize that power is one thing; to draw out its full strategic implications is quite another.

The facts just presented do not mean that distance loses all its importance as a barrier to conflict between the major power centers of the world. It would still loom large in any plans to consolidate an atomic bomb attack by rapid invasion

* See President Truman's speech before Congress on the subject of universal military training, reported in the New York *Times*, October 24, 1945, p. 3.

and occupation. It would no doubt also influence the success
of the bomb attack itself. Rockets are likely to remain of
lesser range than aircraft and less accurate near the limits of
their range, and the weather hazards which still affect aircraft
multiply with distance. Advanced bases will certainly not be
valueless. But it is nevertheless a fact that under existing
technology the distance separating, for example, the Soviet
Union from the United States offers no direct immunity to
either with respect to atomic bomb attack, though it does so
for all practical purposes with respect to ordinary bombs.*

IV. *Superiority in air forces, though a more effective safeguard in itself than superiority in naval or land forces, nevertheless fails to guarantee security.*

This proposition is obviously true in the case of very long
range rockets, but let us continue to limit our discussion to
existing carriers. In his *Third Report to the Secretary of War*,
dated November 12, 1945, General H. H. Arnold, command-
ing the Army Air Forces, made the following statement:
"Meanwhile [i.e., until very long range rockets are devel-
oped], the only known effective means of delivering atomic
bombs in their present stage of development is the very heavy
bomber, and that is certain of success only when the user has
air superiority." †

* Colonel Clarence S. Irvine, who commanded the plane which flew
non-stop from Guam to Washington, was reported by the press as declar-
ing that one of the objects of the flight was "to show the vulnerability
of our country to enemy air attack from vast distances." New York
Times, November 21, 1945, p. 1.

† See printed edition of the *Report*, p. 68. In the sentence following
the one quoted, General Arnold adds that this statement is "perhaps true
only temporarily," but it is apparent from the context that the factor he
has in mind which might terminate its "truthfulness" is the development
of rockets comparable to the V-2 but of much longer range. The present
discussion is not concerned with rockets at all.

This writer feels no inclination to question General Arnold's authority on matters pertaining to air combat tactics. However, it is pertinent to ask just what the phrase "certain of success" means in the sentence just quoted, or rather, how much certainty of success is necessary for each individual bomb before an atomic bomb attack is considered feasible. In this respect one gains some insight into what is in General Arnold's mind from a sentence which occurs somewhat earlier on the same page in the *Report:* "Further, the great unit cost of the atomic bomb means that as nearly as possible every one must be delivered to its intended target." Here is obviously the major premise upon which the conclusion above quoted is based, and one is not disputing General Arnold's judgment in the field of his specialization by examining a premise which lies wholly outside of it.

When the bombs were dropped on Hiroshima and Nagasaki in August, 1945, there were undoubtedly very few such bombs in existence—which would be reason enough for considering each one precious regardless of cost. But the cost of their development and production then amounted to some two billions of dollars, and that figure would have to be divided by the number made to give the cost of each. If, for example, there were twenty in existence, the unit cost would have to be reckoned at $100,000,000. That, indeed, is a staggering sum for one missile, being approximately equivalent to the cost of one *Iowa* class battleship. It is quite possible that there were fewer than twenty at that time, and that the unit cost was proportionately higher. For these and other reasons, including the desirability for psychological effect of making certain that the initial demonstration should be a complete success, one can understand why it was then considered necessary, as General Arnold feels it will remain necessary, to "run a large air operation for the sole purpose of delivering one or two atomic bombs." *

But it is of course clear that as our existing plant is used for the production of more bombs—and it has already been revealed that over three-fourths of the two billion dollars went into capital investment for plants and facilities †—the unit cost will decline. Professor Oppenheimer has estimated that even with existing techniques and facilities, that is, allowing for no improvements whatever in the production processes, the unit cost of the bomb should easily descend to something in the neighborhood of $1,000,000. ‡

Now a million dollars is a large sum of money for any purpose other than war. Just what it means in war may be gauged by the fact that it amounts to substantially less than the cost of two fully equipped Flying Fortresses (B-17's, not B-29's), a considerable number of which were expended in the recent war without waiting upon situations in which each sortie would be certain of success. The money cost of the war to the United States was sufficient to have paid for two or three hundred thousand of such million-dollar bombs. It is evident, therefore, that in the future it will not be the unit cost of the bomb but the number of bombs actually available

* *Report,* p. 68.
† According to the figures provided the McMahon Committee by Major General Leslie R. Groves, the total capital investment spent and committed for plants and facilities as of June 30, 1945, was $1,595,000,000. Total operating costs up to the time the bombs were dropped in August were $405,000,000. The larger sum is broken down as follows:

Manufacturing facilities alone	$1,242,000,000
Research	186,000,000
Housing for workers	162,500,000
Workmen's compensation and medical care	4,500,000
Total	$1,595,000,000

‡ *Loc. cit.*

which will determine the acceptable wastage in any atomic bomb attack.*

Thus, if Country A should have available 5,000 atomic bombs, and if it should estimate that 500 bombs dropped on the cities of Country B would practically eliminate the industrial plant of the latter nation, it could afford a wastage of bombs of roughly 9 to 1 to accomplish that result. If its estimate should prove correct and if it launched an attack on that basis, an expenditure of only five billions of dollars in bombs would give it an advantage so inconceivably overwhelming as to make easy and quick victory absolutely assured—provided it was able somehow to prevent retaliation in kind. The importance of the latter proviso will be elaborated in the whole of the following chapter. Meanwhile it should be noted that the figure of 5,000 bombs cited above is, as will shortly be demonstrated, by no means an impossible or extreme figure for any great power which has been producing atomic bombs over a period of ten or fifteen years.

To approach the same point from another angle, one might take an example from naval warfare. The commander of a battleship will not consider the money cost of his 16-inch shells (perhaps $3,000 each at the gun's breech) when engaging an enemy battleship. He will not hesitate, at least not for financial reasons, to open fire at extreme range, even if he can count on only one hit in thirty rounds. The only con-

* This discussion recalls the often repeated canard that admirals have been cautious of risking battleships in action because of their cost. The thirteen old battleships and two new ones available to us just after Pearl Harbor reflected no great money value, but they were considered precious because they were scarce and irreplaceable. Later in the war, when new battleships had joined the fleet, and when we had eliminated several belonging to the enemy, no battleships were withheld from any naval actions in which they could be of service. Certainly they were not kept out of the dangerous waters off Normandy, Leyte, Luzon, and Okinawa.

sideration which could give him pause would be the fear of exhausting his armor-piercing ammunition before he has sunk or disabled the enemy ship. The cost of each shell, to be sure, is much smaller than the cost of one atomic bomb, but the amount of damage each hit accomplishes is also smaller —disproportionately smaller by a wide margin.

In calculations of acceptable wastage, the money cost of a weapon is usually far overshadowed by considerations of availability; but in so far as it does enter into those calculations, it must be weighed against the amount of damage done the enemy with each hit. A million dollar bomb which can do a billion dollars worth of damage—and that is a conservative figure—is a very cheap missile indeed. In fact, one of the most frightening things about the bomb is that it makes the destruction of enemy cities an immeasurably cheaper process than it was before, cheaper not alone in terms of missiles but also in terms of the air forces necessary to do the job. Provided the nation using them has enough such bombs available, it can afford a large number of misses for each hit obtained.

To return to General Arnold's observation, we know from the experience of the recent war that very inferior air forces can penetrate to enemy targets if they are willing to make the necessary sacrifices. The Japanese aircraft which raided Pearl Harbor were considerably fewer in number than the American planes available at Pearl Harbor. That, to be sure, was a surprise attack preceding declaration of hostilities, but such possibilities must be taken into account for the future. At any rate, the Japanese air attacks upon our ships off Okinawa occurred more than three years after the opening of hostilities, and there the Japanese, who were not superior in numbers on any one day and who did indeed lose over 4,000 planes in two months of battle, nevertheless succeeded in sinking or damaging no fewer than 253 American warships. For that matter, the British were effectively raiding targets deep in Germany, and doing so without suffering great casualties, long before they had overtaken the German lead in numbers of aircraft. The war has demonstrated beyond the shadow of a doubt that the sky is much too big to permit one side, however superior, to shut out enemy aircraft completely from the air over its territories.

The concept of "command of the air," which has been used altogether too loosely, has never been strictly analogous to that of "command of the sea." The latter connotes something approaching absolute exclusion of enemy surface craft from the area in question. The former suggests only that the enemy is suffering losses greater than he can afford, whereas one's own side is not. But the appraisal of tolerable losses is in part subjective, and is also affected by several variables which may have little to do with the number of planes downed. Certainly the most important of those variables is the amount of damage being inflicted on the bombing raids. An air force which can destroy the cities in a given territory has for all practical purposes the fruits of command of the air, regardless of its losses.

Suppose, then, one put to the Army Air Forces the following question: If 3,000 enemy bombers flying simultaneously but individually (i.e., completely scattered) * invaded our skies with the intention of dividing between them as targets

* The purpose of the scattering would be simply to impose maximum confusion on the superior defenders. Some military airmen have seriously attempted to discount the atomic bomb with the argument that a hit upon a plane carrying one would cause the bomb to explode, blasting every other plane for at least a mile around out of the air. That is not why formation flying is rejected in the example above. Ordinary bombs are highly immune to such mishaps, and from all reports of the nature of the atomic bomb it would seem to be far less likely to undergo explosion as a result even of a direct hit.

most of the 92 American cities which contain a population of 100,000 or over (embracing together approximately 29 per cent of our total population), if each of those planes carried an atomic bomb, and if we had 9,000 alerted fighters to oppose them, how much guarantee of protection could be accorded those cities? The answer would undoubtedly depend on a number of technical and geographic variables, but under present conditions it seems to this writer all too easy to envisage situations in which few of the cities selected as targets would be spared overwhelming destruction.

That superiority which results in the so-called "command of the air" is undoubtedly necessary for successful strategic bombing with ordinary bombs, where the weight of bombs required is so great that the same planes must be used over and over again. In a sense also (though one must register some reservations about the exclusion of other arms) General Arnold is right when he says of atomic bomb attack: "For the moment at least, absolute air superiority in being at all times, combined with the best antiaircraft ground devices, is the only form of defense that offers any security whatever, and it must continue to be an essential part of our security program for a long time to come." * But it must be added that the "only form of defense that offers any security whatever" falls far short, even without any consideration of rockets, of offering the already qualified kind of security it formerly offered.

V. *Superiority in numbers of bombs is not in itself a guarantee of strategic superiority in atomic bomb warfare.*

Under the technical conditions apparently prevailing today, and presumably likely to continue for some time to come, the primary targets for the atomic bomb will be cities.

* *Loc. cit.*

One does not shoot rabbits with elephant guns, especially if there are elephants available. The critical mass conditions to which the bomb is inherently subject place the minimum of destructive energy of the individual unit at far too high a level to warrant its use against any target where enemy strength is not already densely concentrated. Indeed, there is little inducement to the attacker to seek any other kind of target. If one side can eliminate the cities of the other, it enjoys an advantage which is practically tantamount to final victory, provided always its own cities are not similarly eliminated.

The fact that the bomb is inevitably a weapon of indiscriminate destruction may carry no weight in any war in which it is used. Even in World War II, in which the bombs used could to a large extent isolate industrial targets from residential districts within an urban area, the distinctions imposed by international law between "military" and "nonmilitary" targets disintegrated entirely.*

How large a city has to be to provide a suitable target for the atomic bomb will depend on a number of variables—the ratio of the number of bombs available to the number of cities which might be hit, the wastage of bombs in respect to each target, the number of bombs which the larger cities can absorb before ceasing to be profitable targets, and, of course, the precise characteristics and relative accessibility of the individual city. Most important of all is the place of the particular

---

* This was due in part to deliberate intention, possibly legal on the Allied side under the principle of retaliation, and in part to a desire of the respective belligerents to maximize the effectiveness of the air forces available to them. "Precision bombing" was always a misnomer, though some selectivity of targets was possible in good weather. However, such weather occurred in Europe considerably less than half the time, and if the strategic air forces were not to be entirely grounded during the remaining time they were obliged to resort to "area bombing." Radar, when used, was far from being an approximate substitute for the human eye.

city in the nation's economy. We can see at once that it does not require the obliteration of all its towns to make a nation wholly incapable of defending itself in the traditional fashion. Thus, the number of *critical* targets is quite limited, and the number of hits necessary to win a strategic decision—always excepting the matter of retaliation—is correspondingly limited. That does not mean that additional hits would be useless but simply that diminishing returns would set in early; and after the cities of, say, 100,000 population were eliminated the returns from additional bombs expended would decline drastically.

We have seen that one has to allow for wastage of missiles in warfare, and the more missiles one has the larger the degree of wastage which is acceptable. Moreover, the number of bombs available to a victim of attack will always bear to an important degree on his ability to retaliate, though it will not itself determine that ability. But, making due allowance for these considerations, it appears that for any conflict a specific number of bombs will be useful to the side using it, and anything beyond that will be luxury. What that specific number would be for any given situation it is now wholly impossible to determine. But we can say that if 2,000 bombs in the hands of either party is enough to destroy entirely the economy of the other, the fact that one side has 6,000 and the other 2,000 will be of relatively small significance.

We cannot, of course, assume that if a race in atomic bombs develops each nation will be content to limit its production after it reaches what it assumes to be the critical level. That would in fact be poor strategy, because the actual critical level could never be precisely determined in advance and all sorts of contingencies would have to be provided for. Moreover, nations will be eager to make whatever political capital (in the narrowest sense of the term) can be made out of superiority in numbers. But it nevertheless remains true that superiority in numbers of bombs does not endow its possessor with the kind of military security which formerly resulted from superiority in armies, navies, and air forces.

VI. *The new potentialities which the atomic bomb gives to sabotage must not be overrated.*

With ordinary explosives it was hitherto physically impossible for agents to smuggle into another country, either prior to or during hostilities, a sufficient quantity of materials to blow up more than a very few specially chosen objectives. The possibility of really serious damage to a great power resulting from such enterprises was practically nil. A wholly new situation arises, however, where such materials as U-235 or Pu-239 are employed, for only a few pounds of either substance are sufficient, when used in appropriate engines, to blow up the major part of a large city. Should those possibilities be developed, an extraordinarily high premium will be attached to national competence in sabotage on the one hand and in countersabotage on the other. The F.B.I. or its counterpart would become the first line of national defense, and the encroachment on civil liberties which would necessarily follow would far exceed in magnitude and pervasiveness anything which democracies have thus far tolerated in peacetime.

However, it would be easy to exaggerate the threat inherent in that situation, at least for the present. From various hints contained in the *Smyth Report* * and elsewhere, † it is clear

* Henry D. Smyth, *Atomic Energy for Military Purposes, The Official Report on the Development of the Atomic Bomb under the Auspices of the United States Government, 1940-1945,* Princeton, Princeton University Press, 1945, paragraphs 12.9-12.22.

† General Arnold, for example, in his *Third Report to the Secretary of War,* asserted that at present the only effective means of delivering the atomic bomb is the "very heavy bomber." See printed edition, p. 68.

that the engine necessary for utilizing the explosive, that is, the bomb itself, is a highly intricate and fairly massive mechanism. The massiveness is not something which we can expect future research to diminish. It is inherent in the bomb. The mechanism and casing surrounding the explosive element must be heavy enough to act as a "tamper," that is, as a means of holding the explosive substance together until the reaction has made substantial progress. Otherwise the materials would fly apart before the reaction was fairly begun. And since the *Smyth Report* makes it clear that it is not the tensile strength of the tamper but the inertia due to mass which is important, we need expect no particular assistance from metallurgical advances.*

The designing of the bomb apparently involved some of the major problems of the whole "Manhattan District" project. The laboratory at Los Alamos was devoted almost exclusively to solving those problems, some of which for a time looked insuperable. The former director of that laboratory has stated that the results of the research undertaken there required for its recording a work of some fifteen volumes.† The detonation problem is not even remotely like that of any other explosive. It requires the bringing together instantaneously in perfect union of two or more subcritical masses of the explosive material (which up to that moment must be insulated from each other) and the holding together of the combined mass until a reasonable proportion of the uranium or plutonium atoms have undergone fission. A little reflection will indicate that the mechanism which can

---

* One might venture to speculate whether the increase in power which the atomic bomb is reported to have undergone since it was first used is not due to the use of a more massive tamper to produce a more complete reaction. If so, the bomb has been increasing in weight rather than the reverse.

† J. Robert Oppenheimer, *op. cit.*, p. 9.

accomplish this must be ingenious and elaborate in the extreme, and certainly not one which can be slipped into a suit case.

It is of course possible that a nation intent upon perfecting the atomic bomb as a sabotage instrument could work out a much simpler device. Perhaps the essential mechanism could be broken down into small component parts such as are easily smuggled across national frontiers, the essential mass being provided by crude materials available locally in the target area. Those familiar with the present mechanism do not consider such an eventuation likely. And if it required the smuggling of whole bombs, that too is perhaps possible. But the chances are that if two or three were successfully introduced into a country by stealth, the fourth or fifth would be discovered. Our federal police agencies have made an impressive demonstration in the past, with far less motivation, of their ability to deal with smugglers and saboteurs.

Those, at any rate, are some of the facts to consider when reading a statement such as Professor Harold Urey was reported to have made: "An enemy who put twenty bombs, each with a time fuse, into twenty trunks, and checked one in the baggage room of the main railroad station in each of twenty leading American cities, could wipe this country off the map so far as military defense is concerned." * Quite apart from the question of whether twenty bombs, even if they were considerably more powerful than those used at Hiroshima and Nagasaki, could produce the results which Professor Urey assumes they would, the mode of distribution postulated is not one which recommends itself for aggressive purposes. For the detection of one or more of the bombs would not

* The *New Republic*, December 31, 1945, p. 885. The statement quoted is that used by the *New Republic*, and is probably not identical in wording with Professor Urey's remark.

merely compromise the success of the entire project but would give the intended victim the clearest and most blatant warning imaginable of what to expect and prepare for. Except for port cities, in which foreign ships are always gathered, a surprise attack by air is by every consideration a handier way of doing the job.

VII. *In relation to the destructive powers of the bomb, world resources in raw materials for its production must be considered abundant.*

Everything about the atomic bomb is overshadowed by the twin facts that it exists and that its destructive power is fantastically great. Yet within this framework there are a large number of technical questions which must be answered if our policy decisions are to proceed in anything other than complete darkness. Of first importance are those relating to its availability.

The manner in which the bomb was first tested and used and various indications contained in the *Smyth Report* suggest that the atomic bomb cannot be "mass produced" in the usual sense of the term. It is certainly a scarce commodity in the sense in which the economist uses the term "scarcity," and it is bound to remain extremely scarce in relation to the number of TNT or torpex bombs of comparable size which can be produced. To be sure, the bomb is so destructive that even a relatively small number (as compared with other bombs) may prove sufficient to decide a war, especially since there will be no such thing as a "near miss"—anything near will have all the consequences of a direct hit. However, the scarcity is likely to be sufficiently important to dictate the selection of targets and the circumstances under which the missile is hurled.

A rare explosive will not normally be used against targets

which are naturally dispersed or easily capable of dispersion, such as ships at sea or isolated industrial plants of no great magnitude. Nor will it be used in types of attack which show an unduly high rate of loss among the attacking instruments —unless, as we have seen, the target is so important as to warrant high ratios of loss provided one or a few missiles penetrate to it. In these respects the effects of scarcity in the explosive materials are intensified by the fact that it requires certain minimum amounts to produce an explosive reaction and that the minimum quantity is not likely to be reduced materially, if at all, by further research.*

The ultimate physical limitation on world atomic bomb production is of course the amount of ores available for the derivation of materials capable of spontaneous atomic fission. The only basic material thus far used to produce bombs is uranium, and for the moment only uranium need be considered.

Estimates of the amount of uranium available in the earth's crust vary between 4 and 7 parts per million—a very con-

* The figure for critical minimum mass is secret. According to the *Smyth Report*, it was predicted in May, 1941, that the critical mass would be found to lie between 2 kg. and 100 kg. (paragraph 4.49), and it was later found to be much nearer the minimum predicted than the maximum. It is worth noting, too, that not only does the critical mass present a lower limit in bomb size, but also that it is not feasible to use very much more than the critical mass. One reason is the detonating problem. Masses above the critical level cannot be kept from exploding, and detonation is therefore produced by the instantaneous assembly of subcritical masses. The necessity for *instant and simultaneous* assembly of the masses used must obviously limit their number. The scientific explanation of the critical mass condition is presented in the *Smyth Report* in paragraphs 2.3, 2.6, and 2.7. One must always distinguish, however, between the chain reaction which occurs in the plutonium-producing pile and that which occurs in the bomb. Although the general principles determining critical mass are similar for the two reactions, the actual mass needed and the character of the reaction are very different in the two cases. See also *ibid.*, paragraphs 2.35, 4.15-17, and 12.13-15.

siderable quantity indeed. The element is very widely distributed, there being about a ton of it present in each cubic mile of séa water and about one-seventh of an ounce per ton (average) in all granite and basalt rocks, which together comprise about 95 per cent by weight of the earth's crust. There is more uranium present in the earth's crust than cadmium, bismuth, silver, mercury, or iodine, and it is about one thousand times as prevalent as gold. However, the number of places in which uranium is known to exist in concentrated form is relatively small, and of these places only four are known to have the concentrated deposits in substantial amounts. The latter deposits are found in the Great Bear Lake region of northern Canada, the Belgian Congo, Colorado, and Joachimsthal in Czechoslovakia. Lesser but nevertheless fairly extensive deposits are known to exist also in Madagascar, India, and Russian Turkestan, while small occurrences are fairly well scattered over the globe.*

The pre-war market was dominated by the Belgian Congo and Canada, who agreed in 1939 to share it in the ratio of 60 to 40,† a proportion which presumably reflected what was then thought to be their respective reserves and productive capacity. However, it now appears likely that the Canadian reserves are considerably greater than those of the Congo. In 1942 the Congo produced 1,021 tons of unusually rich ore containing 695.6 tons of U_3O_8—or about 590 tons of uranium metal. ‡ In general, however, the ores of Canada and the

* See "The Distribution of Uranium in Nature," an unsigned article published in the *Bulletin of the Atomic Scientists of Chicago*, Vol. I, No. 4, February 1, 1946, p. 6. See also U. S. Bureau of Mines, *Minerals Yearbook, 1940, Review of 1939*, p. 766; *ibid., 1943*, p. 828; H. V. Ellsworth, *Rare-Element Minerals of Canada*, Geological Survey (Canada), 1932, p. 39.

† *Minerals Yearbook, 1939*, p. 755.

‡ *Op. cit., 1943*, p. 828. See also A. W. Postel, *The Mineral Resources of Africa*, University of Pennsylvania, 1943, p. 44.

Congo are of a richness of about one ton of uranium in from fifty to one hundred tons of ore. The Czechoslovakian deposits yielded only fifteen to twenty tons of uranium oxide (U_3O_8) annually before the war.* This rate of extraction could not be very greatly expanded even under strained operations— since the total reserves of the Joachimsthal region are far smaller than those of the Congo or Canada or even Colorado.

The quantity of U-235 in metallic uranium is only about .7 per cent (or 1/140th) of the whole. To be sure, plutonium-239, which is equally as effective in a bomb as U-235, is derived from the more plentiful U-238 isotope, but only through a chain reaction that depends on the presence of U-235, which is broken down in the process. It is doubtful whether a given quantity of uranium can yield substantially more plutonium than U-235.† It appears also from the *Smyth Report* that the amount of U-235 which can profitably be extracted by separation of the isotopes is far below 100 per cent of the amount present, at least under present techniques. ‡

What all these facts add up to is perhaps summarized by the statement made by one scientist that there is a great deal more than enough fissionable material in known deposits to

* *The Mineral Industry of the British Empire and Foreign Countries, Statistical Summary, 1935-37*, London, 1938, p. 419.

† The *Smyth Report* is somewhat misleading on this score, in that it gives the impression that the use of plutonium rather than U-235 makes it possible to utilize 100 per cent of the U-238 for atomic fission energy. See paragraph 4.25. However, other portions of the same report give a more accurate picture, especially paragraphs 8.72-73.

‡ Among numerous other hints is the statement that in September, 1942, the plants working on the atomic bomb were already receiving about one ton daily of uranium oxide of high purity (paragraph 6.11). Making the conservative assumption that this figure represented the minimum quantity of uranium oxide being processed daily during 1944-45, the U-235 content would be about 115 pounds. The actual figure of production is still secret, but from all available indices the daily production of U-235 and Pu-239 is even now very considerably below that amount.

blow up all the cities in the world, though he added that there might not be enough to do so if the cities were divided and dispersed into ten times their present number (the size of cities included in that comment was not specified). Whatever solace that statement may bring is tempered by the understanding that it refers to *known* deposits of *uranium* ores only and assumes no great increase in the efficiency of the bombs. But how are these factors likely to change?

It is hardly to be questioned that the present extraordinary military premium on uranium will stimulate intensive prospecting and result in the discovery of many new deposits. It seems clear that some of the prospecting which went on during the war was not without result. The demand for uranium heretofore has been extremely limited and only the richer deposits were worth working—mainly for their vanadium or radium content—or for that matter worth keeping track of.* So far as uranium itself was concerned, no particular encouragement for prospecting existed.

It is true that the radioactivity of uranium affords a very sensitive test of its presence, and that the data accumulated over the last fifty years make it appear rather unlikely that wholly new deposits will be found comparable to those of Canada or the Congo. But it is not unlikely that in those regions known to contain uranium, further exploration will reveal much larger quantities than had previously been suspected. It seems hardly conceivable, for example, that in the great expanse of European and Asiatic Russia no additional workable deposits will be discovered.

In that connection it is worth noting that the cost of mining the ore and of extracting the uranium is so small a fraction of the cost of bomb production that (as is *not* true in the

* "Material for U-235," *The Economist*, London, November 3, 1945, pp. 629-30.

search for radium) even poorer deposits are decidedly usable. Within certain wide limits, in other words, the relative richness of the ore is not critical. In fact, as much uranium can be obtained as the nations of the world really desire. Gold is commonly mined from ores containing only one-fifth of an ounce per ton of rock, and there are vast quantities of granite which contain from one-fifth to one ounce of uranium per ton of rock.

Although the American experiment has thus far been confined to the use of uranium, it should be noted that the atoms of thorium and protoactinium also undergo fission when bombarded by neutrons. Protoactinium can be eliminated from consideration because of its scarcity in nature, but thorium is even more plentiful than uranium, its average distribution in the earth's crust being some twelve parts per million. Fairly high concentrations of thorium oxide are found in monazite sands, which exist to some extent in the United States, Ceylon, and the Netherlands East Indies, but to a much greater extent in Brazil and British India. The *Smyth Report* states merely that thorium has "no apparent advantage over uranium" (paragraph 2.21), but how important are its disadvantages is not stated. At any rate, it has been publicly announced that thorium is already being used in a pilot plant for the production of atomic energy set up in Canada.*

In considering the availability of ores to particular powers, it is always necessary to bear in mind that accessibility is not determined exclusively by national boundaries. Accessibility depends on a combination of geographic, political, and power conditions and on whether the situation is one of war or

* New York *Herald Tribune*, December 18, 1945, p. 4. Incidentally, the Canadian pile is the first one to use the much-discussed "heavy water" (which contains the heavy hydrogen or deuterium atom) as a moderator in place of the graphite (carbon) used in the American piles.

peace. During wartime a great nation will obviously enjoy the ore resources both of allied countries and of those territories which its armies have overrun, though in the future the ores made available only after the outbreak of hostilities may not be of much importance. Because of the political orientation of Czechoslovakia towards the Soviet Union, the latter will most likely gain in peacetime the use of the Joachimsthal ores,* just as the United States enjoys the use of the immensely richer deposits of Canada. The ores of the Belgian Congo will in peacetime be made available to those countries which can either have the confidence of or coerce the Belgian Government (unless the matter is decided by an international instrument to which Belgium is a party); in a time of general war the same ores would be controlled by the nation or nations whose sea and air power gave them access to the region.

Since the atoms of both U-235 and Pu-239 are normally extremely stable (in technical language: possess a long "half-life"), subcritical masses of either material may be stored practically indefinitely. Thus, even a relatively slow rate of production can result over a period of time in a substantial accumulation of bombs. But how slow need the rate of production be? The process of production itself is inevitably a slow one, and even with a huge plant it would require perhaps several months of operation to produce enough fissionable material for the first bomb. But the rate of output thereafter would depend entirely on the extent of the facilities devoted to production, which in turn could be geared to the amount of ores being made available for processing. The eminent Dan-

* However, Mr. Jan Masaryk, Czechoslovak Foreign Minister, asserted in a speech before the Assembly of the UNO on January 17, 1946, that "no Czechoslovak uranium will be used for destructive purposes." New York *Times*, January 18, 1946, p. 8.

ish scientist, Niels Bohr, who was associated with the atomic bomb project, was reported as having stated publicly in October, 1945, that the United States was producing three kilograms (6.6 pounds) of U-235 daily.* The amount of plutonium being concurrently produced might well be considerably larger. Dr. Harold C. Urey, also a leading figure in the bomb development, considers it not unreasonable to assume that with sufficient effort 10,000 bombs could be produced,† and other distinguished scientists have not hesitated to put the figure considerably higher. Thus, while the bomb may remain, for the next fifteen or twenty years at least, scarce enough to dictate to its would-be users a fairly rigorous selection of targets and means of delivery, it will not be scarce enough to spare any nation against which it is used from a destruction immeasurably more devastating than that endured by Germany in World War II.

It is of course tempting to leave to the physicist familiar with the bomb all speculation concerning its future increase in power. However, the basic principles which must govern the developments of the future are not difficult to comprehend, and it is satisfying intellectually to have some basis for appraising in terms of probability the random estimates which have been presented to the public. Some of those estimates, it must be said, though emanating from distinguished scientists, are not marked by the scientific discipline which is so rigorously observed in the laboratory. Certainly they cannot be regarded as dispassionate. It might therefore be profitable for us to examine briefly (a) the relation of increase in power to increase of destructive capacity, and (b) the several factors which must determine the inherent power of the bomb.

* *Time*, October 15, 1945, p. 22.
† New York *Times*, October 22, 1945, p. 4.

As we have seen, the radius of destruction of a bomb increases only as the third root of the explosive energy released. Thus, if Bomb A has a radius of total destruction of one mile, it would take a bomb of 1,000 times the power (Bomb B) to have a radius of destruction of ten miles.* In terms of area destroyed the proportion does not look so bad; nevertheless the *area* destroyed by Bomb B would be only 100 times as great as that destroyed by Bomb A. In other words, the ratio of *destructive efficiency* to energy released would be only one-tenth as great in Bomb B as it is in Bomb A. But when we consider also the fact that the area covered by Bomb B is bound to include to a much greater degree than Bomb A sections of no appreciable military significance (assuming both bombs are perfectly aimed), the military efficiency of the bomb falls off even more rapidly with increasing power of the individual unit than is indicated above.† What this means is that even if it were technically feasible to accomplish it, an increase in the power of the bomb gained only by a proportionate increase in the mass of the scarce and expensive fissionable material within it would be very poor economy. It would be much better to use the extra quantities to make extra bombs.

It so happens, however, that in atomic bombs the total amount of energy released per kilogram of fissionable material (i.e., the efficiency of energy release) *increases* with

* Since the Hiroshima bomb had a radius of total destruction of something under 1¼ miles, its power would have to be increased by some 600 times to gain the hypothetical ten-mile radius.

† The bomb of longer destructive radius would of course not have to be aimed as accurately for any given target; and this fact may prove of importance in very long range rocket fire, which can never be expected to be as accurate as bombing from airplanes. But here again, large numbers of missiles will also make up for the inaccuracy of the individual missile.

the size of the bomb.* This factor, weighed against those mentioned in the previous paragraph, indicates that there is a
theoretical optimum size for the bomb which has perhaps not
yet been determined and which may very well be appreciably
or even considerably larger than the Nagasaki bomb. But it
should be observed that considerations of military economy
are not the only factors which hold down the optimum size.
One factor, already noted, is the steeply ascending difficulty,
as the number of subcritical masses increases, of securing
simultaneous and perfect union among them. Another is the
problem of the envelope or tamper. If the increase of weight
of the tamper is at all proportionate either to the increase in
the amount of fissionable material used or to the amount of
energy released, the gross weight of the bomb might quickly
press against the tactically usable limits. In short, the fact
that an enormous increase in the power of the bomb is theoretically conceivable does not mean that it is likely to occur,
either soon or later. It has always been theoretically possible
to pour 20,000 tons of TNT together in one case and detonate
it as a single bomb; but after some forty years or more of its

* *Smyth Report*, paragraph 12.18. This phenomenon is no doubt due to
the fact that the greater the margin above critical mass limits, the more
atoms split per time unit and thus the larger the proportion of material
which undergoes fission before the heat generated expands and disrupts
the bomb. It might be noted also that even if there were no expansion or
bursting to halt it, the reaction would cease at about the time the fissionable material remaining fell below critical mass conditions, which would
also tend to put a premium on having a large margin above critical mass
limits. At any rate, anything like 100 per cent detonation of the explosive
contents of the atomic bomb is totally out of the question. In this respect
atomic explosives differ markedly from ordinary "high explosives" like
TNT or torpex, where there is no difficulty in getting a 100 per cent reaction and where the energy released is therefore directly proportionate
to the amount of explosive filler in the bomb.

use, the largest amount of it poured into a single lump was about six tons.*

To be sure, greater power in the bomb will no doubt be attained by increasing the efficiency of the explosion without necessarily adding to the quantities of fissionable materials used. But the curve of progress in this direction is bound to flatten out and to remain far short of 100 per cent. The bomb is, to be sure, in its "infancy," but that statement is misleading if it implies that we may expect the kind of progress which we have witnessed over the past century in the steam engine. The bomb is new, but the people who developed it were able to avail themselves of the fabulously elaborate and advanced technology already existing. Any new device created today is already at birth a highly perfected instrument.

One cannot dismiss the matter of increasing efficiency of the bomb without noting that the military uses of radioactivity may not be confined to bombs. Even if the project to produce the bomb had ultimately failed, the by-products formed from some of the intermediate processes could have been used as an extremely vicious form of poison gas. It was estimated by two members of the "Manhattan District" project that the radioactive by-products formed in one day's run of a 100,000-kw. chain-reacting pile for the production of plutonium (the production rate at Hanford, Washington, was from five to fifteen times as great) might be sufficient to make a large area uninhabitable.† Fortunately, however, materials which

---

* In the 10-ton bomb, of which it is fair to estimate that at least 40 per cent of the weight must be attributed to the metal case. In armor-piercing shells and bombs the proportion of weight devoted to metal is very much higher, running above the 95 per cent mark in major-caliber naval shells.

† *Smyth Report*, paragraphs 4.26-28.

are dangerously radioactive tend to lose their radioactivity rather quickly and therefore cannot be stored.

VIII. *Regardless of American decisions concerning retention of its present secrets, other powers besides Britain and Canada will possess the ability to produce the bombs in quantity within a period of five to ten years hence.*

This proposition by-passes the possibility of effective international regulation of bomb production being adopted within that period. A discussion of that possibility is left to subsequent chapters. One may anticipate, however, to the extent of pointing out that it is difficult to induce nations like the Soviet Union to accept such regulation until they can start out in a position of parity with the United States in ability to produce the bomb. The State Department Board of Consultants' report of March 16, 1946, acknowledges as much when it states that "acceleration" of the disappearance of our monopoly must be "inherent in the adoption of any plan of international control."

Statements of public officials and of journalists indicate an enormous confusion concerning the extent and character of the secret now in the possession of the United States. Opinions vary from the observation that "there is no secret" to the blunt comment of Dr. Walter R. G. Baker, Vice-President of the General Electric Company, that no nation other than the United States has sufficient wealth, materials, and industrial resources to produce the bomb.*

Some clarification is discernible in President Truman's message to Congress of October 3, 1945, in which the President recommended the establishment of security regulations and the prescription of suitable penalties for their violation

* New York *Times*, October 2, 1945, p. 6.

and went on to add the following: "Scientific opinion appears to be practically unanimous that the essential theoretical knowledge upon which the discovery is based is already widely known. There is also substantial agreement that foreign research can come abreast of our present theoretical knowledge in time." The emphasis, it should be noted, is on "theoretical knowledge." A good deal of basic scientific data are still bound by rigorous secrecy, but such data are apparently not considered to be crucial. While the retention of such secrets would impose upon the scientists of other nations the necessity of carrying through a good deal of time-consuming research which would merely duplicate that already done in this country, there seems to be little question that countries like the Soviet Union and France and probably several of the lesser nations of Europe have the resources in scientific talent to accomplish it. It is (a) the technical and engineering details of the manufacturing process for the fissionable materials and (b) the design of the bomb itself which are thought to be the critical hurdles.

At a public meeting in Washington on December 11, 1945, Major General Leslie R. Groves permitted himself the observation that the bomb was not a problem for us but for our grandchildren. What he obviously intended that statement to convey was the idea that it would take other nations, like Russia, many years to duplicate our feat. When it was submitted to him that the scientists who worked on the problem were practically unanimous in their disagreement, he responded that they did not understand the problem. The difficulties to be overcome, he insisted, are not primarily of a scientific but of an engineering character. And while the Soviet Union may have first-rate scientists, it clearly does not have the great resources in engineering talent or the industrial laboratories that we enjoy.

Perhaps so; but there are a few pertinent facts which bear on such a surmise. First of all, it has always been axiomatic in the armed services that the only way really to keep a device secret is to keep the fact of its existence secret. Thus, the essential basis of secrecy of the atomic bomb disappeared on August 6, 1945. But a few days later saw the release of the *Smyth Report,* which was subsequently published in book form and widely distributed. Members of the War Department who approved its publication, including General Groves himself, insist that it reveals nothing of importance. But scientists close to the project point out that the *Smyth Report* reveals substantially everything that the American and associated scientists themselves knew up to the close of 1942. It in fact tells much of the subsequent findings as well. In any case, from the end of 1942 it was only two and one-half years before we had the bomb.

The *Smyth Report* reveals among other things that five distinct and separate processes for producing fissionable materials were pursued, and that *all were successful.* These involved four processes for the separation of the U-235 isotope from the more common forms of uranium and one basic process for the production of plutonium. One of the isotope separation processes, the so-called "centrifuge process," was never pushed beyond the pilot plant stage, but it was successful as far as it was pursued. It was dropped when the gaseous diffusion and electromagnetic methods of isotope separation promised assured success.* The thermal diffusion process was restricted to a small plant. *But any of these processes would have sufficed to produce the fissionable materials for the bomb.* Each of these processes presented problems for which generally multiple rather than single solutions were

* See *Smyth Report,* chaps. vii-xi, also paragraph 5.21.

discovered. Each of them, furthermore, is described in the report in fairly revealing though general terms. Finally, the report probably reveals enough to indicate to the careful reader which of the processes presents the fewest problems and offers the most profitable yield. Another nation wishing to produce the bomb can confine its efforts to that one process or to some modification of it.

Enough is said in the *Smyth Report* about the bomb itself to give one a good idea of its basic character. Superficially at least, the problem of bomb design seems a bottleneck, since the same bomb is required to handle the materials produced by any of the five processes mentioned above. But that is like saying that while gasoline can be produced in several different ways, only one kind of engine can utilize it effectively. The bomb is gadgetry, and it is a commonplace in the history of technology that mechanical devices of radically different design have been perfected to achieve a common end. The machine gun has several variants which operate on basically different principles, and the same is no doubt true of dish-washing machines.

Some of those who were associated with the bomb design project came away tremendously impressed with the seemingly insuperable difficulties which were overcome. Undoubtedly they were justified in their admiration for the ingenuity displayed. But they are not justified in assuming that aggregations of talented young men in other parts of the world could not display equally brilliant ingenuity.

We cannot assume that what took us two and one-half years to accomplish, without the certainty that success was possible, should take another great nation twenty to thirty years to duplicate with the full knowledge that the thing has been done. To do so would be to exhibit an extreme form of ethnocentric smugness. It is true that we mobilized a vast amount of talent, but American ways are frequently wasteful.

We were simultaneously pushing forward on a great many other scientific and engineering fronts having nothing to do with the atomic bomb. Another nation which has fewer engineers and scientists than we have could, nevertheless, by concentrating all its pertinent talent on this one job—and there is plenty of motivation—marshal as great a fund of scientific and engineering workers as it would need, perhaps as much as we did. The Japanese, for example, before the recent war, were intent on having a good torpedo, and by concentrating on that end produced a superb torpedo, though they had to accept inferiority to us in practically every other element of naval ordnance. One should expect a similar concentration in other countries on the atomic bomb, and one should expect also comparable results.

It is clear also that the money cost is no barrier to any nation of ordinary substance. The two billion dollars that the bomb development project cost the United States must be considered small for a weapon of such extraordinary military power. Moreover, that sum is by no means the measure of what a comparable development would cost other nations. The American program was pushed during wartime under extreme urgency and under war-inflated prices. Money costs were always considered secondary to the saving of time. The scientists and engineers who designed the plants and equipment were constantly pushing into the unknown. The huge plant at Hanford, Washington, for the production of plutonium, for example, was pushed forward on the basis of that amount of knowledge of the properties of the new element which could be gleaned from the study of half a milligram in the laboratories at Chicago.* Five separate processes for the production of fissionable materials were pushed concurrently, for the planners had to hedge against the possibility of failure in one or more. There was no room for weighing the relative economy of each. Minor failures and fruitless researches did in fact occur in each process.

It is fairly safe to say that another country, proceeding only on the information available in the *Smyth Report*, would be able to reach something comparable to the American production at less than half the cost—even if we adopt the American price level as a standard. Another country would certainly be able to economize by selecting one of the processes and ignoring the others—no doubt the plutonium production process, since various indices seem to point clearly to its being the least difficult and the most rewarding one—an impression which is confirmed by the public statements of some scientists.† General Groves has revealed that about one-fourth of the entire capital investment in the atomic bomb went into the plutonium production project at Hanford. ‡ As fuller

* *Smyth Report,* paragraph 7.3. A milligram is a thousandth of a gram (one United States dime weighs 2½ grams). See also *ibid.,* paragraphs 5.21, 7.43, 8.1, 8.26, and 9.13.

† Dr. J. R. Dunning, Director of Columbia University's Division of War Research and a leading figure in the research which led to the atomic bomb, declared before the American Institute of Electrical Engineers that improvements in the plutonium producing process "have already made the extensive plants at Oak Ridge technically obsolete." New York *Times,* January 24, 1946, p. 7. The large Oak Ridge plants are devoted almost exclusively to the isotope separation processes.

‡ The Hanford, Washington, plutonium plant is listed as costing $350,000,000, and housing for workers at nearby Richland cost an additional $48,000,000. This out of a total country-wide capital investment, including housing, of $1,595,000,000. The monthly operating cost of the Hanford plant is estimated at $3,500,000, as compared with the $6,000,000 per month for the diffusion plant at Oak Ridge and $12,000,000 for the electro-magnetic plant, also at Oak Ridge. These figures have, of course, little meaning without some knowledge of the respective yields at the several plants, but it may be significant that in the projection of future

information seeps out even to the public, as it inevitably will despite security regulations, the signs pointing out to other nations the more fruitful avenues of endeavor will become more abundant. Scientists may be effectively silenced, but they cannot as a body be made to lie. And so long as they talk at all, the hiatuses in their speech may be as eloquent to the informed listener as the speech itself.

operating costs, nothing is said about Hanford. According to General Groves the operating costs of the electro-magnetic plant will diminish, while those of the gaseous diffusion plant will increase only as a result of completion of plant enlargement. Of course, the degree to which less efficient processes were cut back and more efficient ones expanded would depend on considerations of existing capital investment and of the desired rate of current production.

II. IMPLICATIONS FOR MILITARY POLICY

By BERNARD BRODIE

Under conditions existing before the atomic bomb, it was possible to contemplate methods of air defense keeping pace with and perhaps even outdistancing the means of offense. Long-range rockets baffled the defense, but they were extremely expensive per unit for inaccurate, single-blow weapons. Against bombing aircraft, on the other hand, fighter planes and antiaircraft guns could be extremely effective. Progress in speed and altitude performance of all types of aircraft, which on the whole tends to favor the attacker, was more or less offset by technological progress in other fields where the net result tends to favor the defender (e.g., radar search and tracking, proximity-fused projectiles, etc.).

At any rate, a future war between great powers could be visualized as one in which the decisive effects of strategic bombing would be contingent upon the *cumulative effect of prolonged bombardment efforts*, which would in turn be governed by aerial battles and even whole campaigns for mastery of the air. Meanwhile—if the recent war can serve as a pattern—the older forms of warfare on land and sea would exercise a telling effect not only on the ultimate decision but on the effectiveness of the strategic bombing itself. Conversely, the strategic bombing would, as was certainly true against Germany, influence or determine the decision mainly through its effects on the ground campaigns.

70

The atomic bomb seems, however, to erase the pattern described above, first of all because its enormous destructive potency is bound vastly to reduce the time necessary to achieve the results which accrue from strategic bombing—and there can no longer be any dispute about the decisiveness of strategic bombing. In fact, the essential change introduced by the atomic bomb is not primarily that it will make war more violent—a city can be as effectively destroyed with TNT and incendiaries—but that it will concentrate the violence in terms of time. A world accustomed to thinking it horrible that wars should last four or five years is now appalled at the prospect that future wars may last only a few days.

One of the results of such a change would be that a far greater proportion of human lives would be lost even in relation to the greater physical damage done. The problem of alerting the population of a great city and permitting resort to air raid shelters is one thing when the destruction of that city requires the concentrated efforts of a great enemy air force; it is quite another when the job can be done by a few aircraft flying at extreme altitudes. Moreover, the feasibility of building adequate air raid shelters against the atomic bomb is more than dubious when one considers that the New Mexico bomb, which was detonated over 100 feet above the ground, caused powerful earth tremors of an unprecedented type lasting over twenty seconds.* The problem merely of ventilating deep shelters, which would require the shutting out of dangerously radioactive gases, is considered by some scientists to be practically insuperable. It would appear that the only way of safeguarding the lives of city dwellers is to evacuate them from their cities entirely in periods of crisis.

* *Time,* January 28, 1946, p. 75.

But such a project too entails some nearly insuperable problems.

What do the facts presented in the preceding pages add up to for our military policy? Is it worth while even to consider military policy as having any consequence at all in an age of atomic bombs? A good many intelligent people think not. The passionate and *exclusive* preoccupation of some scientists and laymen with proposals for "world government" and the like—in which the arguments are posed on an "or else" basis that permits no question of feasibility—argues a profound conviction that the safeguards to security formerly provided by military might are no longer of any use.

Indeed the postulates set forth and argued in the preceding chapter would seem to admit of no other conclusion. If our cities can be wiped out in a day, if there is no good reason to expect the development of specific defenses against the bomb, if all the great powers are already within striking range of each other, if even substantial superiority in numbers of aircraft and bombs offers no real security, of what possible avail can large armies and navies be? Unless we can strike first and eliminate a threat before it is realized in action— something which our national Constitution apparently forbids—we are bound to perish under attack without even an opportunity to mobilize resistance. Such at least seems to be the prevailing conception among those who, if they give any thought at all to the military implications of the bomb, content themselves with stressing its character as a weapon of aggression.

The conviction that the bomb represents the apotheosis of aggressive instruments is especially marked among the scientists who developed it. They know the bomb and its power. They also know their own limitations as producers of miracles. They are therefore much less sanguine than many laymen or military officers of their capacity to provide the instrument which will rob the bomb of its terrors. One of the most outstanding among them, Professor J. Robert Oppenheimer, has expressed himself quite forcibly on the subject:

"The pattern of the use of atomic weapons was set at Hiroshima. They are weapons of aggression, of surprise, and of terror. If they are ever used again it may well be by the thousands, or perhaps by the tens of thousands; their method of delivery may well be different, and may reflect new possibilities of interception, and the strategy of their use may well be different from what it was against an essentially defeated enemy. But it is a weapon for aggressors, and the elements of surprise and of terror are as intrinsic to it as are the fissionable nuclei." *

The truth of Professor Oppenheimer's statement depends on one vital but unexpressed assumption: that the nation which proposes to launch the attack will not need to fear retaliation. If it must fear retaliation, the fact that it destroys its opponent's cities some hours or even days before its own are destroyed may avail it little. It may indeed commence the evacuation of its own cities at the same moment it is hitting the enemy's cities (to do so earlier would provoke a like move on the opponent's part) and thus present to retaliation cities which are empty. But the success even of such a move would depend on the time interval between hitting and being hit. It certainly would not save the enormous physical plant which is contained in the cities and which over any length of time is indispensable to the life of the national community. Thus the element of surprise may be less important than is generally assumed.†

* "Atomic Weapons and the Crisis in Science," *Saturday Review of Literature*, November 24, 1945, p. 10.

† This idea was first suggested and elaborated by Professor Jacob Viner. See his paper: "The Implications of the Atomic Bomb for Inter-

If the aggressor state must fear retaliation, it will know that even if it is the victor it will suffer a degree of physical destruction incomparably greater than that suffered by any defeated nation of history, incomparably greater, that is, than that suffered by Germany in the recent war. Under those circumstances no victory, even if guaranteed in advance—which it never is—would be worth the price. The threat of retaliation does not have to be 100 per cent certain; it is sufficient if there is a good chance of it, or if there is belief that there is a good chance of it. The prediction is more important than the fact.

The argument that the victim of an attack might not know where the bombs are coming from is almost too preposterous to be worth answering, but it has been made so often by otherwise responsible persons that it cannot be wholly ignored. That the geographical location of the launching sites of long-range rockets may remain for a time unknown is conceivable, though unlikely, but that the identity of the attacker should remain unknown is not in modern times conceivable. The fear that one's country might suddenly be attacked in the midst of apparently profound peace has often been voiced, but, at least in the last century and a half, it has never been realized. As advancing technology makes war more horrible, it also makes the decision to resort to it more dependent on an elaborate psychological preparation. In international politics today few things are more certain than that an attack must have an antecedent hostility of obviously grave character. Especially today, when there are only two or three powers of the first rank, the identity of the major rival would

national Relations," *Proceedings of the American Philosophical Society,* Vol. 90, No. 1 (January 29, 1946), pp. 53ff. The present writer desires at this point to express his indebtedness to Professor Viner for numerous other suggestions and ideas gained during the course of several personal conversations.

be unambiguous. In fact, as Professor Jacob Viner has pointed out, it is the lack of ambiguity concerning the major rival which makes the bipolar power system so dangerous.

There is happily little disposition to believe that the atomic bomb by its mere existence and by the horror implicit in it "makes war impossible." In the sense that war is something not to be endured if any reasonable alternative remains, it has long been "impossible." But for that very reason we cannot hope that the bomb makes war impossible in the narrower sense of the word. Even without it the conditions of modern war should have been a sufficient deterrent but proved not to be such. If the atomic bomb can be used without fear of substantial retaliation in kind, it will clearly encourage aggression. So much the more reason, therefore, to take all possible steps to assure that multilateral possession of the bomb, should that prove inevitable, be attended by arrangements to make as nearly certain as possible that the aggressor who uses the bomb will have it used against him.

If such arrangements are made, the bomb cannot but prove in the net a powerful inhibition to aggression. It would make relatively little difference if one power had more bombs and were better prepared to resist them than its opponent. It would in any case undergo incalculable destruction of life and property. It is clear that there existed in the thirties a deeper and probably more generalized revulsion against war than in any other era of history. Under those circumstances the breeding of a new war required a situation combining dictators of singular irresponsibility with a notion among them and their general staffs that aggression would be both successful and cheap. The possibility of irresponsible or desperate men again becoming rulers of powerful states cannot under the prevailing system of international politics be ruled out in the future. But it does seem possible to erase the idea—if not

among madmen rulers then at least among their military sup-
porters—that aggression will be cheap.

Thus, the first and most vital step in any American security
program for the age of atomic bombs is to take measures to
guarantee to ourselves in case of attack the possibility of
retaliation in kind. The writer in making that statement is not
for the moment concerned about who will *win* the next war
in which atomic bombs are used. Thus far the chief purpose of
our military establishment has been to win wars. From now
on its chief purpose must be to avert them. It can have almost
no other useful purpose.

Neither is the writer especially concerned with whether the
guarantee of retaliation is based on national or international
power. However, one cannot be unmindful of one obvious
fact: for the period immediately ahead, we must evolve our
plans with the knowledge that there is a vast difference between what a nation can do domestically of its own volition
and on its own initiative and what it can do with respect to
programs which depend on achieving agreement with other
nations. Naturally, our domestic policies concerning the
atomic bomb and the national defense generally should not
be such as to prejudice real opportunities for achieving world
security agreements of a worth-while sort. That is an important proviso and may become a markedly restraining one.

Some means of international protection for those states
which cannot protect themselves will remain as necessary in
the future as it has been in the past.* Upon the security of

* The argument has been made that once the middle or small powers
have atomic bombs they will have restored to them the ability to resist
effectively the aggressions of their great-power neighbors—an ability
which otherwise has well-nigh disappeared. This is of course an interesting speculation on which no final answer is forthcoming. It is true that
a small power, while admitting that it could not win a war against a
great neighbor, could nevertheless threaten to use the bomb as a penaliz-

such states our own security must ultimately depend. But only a great state which has taken the necessary steps to reduce its own direct vulnerability to atomic bomb attack is in a position to offer the necessary support. Reducing vulnerability is at least one way of reducing temptation to potential aggressors. And if the technological realities make reduction of vulnerability largely synonymous with preservation of striking power, that is a fact which must be faced. Under those circumstances any domestic measures which effectively guaranteed such preservation of striking power under attack would contribute to a more solid basis for the operation of an international security system.

It is necessary therefore to explore all conceivable situations where the aggressor's fear of retaliation will be at a minimum and to seek to eliminate them. The first and most obvious such situation is that in which the aggressor has a monopoly of the bombs. The United States has a monopoly today, but trusts to its reputation for benignity and—what is more impressive—its conspicuous weariness of war to still the perturbations of other powers. In any case, that special situation is bound to be short-lived. The possibility of a recurrence of monopoly in the future would seem to be restricted to a situation in which controls for the rigorous suppression of atomic bomb production had been imposed by international

ing instrument if it were invaded. But it is also true that the great-power aggressor could make counterthreats concerning its conduct while occupying the country which had used atomic bombs against it. It seems to this writer highly unlikely that a small power would dare threaten use of the bomb against a great neighbor which was sure to overrun it quickly once hostilities began. It seems, on the contrary, much more likely that Denmark's course in the second World War will be widely emulated if there is a third. The aggressor will not "atomize" a city occupied by its own troops, and the opposing belligerent will hesitate to destroy by such an unselective weapon the cities of an occupied friendly state.

agreement but had been evaded or violated by one power without the knowledge of the others. Evasion or violation, to be sure, need not be due to aggressive designs. It might stem simply from a fear that other nations were doing likewise and a desire to be on the safe side. Nevertheless, a situation of concealed monopoly would be one of the most disastrous imaginable from the point of view of world peace and security. It is therefore entirely reasonable to insist that any system for the international control or suppression of bomb production should include safeguards promising practically 100 per cent effectiveness.

The use of secret agents to plant bombs in all the major cities of an intended victim was discussed in the previous chapter, where it was concluded that except in port cities easily accessible to foreign ships such a mode of attack could hardly commend itself to an aggressor. Nevertheless, to the degree that such planting of bombs is reasonably possible, it suggests that one side might gain before the opening of hostilities an enormous advantage in the *deployment* of its bombs. Clearly such an ascendancy would contain no absolute guarantee against retaliation, unless the advantage in deployment were associated with a marked advantage in psychological preparation for resistance. But it is clear also that the relative position of two states concerning ability to use the atomic bomb depends not alone on the number of bombs in the possession of each but also on a host of other conditions, including respective positions concerning deployment of the bombs and psychological preparation against attack.

One of the most important of those conditions concerns the relative position of the rival powers in technological development, particularly as it affects the vehicle for carrying the bombs. At present the only instrument for bombardment at distances of over 200 miles is the airplane (with or without crew). The controlled rocket capable of thousands of miles of range is still very much in the future. The experience of the recent war was analyzed in the previous chapter as indicating that an inferior air force can usually penetrate the aerial defenses of its opponent so long as it is willing to accept a high loss ratio. Nevertheless, the same experience shows also that one side can be so superior quantitatively and qualitatively in both aerial offense and defense as to be able to range practically undisturbed over the enemy's territories while shutting him out largely, even if not completely, from incursions over its own. While such a disparity is likely to be of less importance in a war of atomic bombs than it has been in the past, its residual importance is by no means insignificant.* And in so far as the development of rockets nullifies that type of disparity in offensive power, it should be noted that the development of rockets is not likely to proceed at an equal pace among all the larger powers. One or several will far outstrip the others, depending not alone on the degree of scientific and engineering talent available to each country but also on the effort which its government causes to be channeled into such an enterprise. In any case, the possibilities of an enormous lead on the part of one power in effective use of the atomic bomb are inseparable from technological development in vehicles—at least up to a cer-

* It was stated in the previous chapter, p. 30, that before we can consider a defense against atomic bombs effective, "the frustration of the attack for any given target area must be complete." The emphasis in that statement is on a specific and limited target area such as a small or medium size city. For a whole nation containing many cities such absolute standards are obviously inapplicable. The requirements for a "reasonably effective" defense would still be far higher than would be the case with ordinary TNT bombs, but it would certainly not have to reach 100 per cent frustration of the attack. All of which says little more than that a nation can absorb more atomic bombs than can a single city.

tain common level, beyond which additional development may matter little.

The consequences of a marked disparity between opponents in the spatial concentration of populations and industry are left to a separate discussion later in this chapter. But one of the aspects of the problem which might be mentioned here, particularly as it pertains to the United States, is that of having concentrated in a single city not only the main agencies of national government but also the whole of the executive branch, including the several successors to the presidency and the topmost military authorities. While an aggressor could hardly count upon destroying at one blow all the persons who might assume leadership in a crisis, he might, unless there were considerably greater geographic decentralization of national leadership than exists at present, do enough damage with one bomb to create complete confusion in the mobilization of resistance.

It goes without saying that the governments and populations of different countries will show different levels of apprehension concerning the effects of the bomb. It might be argued that a totalitarian state would be less unready than would a democracy to see the destruction of its cities rather than yield on a crucial political question. The real political effect of such a disparity, however—if it actually exists, which is doubtful —can easily be exaggerated. *For in no case is the fear of the consequences of atomic bomb attack likely to be low.* More important is the likelihood that totalitarian countries can impose more easily on their populations than can democracies those mass movements of peoples and industries necessary to disperse urban concentrations.

The most dangerous situation of all would arise from a failure not only of the political leaders but especially of the military authorities of a nation like our own to adjust to the atomic bomb in their thinking and planning. The possibility of such a situation developing in the United States is very real and very grave. We are familiar with the example of the French General Staff, which failed to adjust in advance to the kind of warfare obtaining in 1940. There are other examples, less well-known, which lie much closer home. In all the investigations and hearings on the Pearl Harbor disaster, there has at this writing not yet been mention of a fact which is as pertinent as any—that our ships were virtually naked in respect to antiaircraft defense. They were certainly naked in comparison to what was considered necessary a brief two years later, when the close-in antiaircraft effectiveness of our older battleships was estimated by the then Chief of the Bureau of Ordnance to have increased by no less than 100 times! That achievement was in great part the redemption of past errors of omission. The admirals who had spent so many of their waking hours denying that the airplane was a grave menace to the battleship had never taken the elementary steps necessary to validate their opinions, the steps, that is, of covering their ships with as many as they could carry of the best antiaircraft guns available.

Whatever may be the specific changes indicated, it is clear that our military authorities will have to bestir themselves to a wholly unprecedented degree in revising military concepts inherited from the past. That will not be easy. They must be prepared to dismiss, as possibly irrelevant, experience gained the hard way in the recent war, during which their performance was on the whole brilliant.

Thus far there has been no public evidence that American military authorities have begun really to think in terms of atomic warfare. The test announced with such fanfare for the summer of 1946, in which some ninety-seven naval vessels will be subjected to the blast effect of atomic bombs, to a degree confirms this impression. Presumably the test is intended mainly to gauge the defensive efficacy of tactical dispersion, since there can be little doubt of the consequences to any one ship of a near burst. While such tests are certainly useful it should be recognized at the outset that they can provide no answer to the basic question of the utility of sea power in the future.

Ships at sea are in any case not among the most attractive of military targets for atomic bomb attack. Their ability to disperse makes them comparatively wasteful targets for bombs of such concentrated power and relative scarcity; their mobility makes them practically impossible to hit with super-rockets of great range; and those of the United States Navy at least have shown themselves able, with the assistance of their own aircraft, to impose an impressively high ratio of casualties upon hostile planes endeavoring to approach them. But the question of how their own security is affected is not the essential point. *For it is still possible for navies to lose all reason for being even if they themselves remain completely immune.*

A nation which had lost most of its larger cities and thus the major part of its industrial plant might have small use for a fleet. One of the basic purposes for which a navy exists is to protect the sea-borne transportation by which the national industry imports its raw materials and exports its finished commodities to the battle lines. Moreover, without the national industrial plant to service it, the fleet would shortly find itself without the means to function. In a word, the strategic issues posed by the atomic bomb transcend all tactical issues, and the 1946 test and the controversy which will inevitably follow it will no doubt serve to becloud that basic point.

Outlines of a Defense Program in the Atomic Age

What are the criteria by which we can appraise realistic military thinking in the age of atomic bombs? The burden of the answer will depend primarily on whether one accepts as true the several postulates presented and argued in the previous chapter. One might go further and say that since none of them is obviously untrue, no program of military preparedness which fails to consider the likelihood of their being true can be regarded as comprehensive or even reasonably adequate.

It is of course always possible that the world may see another major war in which the atomic bomb is not used. The awful menace to both parties of a reciprocal use of the bomb may prevent the resort to that weapon by either side, even if it does not prevent the outbreak of hostilities. But even so, the shadow of the atomic bomb would so govern the strategic and tactical dispositions of either side as to create a wholly novel form of war. The kind of spatial concentrations of force by which in the past great decisions have been achieved would be considered too risky. The whole economy of war would be affected, for even if the governments were willing to assume responsibility for keeping the urban populations in their homes, the spontaneous exodus of those populations from the cities might reach such proportions as to make it difficult to service the machines of war. The conclusion is inescapable that war will be vastly different because of the atomic bomb whether or not the bomb is actually used.

But let us now consider the degree of probability inherent in each of the three main situations which might follow from a failure to prevent a major war. These three situations may be listed as follows:

(a) a war fought without atomic bombs or other forms of radioactive energy;

(b) a war in which atomic bombs were introduced only considerably after the outbreak of hostilities;

(c) a war in which atomic bombs were used at or near the very outset of hostilities.

We are assuming that this hypothetical conflict occurs at a time when each of the opposing sides possesses at least the "know-how" of bomb production, a situation which, as argued in the previous chapter, approximates the realities to be expected not more than five to ten years hence.

Under such conditions the situation described under (a) above could obtain only as a result of a mutual fear of retaliation, perhaps supported by international instruments outlawing the bomb as a weapon of war. It would *not* be likely to result from the operation of an international system for the suppression of bomb production, since such a system would almost certainly not survive the outbreak of a major war. If such a system were in fact effective at the opening of hostilities, the situation resulting would be far more likely to fall under (b) than under (a), unless the war were very short. For the race to get the bomb would not be an even one, and the side which got it first in quantity would be under enormous temptation to use it before the opponent had it. Of course, it is more reasonable to assume that an international situation which had so far deteriorated as to permit the outbreak of a major war would have long since seen the collapse of whatever arrangements for bomb production control had previously been imposed, unless the conflict were indeed precipitated by an exercise of sanctions for the violation of such a control system.

Thus we see that a war in which atomic bombs are not used is more likely to occur if both sides have the bombs in quantity from the beginning than if neither side has it at the outset or if only one side has it.* But how likely is it to occur? Since the prime motive in refraining from using it would be fear of retaliation, it is difficult to see why a fear of reciprocal use should be strong enough to prevent resort to the bomb without being strong enough to prevent the outbreak of war in the first place.

Of course, the bomb may act as a powerful deterrent to direct aggression against great powers without preventing the political crises out of which wars generally develop. In a world in which great wars become "inevitable" as a result of aggression by great powers upon weak neighbors, the bomb may easily have the contrary effect. Hitler made a good many bloodless gains by mere blackmail, in which he relied heavily on the too obvious horror of modern war among the great nations which might have opposed him earlier. A comparable kind of blackmail in the future may actually find its encouragement in the existence of the atomic bomb. Horror of its implications is not likely to be spread evenly, at least not in the form of overt expression. The result may be a series of *faits accomplis* eventuating in that final deterioration of international affairs in which war, however terrible, can no longer be avoided.

* One can almost rule out too the possibility that war would break out between two great powers where both knew that only one of them had the bombs in quantity. It is one of the old maxims of power politics that *c'est une crime de faire la guerre sans compter sur la supériorité,* and certainly a monopoly of atomic bombs would be a sufficiently clear definition of superiority to dissuade the other side from accepting the gage of war unless directly attacked.

Nevertheless, once hostilities broke out, the pressures to use the bomb might swiftly reach unbearable proportions. One side or the other would feel that its relative position respecting ability to use the bomb might deteriorate as the war progressed, and that if it failed to use the bomb while it had the chance it might not have the chance later on. The side which was decidedly weaker in terms of industrial capacity for war would be inclined to use it in order to equalize the situation on a lower common level of capacity—for it is clear that the side with the more elaborate and intricate industrial system would, other things being equal, be more disadvantaged by mutual use of the bomb than its opponent. In so far as those "other things" were not equal, the disparities involved would also militate for the use of the bomb by one side or the other. And hovering over the situation from beginning to end would be the intolerable fear on each side that the enemy might at any moment resort to this dreaded weapon, a fear which might very well stimulate an anticipatory reaction.

Some observers in considering the chances of effectively outlawing the atomic bomb have taken a good deal of comfort from the fact that poison gases were not used, or at least not used on any considerable scale, during the recent war. There is little warrant, however, for assuming that the two problems are analogous. Apart from the fact that the recent war presents only a single case and argues little for the experience of another war even with respect to gas, it is clear that poison gas and atomic bombs represent two wholly different orders of magnitude in military utility. The existence of the treaty outlawing gas was important, but at least equally important was the conviction in the minds of the military policy-makers that TNT bombs and tanks of gelatinized gasoline—with which the gas bombs would have had to compete in airplane carrying capacity—were just as effective as gas if not more so. Both sides were prepared not only to retaliate with gas against gas attack but also to neutralize with gas masks and "decontamination units" the chemicals to which they might be exposed. There is visible today no comparable neutralization agent for atomic bombs.

Neither side in the recent war wished to bear the onus for violation of the obligation not to use gas when such violation promised no particular military advantage. But, unlike gas, the atomic bomb can scarcely fail to have fundamental or decisive effects if used at all. That is not to say that any effort to outlaw use of the bomb is arrant nonsense, since such outlawry might prove the indispensable crystallizer of a state of balance which operates against use of the bomb. But without the existence of the state of balance—in terms of reciprocal ability to retaliate in kind if the bomb is used—any treaty purposing to outlaw the bomb in war would have thrust upon it a burden far heavier than such a treaty can normally bear.

What do these conclusions mean concerning the defense preparations of a nation like the United States? In answering this question, it is necessary first to anticipate the argument that "the best defense is a strong offense," an argument which it is now fashionable to link with animadversions on the "Maginot complex." In so far as this doctrine becomes dogma, it may prejudice the security interests of the country and of the world. Although the doctrine is basically true as a general proposition, especially when applied to hostilities already under way, the political facts of life concerning the United States government under its present Constitution make it most probable that if war comes we will receive the first blow rather than deliver it. Thus, our most urgent military problem is to reorganize ourselves to survive a vastly more destructive "Pearl Harbor" than occurred in 1941. Otherwise we shall not be able to take the offensive at all.

The atomic bomb will be introduced into the conflict only on a gigantic scale. No belligerent would be stupid enough, in opening itself to reprisals in kind, to use only a few bombs. The initial stages of the attack will certainly involve hundreds of the bombs, more likely thousands of them. Unless the argument of Postulates II and IV in the previous chapter is wholly preposterous, the target state will have little chance of effectively halting or fending off the attack. If its defenses are highly efficient it may down nine planes out of every ten attacking, but it will suffer the destruction of its cities. That destruction may be accomplished in a day, or it may take a week or more. But there will be no opportunity to incorporate the strength residing in the cities, whether in the form of industry or personnel, into the forces of resistance or counter-attack. *The ability to fight back after an atomic bomb attack will depend on the degree to which the armed forces have made themselves independent of the urban communities and their industries for supply and support.*

The proposition just made is the basic proposition of atomic bomb warfare, and it is the one which our military authorities continue consistently to overlook. They continue to speak in terms of peacetime military establishments which are simply cadres and which are expected to undergo an enormous but slow expansion *after* the outbreak of hostilities.* Therein lies the essence of what may be called "pre-

* General H. H. Arnold's *Third Report to the Secretary of War* is in general outstanding for the breadth of vision it displays. Yet one finds in it statements like the following: "An Air Force is always verging on obsolescence and, in time of peace, its size and replacement rate will always be inadequate to meet the full demands of war. Military Air Power should, therefore, be measured to a large extent by the ability of the existing Air Force to absorb in time of emergency the increase required

atomic thinking." The idea which must be driven home above all else is that a military establishment which is expected to fight on after the nation has undergone atomic bomb attack must be prepared to fight with the men already mobilized and with the equipment already in the arsenals. And those arsenals must be in caves in the wilderness. The cities will be vast catastrophe areas, and the normal channels of transportation and communications will be in unutterable confusion. The rural areas and the smaller towns, though perhaps not struck directly, will be in varying degrees of disorganization as a result of the collapse of the metropolitan centers with which their economies are intertwined.

Naturally, the actual degree of disorganization in both the struck and non-struck areas will depend on the degree to which we provide beforehand against the event. A good deal can be done in the way of decentralization and reorganization of vital industries and services to avoid complete paralysis of the nation. More will be said on this subject later in the present chapter. But the idea that a nation which had undergone days or weeks of atomic bomb attack would be able to achieve a production for war purposes even remotely comparable in character and magnitude to American production in World War II simply does not make sense. The war of atomic bombs must be fought with stockpiles of arms in finished or semifinished state. A superiority in raw materials will be about as important as a superiority in gold resources

by war together with new ideas and techniques" (page 62). Elsewhere in the *Report* (page 65) similar remarks are made about the expansion of personnel which, it is presumed, will always follow upon the outbreak of hostilities. But *nowhere* in the *Report* is the possibility envisaged that in a war which began with an atomic bomb attack there might be no opportunity for the expansion or even replacement either of planes or personnel. The same omission, needless to say, is discovered in practically all the pronouncements of top-ranking Army and Navy officers concerning their own plans for the future.

was in World War II—though it was not so long ago that gold was the essential sinew of war.

All that is being presumed here is the kind of destruction which Germany actually underwent in the last year of the second World War, only telescoped in time and considerably multiplied in magnitude. If such a presumption is held to be unduly alarmist, the burden of proof must lie in the discovery of basic errors in the argument of the preceding chapter. The essence of that argument is simply that what Germany suffered because of her inferiority in the air may now well be suffered in greater degree and in far less time, so long as atomic bombs are used, even by the power which enjoys air superiority. And while the armed forces must still prepare against the possibility that atomic bombs will not be used in another war—a situation which might permit full mobilization of the national resources in the traditional manner—they must be at least equally ready to fight a war in which no such grand mobilization is permitted.

The forces which will carry on the war after a large-scale atomic bomb attack may be divided into three main categories according to their respective functions. The first category will comprise the force reserved for the retaliatory attacks with atomic bombs; the second will have the mission of invading and occupying enemy territory; and the third will have the purpose of resisting enemy invasion and of organizing relief for devastated areas. Professional military officers will perhaps be less disturbed at the absence of any distinction between land, sea, and air forces than they will be at the sharp distinction between offensive and defensive functions in the latter two categories. In the past it was more or less the same army which was either on the offensive or the defensive, depending on its strength and on the current fortunes of war, but, for reasons which will presently be made clear, a much sharper distinction between offensive and defensive forces seems to be in prospect for the future.

The force delegated to the retaliatory attack with atomic bombs will have to be maintained in rather sharp isolation from the national community. Its functions must not be compromised in the slightest by the demands for relief of struck areas. Whether its operations are with aircraft or rockets or both, it will have to be spread over a large number of widely dispersed reservations, each of considerable area, in which the bombs and their carriers are secreted and as far as possible protected by storage underground. These reservations should have a completely independent system of inter-communications, and the commander of the force should have a sufficient autonomy of authority to be able to act as soon as he has established with certainty the fact that the country is being hit with atomic bombs. The supreme command may by then have been eliminated, or its communications disrupted.

Before discussing the character of the force set apart for the job of invasion, it is necessary to consider whether invasion and occupation remain indispensable to victory in an era of atomic energy. Certain scientists have argued privately that they are not, that a nation committing aggression with atomic bombs would have so paralyzed its opponent as to make invasion wholly superfluous. It might be alleged that such an argument does not give due credit to the atomic bomb, since it neglects the necessity of preventing or minimizing retaliation in kind. If the experience with the V-1 and V-2 launching sites in World War II means anything at all, it indicates that only occupation of such sites will finally prevent their being used. Perhaps the greater destructiveness of the atomic bomb as compared with the bombs used against the V-1 and V-2 sites will make an essential difference in this respect, but it should be remembered that thousands of tons of bombs were dropped òn those sites. At any rate, it is unlikely that any aggressor will be able to count upon eliminating with his initial blow the enemy's entire means of retaliation. If he knows the location of the crucial areas, he will seek to have his troops descend upon and seize them.

But even apart from the question of direct retaliation with atomic bombs, invasion to consolidate the effects of an atomic bomb attack will still be necessary. A nation which had inflicted enormous human and material damage upon another would find it intolerable to stop short of eliciting from the latter an acknowledgment of defeat implemented by a readiness to accept control. Wars, in other words, are fought to be terminated, and to be terminated definitely.

To be sure, a nation may admit defeat and agree to occupation before its homeland is actually invaded, as the Japanese did. But it by no means follows that such will be the rule. Japan was completely defeated strategically before the atomic bombs were used against her. She not only lacked means of retaliation with that particular weapon but was without hope of being able to take aggressive action of any kind or of ameliorating her desperate military position to the slightest degree. There is no reason to suppose that a nation which had made reasonable preparations for war with atomic bombs would inevitably be in a mood to surrender after suffering the first blow.

An invasion designed to prevent large-scale retaliation with atomic bombs to any considerable degree would have to be incredibly swift and sufficiently powerful to overwhelm instantly any opposition. Moreover, it would have to descend in one fell swoop upon points scattered throughout the length and breadth of the enemy territory. The question arises whether such an operation is possible, especially across broad water barriers, against any great power which is not completely asleep and which has sizable armed forces at its disposal. It is clear that existing types of forces can be much more easily reorganized to resist the kind of invasion here envisaged than to enable them to conduct so rapid an offensive.

Extreme swiftness of invasion would demand aircraft for transport and supply rather than surface vessels guarded by sea power. But the necessity of speed does not itself create the conditions under which an invasion solely by air can be successful, especially against large and well-organized forces deployed over considerable space. In the recent war the specialized air-borne infantry divisions comprised a very small proportion of the armies of each of the belligerents. The bases from which they were launched were in every case relatively close to the objective, and except at Crete their mission was always to co-operate with much larger forces approaching by land or sea. To be sure, if the air forces are relieved by the atomic bomb of the burden of devoting great numbers of aircraft to strategic bombing with ordinary bombs, they will be able to accept to a much greater extent than heretofore the task of serving as a medium of transport and supply for the infantry. But it should be noticed that the enormous extension of range for bombing purposes which the atomic bomb makes possible does not apply to the transport of troops and supplies.* For such operations distance remains a formidable barrier.

The invasion and occupation of a great country solely or even chiefly by air would be an incredibly difficult task even if one assumes a minimum of air opposition. The magnitude of the preparations necessary for such an operation might make very dubious the chance of achieving the required measure of surprise. It may well prove that the difficulty of con-

* See above, pp. 36-40.

solidating by invasion the advantages gained through atomic bomb attack may act as an added and perhaps decisive deterrent to launching such an attack, especially since delay or failure would make retaliation all the more probable. But all hinges on the quality of preparation of the intended victim. If it has not prepared itself for atomic bomb warfare, the initial devastating attack will undoubtedly paralyze it and make its conquest easy even by a small invading force. And if it has not prepared itself for such warfare its helplessness will no doubt be sufficiently apparent before the event to invite aggression.

It is obvious that the force set apart for invasion or counter-invasion purposes will have to be relatively small, completely professional, and trained to the uttermost. But there must also be a very large force ready to resist and defeat invasion by the enemy. Here is the place for the citizen army, though it too must be comprised of trained men. There will be no time for training once the atomic bomb is used. Perhaps the old ideal of the "minute man" with his musket over his fireplace will be resurrected, in suitably modernized form. In any case, provision must be made for instant mobilization of trained reserves, for a maximum decentralization of arms and supply depots and of tactical authority, and for flexibility of operation. The trend towards greater mobility in land forces will have to be enormously accelerated, and strategic concentrations will have to be achieved in ways which avoid a high spatial density of military forces. And it must be again repeated, the arms, supplies, and vehicles of transportation to be depended upon are those which are *stockpiled* in as secure a manner as possible.

At this point it should be clear how drastic are the changes in character, equipment, and outlook which the traditional armed forces must undergo if they are to act as real deterrents to aggression in an age of atomic bombs. Whether or not the ideas presented above are entirely valid, they may perhaps stimulate those to whom our military security is entrusted to a more rigorous and better-informed kind of analysis which will reach sounder conclusions.

In the above discussion the reader will no doubt observe the absence of any considerable role for the Navy. And it is indisputable that the traditional concepts of military security which this country has developed over the last fifty years—in which the Navy was quite correctly avowed to be our "first line of defense"—seem due for revision, or at least for reconsideration.

For in the main sea power has throughout history proved decisive only when it was applied and exploited over a period of considerable time, and in atomic bomb warfare that time may well be lacking. Where wars are destined to be short, superior sea power may prove wholly useless. The French naval superiority over Prussia in 1870 did not prevent the collapse of the French armies in a few months, nor did Anglo-French naval superiority in 1940 prevent an even quicker conquest of France—one which might very well have ended the war.

World War II was in fact destined to prove the conflict in which sea power reached the culmination of its influence on history. The greatest of air wars and the one which saw the most titanic battles of all time on land was also the greatest of naval wars. It could hardly have been otherwise in a war which was truly global, where the pooling of resources of the great Allies depended upon their ability to traverse the highways of the seas and where American men and materials played a decisive part in remote theaters which could be reached with the requisite burdens only by ships. That period of greatest influence of sea power coincided with the emergence of the United States as the unrivaled first sea power of the world. But in many respects all this mighty power seems at the moment of its greatest glory to have become redundant.

Yet certain vital tasks may remain for fleets to perform even in a war of atomic bombs. One function which a superior fleet serves at every moment of its existence—and which therefore requires no time for its application—is the defense of coasts against sea-borne invasion. Only since the surrender of Germany, which made available to us the observations of members of the German High Command, has the public been made aware of something which had previously been obvious only to close students of the war—that it was the Royal Navy even more than the R.A.F. which kept Hitler from leaping across the Channel in 1940. The R.A.F. was too inferior to the Luftwaffe to have stopped an invasion by itself, and was important largely as a means of protecting the ships which the British would have interposed against any invasion attempt.

We have noticed that if swiftness were essential to the execution of any invasion plan, the invader would be obliged to depend mainly if not exclusively on transport by air. But we also observed that the difficulties in the way of such an enterprise might be such as to make it quite impossible of achievement. For the overseas movement of armies of any size and especially of their larger arms and supplies, sea-borne transportation proved quite indispensable even in an era when gigantic air forces had been built up by fully mobilized countries over four years of war. The difference in weight-carrying capacity between ships and planes is altogether too great to permit us to expect that it will become militarily unimportant in fifty years or more.* A force which is able to keep the enemy from using the seas is bound to remain for a long time an enormously important defense against overseas invasion.

However, the defense of coasts against sea-borne invasion is something which powerful and superior air forces are also able to carry out, though perhaps somewhat less reliably. If that were the sole function remaining to the Navy, the maintenance of huge fleets would hardly be justified. One must consider also the possible offensive value of a fleet which has atomic bombs at its disposal.

It was argued in the previous chapter that the atomic bomb enormously extends the effective range of bombing aircraft, and that even today the cities of every great power are inside effective bombing range of planes based on the territories of any other great power. The future development of aircraft will no doubt make bombing at six and seven thousand miles range even more feasible than it is today, and the tendency towards even higher cruising altitudes will ultimately bring planes above the levels where weather hazards are an important barrier to long flights. The ability to bring one's planes relatively close to the target before launching them, as naval carrier forces are able to do, must certainly diminish in military importance. But it will not wholly cease to be important, even for atomic bombs. Apparently today's carrier-borne aircraft cannot carry the atomic bomb, but no one would predict that they will remain unable to do so. And if the emphasis in vehicles is shifted from aircraft to long-range rockets, there will again be an enormous advantage in having one's missiles close to the target. It must be remembered that in so far as

* See Bernard Brodie, *A Guide to Naval Strategy*, 3rd ed., Princeton, Princeton University Press, 1944, p. 215.

advanced bases remain useful for atomic bomb attack, navies are indispensable for their security and maintenance.

Even more important, perhaps, is the fact that a fleet at sea is not easily located and even less easily destroyed. The ability to retaliate if attacked is certainly enhanced by having a bomb-launching base which cannot be plotted on a map. A fleet armed with atomic bombs which had disappeared into the vastness of the seas during a crisis would be just one additional element to give pause to an aggressor. It must, however, be again repeated that the possession of such a fleet or of advanced bases will probably *not be essential* to the execution of bombing missions at extreme ranges.

If there should be a war in which atomic bombs were not used—a possibility which must always be taken into account —the fleet would retain all the functions it has ever exercised. We know also that there are certain policing obligations entailed in various American commitments, especially that of the United Nations Organization. The idea of using atomic bombs for such policing operations, as some have advocated, is not only callous in the extreme but stupid. Even general bombing with ordinary bombs is the worst possible way to. coerce states of relatively low military power, for it combines the maximum of indiscriminate destruction with the minimum of direct control.*

At any rate, if the United States retains a strong navy, as

* There has been a good deal of confusion between automaticity and immediacy in the execution of sanctions. Those who stress the importance of bringing military pressure to bear *at once* in the case of aggression are as a rule really less concerned with having sanctions imposed quickly than they are with having them appear certain. To be sure, the atomic bomb gives the necessity for quickness of military response a wholly new meaning; but in the kinds of aggression with which the UNO is now set up to deal, atomic bombs are not likely to be important for a very long time.

it no doubt will, we should insist upon that navy retaining the maximum flexibility and adaptability to new conditions. The public can assist in this process by examining critically any effort of the service to freeze naval armaments at high quantitative levels, for there is nothing more deadening to technological progress especially in the navy than the maintenance in active or reserve commission of a number of ships far exceeding any current needs. It is not primarily a question of how much money is spent or how much manpower is absorbed but rather of how efficiently money and manpower are being utilized. Money spent on keeping in commission ships built for the last war is money which might be devoted to additional research and experimentation, and existing ships discourage new construction. For that matter, money spent on maintaining a huge navy is perhaps money taken from other services and other instruments of defense which may be of far greater relative importance in the early stages of a future crisis than they have been in the past.

The Dispersion of Cities as a Defense Against the Bomb

We have seen that the atomic bomb drastically alters the significance of distance *between* rival powers. It also raises to the first order of importance as a factor of power the precise spatial arrangement of industry and population *within* each country. The enormous concentration of power in the individual bomb, irreducible below a certain high limit except through deliberate and purposeless wastage of efficiency, is such as to demand for the full realization of that power targets in which the enemy's basic strength is comparably concentrated. Thus, the city is a made-to-order target, and the degree of urbanization of a country furnishes a rough index of its relative vulnerability to the atomic bomb.

And since a single properly aimed bomb can destroy a

city of 100,000 about as effectively as it can one of 25,000, it is obviously an advantage to the attacker if the units of 25,000 are combined into units of 100,000. Moreover, a city is after all a fairly integrated community in terms of vital services and transportation. If half to two-thirds of its area is obliterated, one may count on it that the rest of the city will, under prevailing conditions, be effectively prostrated. Thus, the more the population and industry of a state are concentrated into urban areas and the larger individually those concentrations become, the fewer are the atomic bombs necessary to effect their destruction.*

In 1940 there were in the United States five cities with 1,000,000 or more inhabitants (one of which, Los Angeles, is spread out over more than 400 square miles), nine cities between 500,000 and 1,000,000, twenty-three cities between 250,000 and 500,000, fifty-five between 100,000 and 250,000, and one hundred and seven between 50,000 and 100,000 population. Thus, there were ninety-two cities with a population of 100,000 and over, and these contained approximately 29 per cent of our total population. Reaching down to the level of 50,000 or more, the number of cities is increased to 199 and the population contained in them is

---

* In this respect the atomic bomb differs markedly from the TNT bomb, due to the much smaller radius of destruction of the latter. The amount of destruction the TNT bomb accomplishes depends not on what is in the general locality but on what is in the immediate proximity of the burst. A factory of given size requires a given number of bombs to destroy it regardless of the size of the city in which it is situated. To be sure, the "misses" count for more in a large city, but from the point of view of the defender there are certain compensating advantages in having the objects to be defended gathered in large concentrations. It makes a good deal easier the effective deployment of fighter patrols and antiaircraft guns. But the latter advantage does not count for much in the case of atomic bombs, since, as argued in the previous chapter, it is practically hopeless to expect fighter planes and antiaircraft guns to stop atomic attack so completely as to save the city.

increased to some 34 per cent. Naturally, the proportion of the nation's factories contained in those 199 cities is far greater than the proportion of the population.

This is a considerably higher ratio of urban to non-urban population than is to be found in any other great power except Great Britain. Regardless of what international measures are undertaken to cope with the atomic bomb menace, the United States cannot afford to remain complacent about it. This measure of vulnerability, to be sure, must be qualified by a host of other considerations, such as the architectural character of the cities,* the manner in which they are individually laid out, and above all the degree of interdependence of industry and services between different parts of the individual city, between the city and its hinterland, and between the different urban areas. Each city is, together with its hinterland,

* The difference between American and Japanese cities in vulnerability to bombing attack has unquestionably been exaggerated. Most commentators who stress the difference forget the many square miles of predominantly wooden frame houses to be found in almost any American city. And those who were impressed with the pictures of ferro-concrete buildings standing relatively intact in the midst of otherwise total devastation at Hiroshima and Nagasaki will not be comforted by Dr. Philip Morrison's testimony before the McMahon Committee on December 6, 1945. Dr. Morrison, who inspected both cities, testified that the interiors of those buildings were completely destroyed and the people in them killed. Brick buildings, he pointed out, and even steel-frame buildings with brick walls proved extremely vulnerable. "Of those people within a thousand yards of the blast," he added, "about one in every house or two escaped death from blast or burn. But they died anyway from the effects of the rays emitted at the instant of explosion." He expressed himself as convinced that an American city similarly bombed "would be as badly damaged as a Japanese city, though it would look less wrecked from the air."

No doubt Dr. Morrison is exaggerating in the opposite direction. Obviously there must be a considerable difference among structures in their capacity to withstand blast from atomic bombs and to shelter the people within them. But that difference is likely to make itself felt mostly in the peripheral portions of a blasted area. Within a radius of one mile from the center of burst it is not likely to be of consequence.

an economic and social organism, with a character somewhat distinct from other comparable organisms.

A number of students have been busily at work evolving plans for the dispersal of our cities and the resettlement of our population and industries in a manner calculated to reduce the number of casualties and the amount of physical destruction that a given number of atomic bombs can cause. In their most drastic form these plans, many of which will shortly reach the public eye, involve the redistribution of our urban concentrations into "linear" or "cellular" cities.

The linear or "ribbon" city is one which is very much longer than it is wide, with its industries and services as well as population distributed along its entire length. Of two cities occupying nine square miles, the one which was one mile wide and nine long would clearly suffer less destruction from one atomic bomb, however perfectly aimed, than the one which was three miles square. The principle of the cellular city, on the other hand, would be realized if a city of the same nine-square-miles size were dispersed into nine units of about one square mile each and situated in such a pattern that each unit was three to five miles distant from another.

Such "planning" seems to this writer to show a singular lack of appreciation of the forces which have given birth to our cities and caused them to expand and multiply. There are always important geographic and economic reasons for the birth and growth of a city and profound political and social resistance to interference with the results of "natural" growth. Cities like New York and Chicago are not going to dissolve themselves by direction from the government, even if they could find areas to dissolve themselves into. As a linear city New York would be as long as the state of Pennsylvania, and would certainly have no organic meaning as a city. "Solu-

tions" like these are not only politically and socially un-
realistic but physically impossible.

Nor does it seem that the military benefits would be at
all commensurate with the cost, even if the programs were
physically possible and politically feasible. We have no way
of estimating the absolute limit to the number of bombs which
will be available to an attacker, but we know that unless
production of atomic bombs is drastically limited or completely suppressed by international agreement, the number
available in the world will progress far more rapidly and
involve infinitely less cost of production and use than any
concurrent dissolution or realignment of cities designed to
offset that multiplication. If a city three miles square can be
largely destroyed by one well aimed bomb, it will require
only three well spaced bombs to destroy utterly a city nine
miles long and one mile wide. And the effort required in producing and delivering the two extra bombs is infinitesimal
compared to that involved in converting a square city into a
linear one.

Unquestionably an invulnerable home front is beyond
price, but there is no hope of gaining such a thing in any
case. What the city-dispersion-planners are advocating is a
colossal effort and expenditure (estimated by some of them
to amount to 300 billions of dollars) and a ruthless suppression of the inevitable resistance to such dispersion in order to
achieve what is at best a marginal diminution of vulnerability.
No such program has the slightest chance of being accepted.

However, it is clear that the United States can be made a
good deal less vulnerable to atomic bomb attack than it is at
present, that such reduction can be made great enough to
count as a deterrent in the calculations of future aggressors,
and that it can be done at immeasurably less economic and

social cost and in a manner which will arouse far less resistance than any of the drastic solutions described above.

But first we must make clear in our minds what our ends
are. Our first purpose, clearly, is to reduce the likelihood that
a sudden attack upon us will be so paralyzing in its effects as
to rob us of all chance of effective resistance. And we are
interested in sustaining our power to retaliate primarily to
make the prospect of aggression much less attractive to the
aggressor. In other words, we wish to reduce our vulnerability
in order to reduce the chances of our being hit at all. Secondly, we wish to reduce the number of casualties and of
material damage which will result from an attack upon us
of any given level of intensity.

These two ends are of course intimately interrelated, but
they are also to a degree distinguishable. And it is necessary
to pursue that distinction. We should notice also that while
most industries are ultimately convertible or applicable to
the prosecution of war, it is possible to distinguish between
industries in the degree of their immediate indispensability
for war purposes. Finally, while industries attract population
and vice versa, modern means of transportation make possible
a locational flexibility between an industry and those people
who service it and whom it serves.

Thus it would seem that the first step in reducing our
national vulnerability is to catalog the industries especially
and immediately necessary to atomic bomb warfare—a relatively small proportion of the total—and to move them out
of our cities entirely. Where those industries utilize massive
plants, those plants should as far as possible be broken up
into smaller units. Involved in such a movement would be the
labor forces which directly service those industries. The great
mass of remaining industries can be left where they are within
the cities, but the population which remains with them can be

encouraged, through the further development of suburban building, to spread over a greater amount of space. Whole areas deserving to be condemned in any case could be converted into public parks or even airfields. The important element in reducing casualties is after all not the shape of the individual city but the spatial density of population within it.

Furthermore, the systems providing essential services, such as those supplying or distributing food, fuel, water, communications, and medical care, could and should be rearranged geographically. Medical services, for example, tend to be concentrated not merely within cities but in particular sections of those cities. The conception which might govern the relocation of services within the cities is that which has long been familiar in warship design—*compartmentation.* And obviously where essential services for large rural areas are unnecessarily concentrated in cities, they should be moved out of them. That situation pertains especially to communications.

It would be desirable also to initiate a series of tests on the resistance of various kinds of structures to atomic bomb blast. It might be found that one type of structure has far greater resistance than another without being correspondingly more costly. If so, it would behoove the government to encourage that kind of construction in new building. Over a long period of years, the gain in resistance to attack of our urban areas might be considerable, and the costs involved would be marginal.

So far as safeguarding the lives of urban populations is concerned, the above suggestions are meaningful only for the initial stages of an attack. They would permit a larger number to survive the initial attacks and thereby to engage in that exodus from the cities by which alone their lives can be safeguarded. And the preparation for such an exodus would involve a vast program for the construction of temporary shelter in the countryside and the planting of emergency stores of food. What we would then have in effect is the dispersal not of cities but of air-raid shelters.

The writer is here presenting merely some general principles which might be considered in any plan for reducing our general vulnerability. Obviously, the actual content of such a plan would have to be derived from the findings of intensive study by experts in a rather large number of fields. It is imperative, however, that such a study be got under way at once. The country is about to launch into a great construction program, both for dwellings and for expanding industries. New sources of power are to be created by new dams. The opportunities thus afforded for "vulnerability control" are tremendous, and should not be permitted to slip away—at least not without intensive study of their feasibility.

Those who have been predicting attacks of 15,000 atomic bombs and upward will no doubt look with jaundiced eye upon these speculations. For they will say that a country so struck will not merely be overwhelmed but for all practical purposes will vanish. Those areas not directly struck will be covered with clouds of radioactive dust under which all living beings will perish.

No doubt there is a possibility that an initial attack can be so overwhelming as to void all opportunity of resistance or retaliation, regardless of the precautions taken in the target state. Not *all* eventualities can be provided against. But preparation to launch such an attack would have to be on so gigantic a scale as to eliminate all chances of surprise. Moreover, while there is perhaps little solace in the thought that the lethal effect of radioactivity is generally considerably delayed, the idea will not be lost on the aggressor. The more horrible the results of attack, the more he will be deterred by even a marginal chance of retaliation.

Finally, one can scarcely assume that the world will remain either long ignorant of or acquiescent in the accumulations of such vast stockpiles of atomic bombs. If existing international organization should prove inadequate to cope with the problem of controlling bomb production—and it would be premature to predict that it will prove inadequate, especially in view of the favorable official and public reception accorded the Board of Consultants' report of March 16, 1946—a runaway competition in such production would certainly bring new forces into the picture. In this chapter and in the preceding one, the writer has been under no illusions concerning the adequacy of a purely military solution.

Concern with the efficiency of the national defenses is obviously inadequate in itself as an approach to the problem of the atomic bomb. In so far as such concern prevails over the more fundamental consideration of eliminating war or at least of reducing the chance of its recurrence, it clearly defeats its purpose. That has perhaps always been true, but it is a truth which is less escapable today than ever before. Nations can still save themselves by their own armed strength from subjugation, but not from a destruction so colossal as to involve complete ruin. Nevertheless, it also remains true that a nation which is as well girded for its own defense as is reasonably possible is not a tempting target to an aggressor. Such a nation is therefore better able to pursue actively that progressive improvement in world affairs by which alone it finds its true security.

THE SECURITY PROBLEM IN THE LIGHT
OF ATOMIC ENERGY

By BERNARD BRODIE[1]

THE last time I had the honor of leading one of the Harris Institute round tables, I was the first speaker in five round tables who turned up with a formal paper. This time I came prepared to give some informal comments, and I find that again, unwillingly, I am making a departure from the normal. Of course I am solaced by the fact that Mr. deKiewiet was able yesterday to do quite as well without a paper as he did with one.

I was also very much taken yesterday with Mr. deKiewiet's remark that there is at present no strategy. I think that is true not only as concerns the literature and doctrine inherited from the past and the political policy based thereon but also as concerns the very goals and purposes of strategy. In other words, strategy seems to have lost its entire reason for being. Certainly, the famous remark of Clausewitz, that "war is a continuation of policy," has now become a complete absurdity.

In a war in which both sides use the atomic bomb it is hardly conceivable that the victor, if there is one, can derive any benefits, even negative ones, at all commensurate with the costs. Whether that was true or not before is arguable; it is now inescapable.

General Walter Bedell Smith in a recent series of articles appearing in the *Saturday Evening Post* pointed out that the American Army in Germany was following the age-old policy, which has always been basic to strategy, of destroying the enemy's armed forces—and there again we see one of the basic tenets of strategy collapsing. Notice, however, that the situation is very different if one side has a monopoly of the bomb or if, by its initiative in using it, that side gains a monopoly of the ability to use it.

That last point illustrates one justification of the effort to conceive of what it is which replaces strategy in the atomic age. We want to know, first of all, whether the atomic bomb does or does not facilitate

[1] Institute of International Studies, Yale University.

[89]

aggression and what we can do about it. The bomb might under some circumstances facilitate aggression; but if certain adjustments to it are made, it might also have the contrary effect.

We want to know, second, the minimum requirements of any international system for the control of atomic energy. I hope Mr. Fox will be present with us before very long, because he has been doing a lot of work on just that problem.

I think we want to know, third, whether there is any useful course of defense policy left to us in the event of a failure to attain a system possessing those minimum requirements. In that connection it seems to me that the Lilienthal plan, when considered as a sample of human ingenuity applied to a great social and political problem, is not only an admirable achievement but a magnificent one. However, before we lose ourselves in rejoicing, we should consider that many aspects of that plan are of such nature that one can hardly be optimistic concerning acceptance of the plan on the part of certain powers whose co-operation is indispensable.

Last night I was much interested in the discussion concerning the allaying of suspicion in negotiations with Russia. It seems to me that it is one thing to talk in the abstract about allaying suspicion, in which case you do not have a very profound problem; it is quite another thing when you consider that you always have to deal with that problem in connection with the discussion of very vital and crucial issues. And I can think of no issue more likely to provoke suspicion than our proposal that we and a number of other countries send representatives into the Soviet Union to conduct large-scale industrial, exploratory, and even policing operations. And it does not help one bit that while we make that proposal we have in our left hand a sizable quantity of atomic bombs and are also continuing to produce them. I will admit that we could rectify that latter liability if we wanted to and if we felt the circumstances warranted it; but I think you would still have a very grave problem of persuading the Russians that there was not a very serious "Mickey Finn" in there somewhere.

Another problem which we must consider is: What do we do in the event of, and how do we prepare against, the possible collapse of a system which is put into operation? And that includes also the whole question of sanctions, something which Mr. Baruch added to the Lilienthal report when he presented it before the Atomic Energy Commission. A corollary to that question is: How can we by our

[90]

domestic policy effectively implement the kind of international system which may be devised? It is clear, for example, that if we can so organize our own defenses that the aggressor needs a large number of bombs in order to achieve a decisive end, and if we achieve a situation also where the secret manufacture of only a few bombs is of rather small consequence, there is a much firmer foundation for an international security system than exists in a situation in which only a few bombs might have decisive effects.

A final question which I think is presented is: What aspects of our present diplomacy are based on tenets inherited from the past and are now clearly obsolete?

These and comparable questions can be answered, if at all, only by a study of the bomb as a weapon of war. To put the issue epigrammatically, war is unthinkable but not impossible, and therefore we must think about it.

Now I turn to a few basic propositions which I have already presented and expatiated on elsewhere and which some of you may be somewhat familiar with already. The first is that in the atomic bomb we have a weapon of which one to ten units is sufficient to destroy any city in the world.

I had a bit of a conversation with Mr. Pasvolsky yesterday afternoon, and he objected to our use of the term the "absolute weapon" in speaking of the atomic bomb, and I think I might take a minute to explain why we use the term.

When you have a weapon as effective as this one is, it does not make much difference whether you succeed in devising one which is more effective. I have been completely unimpressed by the discussion that this bomb is only a beginning and that ten or twenty years from now we shall have one a hundred times more powerful. I do not think the order of difference between that situation and the present one is at all comparable to the difference between the atomic bomb and the preatomic-bomb era. If someone challenged my figures about one to ten bombs—if he said it would take not ten bombs to destroy New York but only two—I would say that that is a matter of indifference militarily. If he said it took not ten but twenty, I would say that that also is a matter of relative indifference militarily, because an enemy could deliver twenty bombs about as easily as he could deliver two, assuming he had a large number of bombs to begin with.

One of the implications of the proposition I have just made about one to ten bombs being sufficient to destroy any city is that, with air

[91]

forces no greater than those which existed in the recent war, it is at least physically possible for any power to destroy all, or at least most, of the cities of any other great power; and the second implication is that industry as now organized would be the first casualty of such an attack. In other words, the kind of warfare which we have conducted in the past, which relied very heavily on war-expanded industries, would not be possible under such conditions.

The second proposition is that no defense against the atomic bomb is known, and the possibilities of its existence in the future are exceedingly remote. That latter point sounds as though one were putting on the astrologer's cap. We certainly cannot be dogmatic about the future, but what we can say very definitely is that the experience of the past, which superficially leads one to believe that aggressive weapons have always been successfully countered, breaks down under analysis as misleading or irrelevant.

I have in mind Admiral Nimitz' speech before the Washington Monument on last Navy Day, in which he admonished his hearers to remember that there never has been a weapon to which man has been unable to devise a counterweapon. I think, if you look at history very carefully, you will find that, regardless of its relevance to the future, that statement itself is not true. What we have always had in the past is an adjustment to new weapons which tended to qualify those weapons, and such adjustments will not be sufficient in terms of the atomic bomb.

I could give one example. The British congratulated themselves that their defense against the V-1 weapon was, on the whole, quite effective, and I think it was. On the banner day, so far as concerns the British, they succeeded in shooting down 97 out of 101 bombs launched against England. But if the other four had been atomic bombs, then the survivors in London would have had little cause to congratulate themselves.

The third proposition is that superiority neither in numbers of bombs nor in numbers of air forces, let alone armies and navies, is sufficient to guarantee security. We know, for example, that if one side has five hundred bombs and has reasonable expectation of being able to deliver a large part of those five hundred, the opponent is not protected by the fact that he may himself have five thousand. We know also that inferior air forces, if they are willing to pay the cost, can usually penetrate to a target—at least, a certain proportion of their numbers can succeed in penetrating. That was demonstrated over

[92]

and over again in the recent war. The concept of command of the air, in other words, breaks down.

Of course, a great many persons have often questioned in the past whether armed forces really guaranteed the security of the country which possessed them, even superior armed forces. Naturally, that is a large problem, with all kinds of ramifications; but I would say that, if we put it in a limited context and take at least one important historical example, namely, Britain, it seems pretty clear that the record there is that her command of the sea protected her territory from invasion from 1066 to the present, during which time she succeeded in invading the Continent a large number of times.

You might say that England was engaged in a lot of wars during that period, which is true. Some of those wars had imperial motives, but others were designed to *maintain on an economical level* those defenses which Britain found sufficient to her security—which is what I conceive to have been the purpose of the balance-of-power principle.

The British experience is certainly relevant to the American case, and I think that this country prior to the atomic bomb could have felt some assurance that, with the armaments it was capable of building, it had a fairly effective guaranty against devastation or invasion of its homeland. That does not mean, of course, that we should have been ready and willing to live in the kind of world that would have existed if we had retired to our own defenses.

The next proposition I want to bring in is the effect of the atomic bomb on the ranges even of existing aircraft, not to mention long-range rockets, which are certain to be developed within the next several decades. For various technical reasons which I do not think it profitable to go into at this point, with ordinary bombs the effective bombing range of an aircraft is about one-quarter or less of its straight-line cruising radius. With the atomic bomb, on the other hand, the effective bombing radius is extended to practically its entire straight-line cruising radius without pay load. In other words, the B-29, for example, to be effective in day-to-day strategic bombing with ordinary bombs, has to be located within at least 1,500 miles of its target. With an atomic bomb I should expect it to be able to deliver the missile at a distance of nearly the 8,000 miles which it has already succeeded in flying. That, of course, would involve sacrifice of the plane and crew; but in the callously utilitarian standards of military bookkeeping, it is not likely that belligerents using the

[93]

atomic bomb and delivering it by aircraft would be particularly interested in getting back after each mission the particular plane or crew which delivered it. Rear Admiral Parsons, Admiral Blandy's deputy, rejected that idea when it was first suggested to him; but I noticed recently that in a speech in Honolulu, Assistant Secretary of War for Air, Mr. Symington, was advancing exactly that idea.

The final proposition, the fifth, scarcely needs discussion at this time. It is pretty clear by now that there is no question at all of world-wide scarcity of the materials for producing the bomb. Relative to the tremendous destructive powers of the bomb, such materials are not scarce, though their distribution is still incompletely known.

Finally, we all know that it is only a matter of time before there is multiple possession of the bomb among the great powers. How much time it will take is still in question, but the estimates range from three to about twenty years.

These propositions have led me to the conclusion that military forces can no longer defend a territory in the sense of offering protection; the only defense possible is of the deterrent type. In other words, defense becomes synonymous with measures to guarantee the ability to retaliate if attacked and also of measures to diminish the ease with which the enemy can overwhelm the country by his attack.

Many people have reacted violently against this suggestion, not least the chancellor of the University of Chicago. It is true that a defense based on deterrence is of less than no value if it fails to deter. It is also true that the reign of mutual fear which such a system implies would unquestionably produce psychoses, which, in turn, would have effects, the direction and magnitude of which are unpredictable, almost unimaginable. On the other hand, I think we should not for those reasons too readily write off the real deterrent value of the ability to retaliate against an aggressor, provided that that ability is somehow maintained.

What, then, are the final effects on policy? Of course, they are numerous, but I have noted down for submission to you only three.

The first of these is that the kind of analysis which the foregoing represents in brief form indicates that in an atomic-bomb war there would be almost no scope whatever for sea power. In that connection the tests at Bikini are completely beside the point. They represent an effort to gauge tactical effects when we are interested in strategic effects. It seems to me that it is a matter of no consequence at all that

[94]

a navy is completely immune to the atomic bomb if the whole reason for its existence collapses; and it seems to me also that a navy which is operating from a country which has lost its entire industry will soon lose both its ability to operate and its reason for operating.

That is an issue of tremendous significance for the United States. The United States has just inherited from Great Britain the mantle of leading sea power of the world. I think also, contrary to the opinions of a great many observers, that sea power reached its apogee in the war just ended. It was often spoken of as an obsolescent force, of less importance than other forces, especially air power. I can think of no war in history in which sea power played a greater role. I think there was very little in the way of competition with air force. I would submit merely that the Allied air attack on Germany and the Allied air attack on Japan would both have been impossible without British-American command of the seas. The ability of the three major powers to marshal and combine their forces and choose first one enemy to concentrate against and then the other was also a function of their command of the seas; and, of course, a large amount of the relatively high degree of security which the United States enjoyed was the result of its great sea power.

The second point is that geographical distance loses much of its importance as a barrier against attack. In his book, *The Super Powers*, my colleague Mr. Fox pointed out that the great distance separating the Soviet Union from the United States was such as to render war between them unlikely to achieve decisive results. That fact was itself a considerable impedance or obstacle to any outbreak of conflict. I think that that statement not only was true for the time at which he wrote it but would have remained true indefinitely for as long as we can foresee—if it were not for the development of the atomic bomb. I think also that that proposition is not entirely obliterated by the appearance of the atomic bomb, but I am sure Mr. Fox, who is now with us, would be the first to admit that it has been very vitally affected.

Third, I should like to call your attention to the consequences of the collapse of the threat of war as an instrument of policy on the part of responsible governments. Or, to put it in another way, which is perhaps less offensive to our consciences, the threat of war now becomes a much greater instrument in the hands of irresponsible governments and is an instrument of which responsible governments are practically deprived.

[95]

The threat of war, it seems to me, on the part of responsible governments has had a tremendous utility in the past. It has prevented a lot of instances of rape which would otherwise have occurred. It obviously has not prevented war, though it probably did reduce the frequency of wars. Now we have the situation in which a government comparable to the Hitler government could pursue a line of policy comparable to that pursued by the Hitler government in 1938, and the cards would be stacked even more in its favor than was true in the past. In other words, the war with atomic bombs becomes so unthinkable that a government possessed of its senses and possessed also of some feeling of responsibility both to its own people and to the world could be nothing but appalled at even the thought of using a threat of force, in the knowledge that such a threat, if realized, might provoke an atomic war.

DISCUSSION OF GENERAL SECURITY

THE discussion of the problem of general security centered about the effects of atomic energy in military strategy and world politics and the method for preventing the use of that energy in war. The problem of general security also arose in connection with the discussion of the relations of the great powers and the situation in particular parts of the world, considered in other sections of this volume. There was no detailed discussion of the United Nations, but the role of that organization in channeling, or perhaps eventually superseding, "power politics," in effecting a regulation of armaments, and in contributing to the development of a sense of world community were considered.

The participants varied in the optimism with which they envisaged future security. Some leaned to the view that the atomic bomb had made the power equilibrium less stable but that a system of effective international or world control was not to be anticipated. Others were more confident that the technical problems of atomic energy control could be solved, that the political problem of winning acceptance for a control system was not hopeless, that the germs of world community were to be found and could be stimulated by the exigencies of the present situation, and that, in any case, the increasing destructiveness of war even to a victor made its initiation less probable.

FINANCE AND COLLECTIVE SECURITY

Mr. WILLIAM ROGERS: What would be the effect of channeling American wealth into the specialized agencies of the United Nations which would work toward international reconstruction and development as opposed to a policy of using our wealth by granting conditional loans to Great Britain and France and making that wealth an instrument of national policy, supporting the Western world as against Russia or something of that sort? Do we not have those two choices of using our wealth to develop a stable world, which is presumably what the United States desires?

Mr. deKiewiet: That is a searching question. The answer, I suppose, would have to lie in our lack of assurance—I won't say confi-

[97]

dence as yet—but our lack of assurance in the United Nations, in the lack of compatible policies between the co-operating powers. If, for example—and I think most of us would be very happy to see a development of that sort—the United States were to put considerable amounts of money at the disposal of instrumentalities of the United Nations, it would be necessary, of course, that the Russians and the British, the Russians certainly, make a comparable contribution, not in amount but in spirit. We would also have to have the assurance that the money would be used in a manner generally acceptable to United States policies; and, as long as the United Nations organization is in its critical, unbalanced position, I suppose some doubt would attach to that policy—at least it would in my own mind. I can see very clearly the disadvantage in using American funds and devoting them to policies over which America has only indirect influence.

MR. BRODIE: This is something about which the State Department itself can do extremely little; but it seems to me that, when we talk about the economic role which the United States must play, we always have to keep in mind the very close connection between our foreign policy and economic events in this country. It seems to me, for example, that one of the great dangers to our foreign relations today is the inflation which is now proceeding in this country, which, first of all, makes more acute the threat of future domestic instability —which will have its repercussions abroad—and which also makes it very difficult for this country to offer the kind of assistance that the government as such might be meaning to offer.

POWER POLITICS AND COLLECTIVE SECURITY

MR. LEO PASVOLSKY: Someone said in one of our sessions that Britain has lost her security. I think that is true. In a sense we have all lost our sense of security, not only Britain. But that raises a question in my mind as to what we mean by the term "security system"—"Eastern security system," "Western security system," and things of that sort—and particularly what we mean when we talk about Britain's having an alternative as between a Western security system and something else.

As I understood the speaker, the thought goes back to Churchill's proposal to France, to the Smuts plan, and things of that sort as an attempt to build a broader industrial and economic base for British power. I, myself, never put much stock in that. I think that means even less today than it did at that time.

[98]

There was some mention made in the discussion as to the different status of nationalism in eastern and in western Europe. I think that is rather important. I wonder whether our speaker really thinks that nationalism has evolved in eastern Europe. I am not satisfied that the Russian experiment of forcible abatement of nationalism is really going to go deep.

I would like to suggest that it is not nationalism as such that is our difficulty; it is lack of a concept of responsibility attaching to nationalism. I think our trouble before the war was not that there were national units but that there were too many national units which were irresponsible in their international relations. That was true of the big powers, and it was true of small powers.

If our problem is the channeling of nationalism into terms of international responsibility, then it is a little difficult for me to see how a Western system of security can be created, or how what we call an Eastern system of security is really a system of security. Security for whom? After all, we do have to consider that, when we talk about a group seeking security, it is not merely the big partner in that group that is interested in security but the small partners, too. If we start with the central thesis that even Great Britain, with her still great resources, still great potentiality in the world of today, has lost a feeling of security, I think it is rather easy to see what is happening to the other countries.

MR. deKiewiet: Wouldn't you have to admit, Mr. Pasvolsky, that the smaller powers, particularly, have to define their international responsibility in response to clear policies enunciated by the larger powers? If, for example, there has been some awakening of nationalism in eastern Europe, the governments concerned there, on the whole, recognize that they can have no effective foreign policy independent of that of Russia.

My suggestion that we might be interested in a Western security system was not that we should impose the Russian equivalent of an Eastern system in western Europe but that we missed an opportunity during the war of getting a voluntary acceptance of those interests.

MR. Pasvolsky: You notice what the Swedes have said about joining the United Nations: they want to join the United Nations, but they don't want to join blocs within the United Nations. I think it was a rather enlightening statement.

The whole United Nations idea is based on the proposition that there is no security for anybody except in a general system—and not

[99]

105

too much there, unless certain conditions are fulfilled. If the countries of western Europe are to seek their security in Britain, they won't have it; if they are going to go beyond Britain and seek their security in the United States, they may have it only to the extent that the United States and Russia are not in conflict. The same thing is true of the countries of eastern Europe, all due allowance being made for the myth of creating the "security zone."

I think what you said about nineteenth-century conceptions applied to twentieth-century reality ought to be applied to the whole concept of regional security groups. We have a new situation from the security point of view.

I am afraid that the more we talk about the possibility of these balanced systems of security, the more difficulty we are going to get into. Remember that the British and French governments last December signed an agreement, in connection with the Syrian government, in which they used precisely that terminology: that they will withdraw their troops as soon as a regional system of security for the Near East is established by the United Nations. Even the little Syrians and Lebanese came back and said: "You are setting down conditions which are unfulfillable because that concept has no meaning." And from their point of view it certainly had no meaning.

Mr. deKiewiet: If I may interrupt, aren't you using "security" in two definitions? You are referring to security as an absolute thing, in which case we will agree with you immediately that there is no such thing as security for the United States, Great Britain, or Lebanon. On the other hand, I suppose we are more accustomed to using the term "security" in a more relative sense.

Mr. Pasvolsky: There is no such thing as security in an absolute sense, because we do not have it in our internal relations and we do not have it in the best-governed country in the world. There is always an element of insecurity, of course; it is a question of degree. I think our big problem, Britain's big problem, and Russia's big problem is whether there is going to be more or less insecurity; and I have no doubt in my mind that the more Russia talks about an Eastern system of security and Britain talks about a Western system of security and we talk about a Western Hemisphere system of security and the British and French talk about a Near Eastern system of security, the more we create insecurity because we fail to get to the root of the whole matter.

Mr. deKiewiet: Which is?

[100]

MR. PASVOLSKY: Which is that there is going to be security in the world, there is going to be peace in the world, if the "big fellows" behave, and if the "little fellows" do not provide a pretext for the "big fellows" to misbehave. If we can't get that—and we can't legislate it—we just can't get security. We shall just have to live from hand to mouth as we have for a long time.

I was very much interested in the discussion of identity and disparity of our interests with Britain. Somebody said that there are disparities but there are bigger identities. To me that would be very important. Of course, there are going to be disparities. Of course, at every point we shall have to make the judgment, as was brought up here a while ago, as to whether a particular proposition, a particular point, is essential. There is, however, a great danger in carrying that too far, because when you start grading interests you may fall into a very difficult error of underestimating or overestimating, particularly underestimating.

It would not hurt us to say that we are so much involved in everything that happens in the world that we never know what a little spark might do somewhere because there are no longer any divisions, because each country has at least two frontiers, and when something starts at one frontier somebody else is affected on the next frontier. A little war may start a chain of war.

MR. BRODIE: I agree entirely with Mr. Pasvolsky's remark that there is no such condition as absolute security today. I would go further and say that relative security as we have known it in the past no longer exists. I would agree also with Mr. deKiewiet, that there is no longer any such thing as strategy. But, because there is no such thing as strategy, nations are bound, in so far as it does not look too ridiculous to them, to pursue their security in somewhat accustomed paths. I say that, not with approval or disapproval but merely as a statement of fact; but I think there is some justification for it in any case, particularly as we are discussing Great Britain. Britain, I think, is justified in feeling that a domination of the entire European Continent by Russia means less security than she has today, even if what she has today is very little indeed.

Second, it is the very expansionist character of what appears at least to be the Russian policy, or at least certain aspects of it, which prevents the working of the United Nations which Mr. Pasvolsky adduces as the only kind of security we can possibly have.

[101]

So I submit that one way in which to retard or halt that chain reaction to which Mr. Pasvolsky refers is in a large measure by concerning ourselves with the territorial expansion of those nations which seem to be going about it in an aggressive fashion. I should not say it is the only way but that it is the essential ingredient of any policy we might follow.

MR. FOX: I want to clarify my own position, just to indicate how completely I agree with Mr. Pasvolsky. I have said that I regarded a grouping of the Western bloc as something which would spontaneously occur when the other thing had failed—when the time had come that we no longer had diplomatic relations with the Soviet Union, if that time should come. It is true that our policy vis-à-vis Russia has to be firm enough so that the Russians see the need of coming to some agreement. It may be a very long time before we come to the position where we must say that every other way is closed and we must seek regional security. The only circumstances in which we would make that choice would be when the bigger prize had already been lost.

MR. DE KIEWIET: My remarks were not intended to be identified simply with an interest in a present or future security problem. Had a Western bloc been brought about at an earlier moment, it would not have been brought about as a counter to Russian policies. Now there is that danger, and I would agree with you. There might have been, however, an economic undertaking as well as a political undertaking very much more promising than we could possibly expect now. If there is anything that we need at the present moment it is an increase in production under harmonious conditions, and it was the harmony and productive quality of that association that we have lost, which is my principal regret.

MR. PASVOLSKY: I doubt whether it would have worked. There is a very curious limitation there.

MR. DE KIEWIET: It may well be, although I think the prostration of those elements inclined to resist its working would have favored its success.

MR. PRICE: Did Mr. deKiewiet have in mind the rather elaborate national arrangements, like the combined boards and combined chiefs of staff, as the machinery of the Western group?

MR. DE KIEWIET: I had not thought of it institutionally. I am the sort of person who liked very much the suggestion that France and England join, partly because of my liking of the unusual and partly

[102]

because I think it is one of the responsibilities of statesmen to be creative, and there was an act of creativeness there that appealed to me very much, although what England would have done with its monarchy and France with its republic I would not attempt to answer.

THE ATOMIC BOMB AND SECURITY

MR. WRIGHT: As I understand, with present airplanes it is possible to launch atomic bombs for attack 8,000 miles from their destination. I believe that in that radius practically every large city in the world would be included from the mainland of the United States; and, reciprocally, practically every large city would be included from the Soviet territory.

MR. BRODIE: Yes, I think so. Practically all the great cities of the world are in the Northern Hemisphere, and especially when you consider that, in a Soviet-American conflict, the United States would probably have bases in northern Canada and the Soviet Union in northern Russia and Siberia, there is no question there. That is true even with planes actually in existence, let alone those now being produced, such as the B-36, which has a longer range and larger carrying capacity than the B-29.

MR. PRICE: I was sorry that Mr. Brodie confined most of his remarks to what I believe Mr. Pasvolsky has called "problems of strategy" rather than of security. It seems to me, perhaps because of the atomic bomb, that we are talking much less aggressively about what kind of world machinery we want to create than we were a year ago, or even two or three years ago, perhaps far less than we were four or five years ago.

I thought Mr. Brodie dismissed the possibility of a real international agency to control the bomb a little bit too casually, when he talked about the suspicion that the Russians would have on admitting inspectors from an atomic energy authority, because the only concession that we would be making would be to quit making atomic bombs. After all, we would be making the parallel concession of admitting inspectors to our properties and we have more atomic energy properties now than they have.

That does not dispose of the psychological points that Mr. Hazard mentioned last night. I think there is undoubtedly suspicion of strangers in Russia, and that is a great handicap; but are we, on that account, ready to give up our hope of an international system by which, especially in the field of atomic energy, some international

[103]

authority is going to deal, not with the governments concerned but with persons or lesser agencies? That is the question that seems to me the nub of the security problem in the future.

MR. BRODIE: The mere fact that we have evolved this plan does not in itself give us cause for great rejoicing. I think it was a great accomplishment of ingenuity. I think it looks like the kind of plan which would be workable, if accepted. I was simply giving reasons for restraint of optimism for its acceptance.

I would also submit that the Lilienthal plan, which, in substance, is the official American proposal, is only the bare outline of a plan; and in filling in that outline numerous great problems arise which, so far as I can see, we have not even explored in our own minds. I don't know how far the State Department has gone on that. I mean such questions, for example, as those relating to the distribution of the primary production plants. But the basic point is that the plan involves large-scale activities within Russia on the part of an international authority, of a nature which our experience thus far in comparable issues certainly does not lead us to have extravagant hope will be acceptable to them.

MR. PRICE: No more to us.

MR. BRODIE: Right, but I think there is a difference of degree there.

MR. WRIGHT: You have this psychological question: Is it possible that the countries that are members of the United Nations or of the atomic development authority could regard that authority as "us" rather than as a foreigner? I suppose the state of Illinois does not regard it as invasion if the federal government establishes a post office or even maintains federal troops here. I must say that the reaction that some of the inhabitants of western Connecticut had to the invasion of the United Nations is not entirely hopeful on this.

MR. BRODIE: And they are all mild men, too.

ROLE OF RETALIATION IN CONTROL

MR. FOX: Mr. Brodie suggested that defense can be thought of only in terms of deterrents. There has been considerable objection in certain quarters to erecting a system of atomic energy control on the substratum of retaliation. It occurs to me that we might clarify the discussion if we distinguished between a system which, in its first instance, simply depends on a broad distribution of bombs so that if one party shoots them off he will be sure to get a lot of them back

[104]

that afternoon—what you might call a planned system for retaliation—and a system which sets up a true international control but keeps in the background as an incentive for not permitting the international control to break down the deterrent possibilities of ultimate retaliation if there is a gross violation or if the scheme defaults.

When we are talking about the United Nations in general, we keep saying that, so long as the great powers are in agreement, the scheme will work. We don't always ask why they should agree. One reason why they jointly ought to have an incentive to keep agreeing is that if they don't agree there are certain deterrent possibilities that will be invoked. The penalty for noncollective action is mutual destruction, and it is especially mutual destruction with the invention of the atomic bomb. Any prolonged war would be sure to have it used, whether there were any bombs in existence on the first day or not. Therefore, it seems to me to make some sense, if you are going to set up any effective atomic energy control scheme, to build up incentives along with all the other things one tries to harness up. It is simply another way by which you use the balance of power to underwrite the collective system.

I think it may very well be possible to have a system which permits no bombs anywhere and still is made more likely to work because it was organized so that in the event of its breakdown there would be some swift and effective punitive action against the violator and in the event of its breakdown there would be a stock pile of bombs created on the side of the nonaggressors rather more quickly than on the side of the aggressors.

Mr. Wilbur W. White: Wouldn't it be better to have that stock pile in existence under control of, let us say, the United Nations?

Mr. Fox: I think that is a real question, one that ought to be discussed. I think I can see certain dangers in having it in existence under the control of the United Nations, the chief one being that the bombs have to be located somewhere; and, since they have to be located somewhere, the phrase "under the control of the United Nations" simply masks the fact that you have set up a system which depends for its operation on a balanced distribution of bombs among the great powers.

Mr. Gurian: Permit me, first, to enumerate some points about which there is, I think, no disagreement.

First, I think that the atomic-bomb weapon has such an enormous destructive power that it cannot be compared with any other weap-

[105]

on. To put it into terms of Hegelian logic, in this case quantity has developed into a change of quality. I think this point is beyond dispute.

The second point, which is perhaps less accepted, is the fact that at the present time only the United States can use atomic bombs. I think that can be taken for granted.

Third, this situation will not continue to exist; after a few years—I don't know whether after three years or after ten years—other powers will be able to produce atomic bombs.

Therefore, the practical question is simple: What must be done in the time between now and the year in which other powers, particularly Russia, will be able to produce atomic bombs? That is the decisive question. How may we use this force for the salvation of humanity?

I am afraid that even the best-worked-out proposals of international control do not have in themselves the guaranty that they will be even accepted. I think it would be somewhat dangerous to assume that all powers will act as "responsible powers." There will perhaps be powers which will believe that they can wait until they have atomic bombs. I don't know whether, for instance, Russia, or perhaps a minor group which would be able to produce atomic bombs, would be impressed by the threat of punitive action. I am afraid that the term "punitive action" has become comparatively meaningless in the age of the atomic bomb.

Could we not make the following calculations? Someone starts an atomic war; the start is so effective that the punitive action would be perhaps impossible, or at least would become extremely difficult. Therefore, we are in a most serious situation unless one makes the optimistic assumption that all powers must necessarily agree and that all men will act like reasonable beings.

What can be done about this situation? It is extremely unlikely, I think, that the Baruch plan will be accepted in its decisive parts, and how will you compel those powers which are not willing to accept this plan? Will you start against them in a public war in order to impose upon them acceptance of such a plan? Therefore, would it not be necessary to create something to be popularly known as world government? Is it not the single possible solution? I personally do not believe that, but I ask the question.

Mr. Brodie mentioned in his remarks the book review which Chancellor Hutchins published in the *New York Times* and which is

[106]

written from the point of view of world government. The Chancellor championed the argument that only world government can help. I cannot see how that would help very much, because, in order to establish world government, one has to compel the powers which are not willing to accept the authority of world government to accept this authority; therefore world government would be nothing else than, to use a historical term, *Pax Romana*. World government would be possible only if the power which has the monopoly of the atomic bomb would really use this monopoly, or would threaten to use this monopoly, against governments which would not accept world government.

Therefore, I think the question by which we are faced is simple. From a reasonable point of view it would be ideal for all powers to agree; but, unfortunately, the reasonable point of view does not prevail, and I cannot see any other solution than the very precarious and dangerous solution of the balance-of-power system. The atomic bomb has not changed the basic features of the world policies. The balance-of-power system is nothing particularly new, and I cannot see any other way out than the application of that system, perhaps with some pious sentences, with some application of collective security in order to impress public opinion, which likes such statements.

STABILITY OF THE BALANCE OF POWER

MR. WRIGHT: May I ask Mr. Gurian whether he thinks the invention of the atomic bomb has rendered the balance of power more stable or less stable than it was before?

MR. GURIAN: I would say less stable, more precarious; but at least I can see the working of the balance-of-power system. I cannot say that this balance-of-power system will guarantee eternal peace; it has not guaranteed lasting peace in the past. But I cannot see, on the other hand, how the Baruch plan will work; and I cannot see, if one accepts the criticism of Chancellor Hutchins, how his belief in world government can be realized. As I wrote to him, I believe that humanity will rather destroy itself than accept world government.

MR. BRODIE: I would like to take up some of your points in inverse order. First, about balance of power, I would add that it is not only likely to be less stable but that it has become a much more ambiguous concept; that is, the old calculus of what constitutes power largely falls to the ground. Certainly, industrial strength does not mean a great deal if you assume that the industry of a nation will be the first

[107]

thing to go, that is, if that assumption is valid. Size of population ceases to have the importance it had before. Various other factors which it has lately become fashionable to add up in a calculus of power have to be considered completely anew.

About world government, I think a great deal can be said against the idea. I will confine myself to only one remark. I think that the preaching of world government as a solution to the problem is really a rejection of the problem, because even the proponents concede, as Mr. Hutchins did in that article you mentioned, that this is, after all, a long-term proposal, not a short-term one. I am not interested in whether or not it is valid even for the long term. I am thinking only of the proposition which I think the late Lord Keynes originated, that in the long term we are all dead. I would now add to that: In the short term we may all be killed. So it seems to me much more profitable to consider solutions which, if possible at all, can be attained within the next two decades, let us say.

In connection with your remarks that a world government could be attained at present only by conquest, I would say that at present only two powers appear to have anything like the strength necessary to effect such conquest, and of those two only one appears prepared to carry through with the administration and policing of conquered territories, especially if those territories are world-wide. It is prepared and to some degree equipped to do so. I obviously do not have in mind the United States, which is having trouble enough staffing its occupation armies in Germany and Japan.

Finally, your initial remark about the necessity of finding some kind of solution before other countries, especially Russia, have the bomb. I think that Mr. Fox observed yesterday in his speech that the possession of the bomb by us, so long as we are obviously not ready to use it, is the reverse of an advantage in bargaining relative to a security system.

Mr. WHITE: Mr. Brodie, you were talking about the balance of power. Isn't it true that what you said about the balance of power is the case only if there is a monopoly of the bombs? If the bombs are fairly equally distributed among the great powers, won't they tend to offset each other in terms of destruction of each other's cities, populations, and so on, much as high-powered air power has done?

Mr. BRODIE: Except that under the old system you could always depend on a certain duration of time, a rather long time, before your instruments could take decisive effect. Even if you had a monopoly

[108]

of air power, you could not depend on bringing a great power to its knees within a term of weeks; you would need a lot more time, during which all sorts of other things could happen.

MR. WHITE: No, but some people said you did have a monopoly of air power.

MR. BRODIE: At present we have the testimony of experience. In the latter stages of the war the Allied superiority in the air over Germany was so extreme that one could almost speak of monopoly of air power. You could never expect a war to begin with a greater monopoly. Yet it took a pretty long time to destroy her industry, even if we consider only the period during which the most effective bombing was carried on—which was the last year. During that year a nation might conceivably, if it had the resources, be able to marshal those resources and resist the attack. Where you have a situation in which the decisive phases of the war may take only days or hours, you have something new and almost completely unknown. I don't think I would approach a solution of what would happen under such circumstances by a study of past situations. One would have to start anew to think it through.

MR. WHITE: My question was this: If both sides have the power to do that, aren't you on Monday of the second week of a war starting with two states that are still of relatively equal strength even as they were the week before; though, of course, at the later date all cities and all industries are gone in both states?

MR. BRODIE: That would perhaps be true if you assume that the power which is the first one hit will nevertheless retain the ability to hit back. Of course, that itself is in some question; in fact, it is one of the basic questions. I was saying, even if you imagine a situation in which both sides have, let us say, their cities wiped out, you certainly don't have equality. You have all kinds of factors entering into the situation, such as relative degrees of panic and disintegration. In one case, you might have a readiness to capitulate on the part of those who remain who have the authority to do so; on the other side, you may have a readiness to conduct guerrilla warfare, which would require an invasion.

MR. WRIGHT: Is Mr. White suggesting that we have a stable balance of power, because it would be a stable balance of power after all the cities of the world had been wiped out? A peace that contemplated that presently all the cities of the world were going to be wiped out would not be a very satisfactory peace.

[109]

I was very much interested in Mr. Brodie's introduction of the time element, which seems to me the crucial thing. The problem is to make it impossible for any government to prepare for atomic war without giving unequivocal evidence of its intentions and to prolong to a maximum the period of time prior to the possible outbreak of an atomic war after that unequivocal signal of its intentions. If you can create conditions so that it would be absolutely impossible for any government to start an atomic war until at least a year after there had been some unequivocal signal that the government intended to start such a war, measures could probably be devised to prevent the war altogether. On the other hand, if that period of time is something on the order of ten minutes or an hour, the world will be in a continuous state of jitters, very hazardous to peace.

It seems to me that that consideration is a major argument for trying to eliminate all atomic bombs in being. If atomic bombs, as Mr. Fox said, are in being anywhere, they are in some country, and that always presents the possibility of that country's seizing them, whatever its obligations may be, and starting an atomic-bomb war immediately. In other words, if atomic bombs are in being, that period of time is reduced to the minimum. If, however, you can assure that there are no such bombs and, consequently, that a long process of mining uranium, developing plants, manufacturing fissionable materials, and assembling bombs is necessary before an atomic-bomb attack could be launched, then you've got a fairly long period of time.

That seems to me the center of the Baruch report. If the operations all over the world which have anything to do with atomic energy, including mining uranium and operating plants which produce fissionable materials for peaceful purposes, are in the hands of an international authority, there could be no preparation for atomic war without a seizure of mines or plants from that international authority, and such seizure would give the unequivocal signal which I referred to. Even if some country did seize all the plants of the international authority in its territory, still it would be a considerable time before it could make atomic bombs.

MR. CHARLES E. MERRIAM: What is this unequivocal signal they would flash? How could you be sure they would flash it until the day after?

MR. WRIGHT: I would say it would be impossible for any government to seize a plant or a mine which was owned and operated by an

[110]

116

international authority with personnel largely foreigners and keep it dark for any length of time. If it were a plant operated in the middle of Russia by American and other non-Soviet citizens, I would think that the news of the seizure of that plant by the Russian government would leak out very rapidly.

MR. JOSEPH W. BALLANTINE: There is another problem in connection with this distribution. If you had bombs distributed in equal quantities among the powers as a means of insuring a balance of power, you would put a disproportionate advantage on a power that would be ruthless, that has a disregard for life, that has a disregard for property, that would be willing to take action the way Germany did in invading Russia or as Japan did in attacking Pearl Harbor. The more responsible governments would be at a disadvantage compared with a country that is ruthless.

MR. FOX: I simply want to add a footnote to your remark. There are two kinds of violations. One would be the seizure of the primary plutonium plants, in which case the technical problem would be to try to figure out whether the plutonium that was in the pipeline of production was enough to produce quickly a stock pile of bombs to cause real trouble. The other would be the illicit development of completely independent production from uranium extraction to plutonium production, which would not involve seizure of the atomic development authority's plutonium plants. The period of grace which might be vouchsafed us after the unmistakable warning signal had been given might be different in those two cases, but I think we ought to keep them separated.

MR. WRIGHT: You mean in the second case that there has been an evasion—illegitimate mining and manufacture.

MR. FOX: Yes. It seems to me an admirable feature of the Lilienthal-Baruch proposals that it gives to the atomic development authority a monopoly of all kinds of atomic energy activities. Mere performance of uranium extraction and any of these other things convicts the power.

MR. BRODIE: I think you can put that another way and say that the great merit of the plan is that it minimizes the inspection problem, which otherwise appeared to a great many persons, especially some of the physical scientists, as an insuperable one. However, it does not by any means obliterate the inspection problem. A very sizable inspection function remains, which has to be considered when we attempt to evaluate its acceptability. Also, the minimizing of the

[111]

inspection problem is at the cost of requiring nations to permit foreign agencies—call them "international" if you will, but nevertheless looked upon as foreign—to carry on large exploratory, industrial, and even policing activities within its country, which is an enormous abatement of sovereignty. However desirable such abatement may appear in the abstract, the question is: Is a nation like Russia prepared to relinquish that much of its authority?

MR. WRIGHT: Would a nation resent more having an industrial operation carried on by an international authority in its territory than having a corps of inspectors in all its plants, factories, and mines?

MR. BRODIE: I think not. I think that is why the plan has such merit. Obviously, an agency whose sole job is inspection has saddled upon it a function which is bound to result in innumerable frictions and dissatisfactions on the part of both sides, and, as I say, the great merit of the plan is that it minimizes those sources of friction.

RELIABILITY OF INTERNATIONAL LAW

MR. HAZARD: Mr. Brodie and most commentators talk about the atomic bomb in terms of production and refer to inspection and what not. Up until the atomic bomb, there was some reliance upon what we used to call "international law." All conferences after the last war that discussed problems of armament talked in terms of limitation of armament and nonuse of armaments. Have we entirely passed beyond that stage?

MR. BRODIE: I believe the best observation on that was contained in a recent article of the *London Economist*, which, unfortunately, I do not have here, but it ran something like this: It is not that nations can be expected to violate their word. In this case they would probably keep their word, but in an issue so critical the probability is not enough. Each nation has to be sure, or as sure as human ingenuity permits it to be, that there is no violation or evasion. In other words, the evasion or violation has to be practically *impossible*, not merely *improbable*, and that is a very different situation from what we have had before.

Incidentally, as far as I can recall, the only really effective disarmament programs of the past have pertained to naval disarmaments, and those, of course, are units which are extremely difficult to hide, battleships especially.

MR. HAZARD: There have been some relatively effective agreements not to use bacteriological warfare.

[112]

MR. BRODIE: Or gas. I think there is another issue there, especially in relation to gas. You have a very different order of military utility between gas and atomic bombs. I know there happens to be a very marked difference of opinion in respect to gas within the armed services themselves. There are officers who believe that, if gas had been used in the recent war, it would have been a decisive weapon, particularly if used by us against the Japanese. On the other hand, I also know that the policy-makers were persuaded that they had other instruments which were not barred by law, such as tanks of gelatinized gasoline, etc., which were at least as effective on the weight-for-weight basis. That is, an airplane would be just as effective carrying so many pounds of that material as it would be carrying an equal number of pounds of gas. Also, we know that in the case of gas you have such things as gas masks and decontamination units, etc. In other words, you have not only the ability to retaliate but also actual protection.

I am not discounting the value of the convention which prohibited gas. I think that was decisive in the sense that it was the element which crystallized the existing balance arguing against its use; but without that balance I don't think the convention would have been observed, because, after all, a good many legal requirements were not observed when they did not fall under that character of equality.

MR. WRIGHT: I think experience with disarmament conventions emphasizes the time element which I referred to. A capital ship takes several years to make, and it is very difficult to conceal the fact that one has been started. Consequently, there is a signal that the convention is being violated long before the capital ship is constructed, a period of a year or two. With such a long lag between the known violation and the maturing of the results of violation, there probably won't be any violation at all. On the other hand, when it was a question of disarmament affecting size of contingents, budgetary expenditures, small arms, airplanes, the lag would be less; and the disarmament conferences recognized that an effective system of inspection was necessary before they could expect such limitations to be accepted. There was a great deal of discussion at the disarmament conference of 1932 in regard to setting up a system of inspection which would prolong as much as possible that period of time.

MR. HAZARD: I take it from what you both have said that there is no possibility whatever in the Soviet proposal, which is just this: disarmament plus agreement not to use.

[113]

MR. BRODIE: It seems pretty transparent that that proposal, and I think it is reasonable on their part, is, in effect, a proposal that we disarm ourselves of bombs before we go on with this negotiating.

MR. HAZARD: We have to agree at the same time never to use them.

MR. BRODIE: May I add a footnote to what Mr. Wright said: rumors before the war that Japan was secretly building a lot of naval vessels turned out not to be true.

MR. GURIAN: The atomic bomb is a deadly weapon, but previous struggles among nations for power continue, even in an intensified degree. Would it, therefore, not be somewhat dangerous (though I think Mr. Brodie proved his point) to accept simply as a consequence of the atomic weapon the fact that other weapons, sea power and so on, are less important today than they ever were before? Such observations are surely correct from the point of view of atomic war, but from the point of view of continuation of traditional policies which you observe today, I think such observations cannot be completely proved. Therefore, we observe that traditional power policies continue, even intensified and poisoned by the threat of atomic war.

A second question: What would happen if we should, for instance, hear tomorrow or in a few months a radio broadcast in which it would be said, "Stalin has received a group of physicists and has given them five million rubles for discovery of a new, improved method for production of atomic bombs"? Would our whole discussion here be somewhat out of date? Are not all these proposals based on the assumption that we have time, that we have a monopoly?

MR. BRODIE: I think in regard to the latter question that it is likely that a radical change in thinking would take place in this country. I think there would be an even greater feeling of urgency and even of desperation.

In regard to your first point, however, I think there are two things to be said. One is that, even if the world happily finds some way of actually prohibiting production of the atomic bomb, that in itself does not necessarily furnish a guaranty that there will be no more war. In other words, you have an isolation, an insulation, a sealing-off of the bomb, and other things remain pretty much as they are. It seems to me that the military leader today has to worry himself about two extremely different kinds of military activities.

In line also with that point, I think it was in 1794 that the Earl of Stanhope pointed out in a letter to one of Pitt's friends that the

[114]

120

recent invention of the steamship—notice that that was considerably before Fulton produced his "Clermont," although Stanhope also had been experimenting with steam—had nullified the purpose of Britain's concern with who possessed the Low Countries, because the possession of the Low Countries had meant one thing under sail and they meant something entirely different under steam. Notice, also, that Britain did not for over a hundred years abandon the policy of being concerned with who possessed the Low Countries. I am not implying that her policy was backward or stupid; it had some justification even after steam had progressed not only into the merchant marine but also into the navy. But, nevertheless, you do have that tendency for pursuit of security to follow traditional paths, whether or not they become absurd. This suggests that we might take stock of our foreign policy in respect to distant bases and see what it is that we are striving for which means a lot of friction with other countries but which may have no intrinsic benefit in terms of strategic use for the future.

THE LILIENTHAL-BARUCH PLAN

MR. PRICE: Regarding this time period that Mr. Wright and Mr. Brodie both talked about, it seems to me it is worth remarking that, as long as there is going to be any peaceful use of atomic energy on a national basis, the time limit for conversion of plutonium or U-235 to use as weapons is very short indeed. If, however, you have the international authority, as proposed in the Lilienthal-Baruch report, with this denaturing process, which scientists set great store by, you very greatly increase the time limit and decrease the danger.

There are a lot of arguments about this. There are those who are in favor of an international authority if you can get it effected. How many share Mr. Gurian's belief that you cannot get it effected? It is difficult not only in Russia but also in the United States. After all, we have had one senator say that this is a gift from God to the only peace-loving nation of the world, and we have had one or two other congressmen introduce measures that would provide that, even if we had a United Nations agreement, we would go on letting the Army control our atomic bombs. Obviously, that is a temporary political tactic, but I can imagine how that would look to Russia, even if they weren't suspicious.

Do other people here think the hope is utterly past for getting acceptance in, say, the next two or three years? Is there any hope of getting an interchange of scientists between countries? Mr. Hazard

[115]

set considerable store last night on increasing the possibilities of peace by not attacking the problems directly but by collateral means. I was going to add U.N.E.S.C.O. If you have an understanding among physical scientists and atomic physicists, I think you considerably increase the possibility of an international administration that would let a mixed personnel in different countries increase this time limit to a point where it would become practicable to put some reliance on it.

MR. WRIGHT: Atomic scientists have given major consideration to this question of increasing the time lag, and many of them have reached the conclusion that, with a system such as the Lilienthal-Baruch report contemplates, a lag of nine months or a year could be assured, but without international operation the lag would be very short.

They do not attach too much importance to the denaturing process. The statement on that in the Lilienthal report received exaggerated attention in the press and a modifying explanation was subsequently issued by the State Department.

It seems to me that the potentialities of atomic energy for peaceful power purposes is the crux of the technical problem. If atomic energy did not have such potentialities, the technical problem would be much simpler. If a large number of power plants based on atomic energy exist throughout the world, there is bound to be a certain danger; but atomic scientists think that, even in that situation, a time of nine months to a year could be assured after an illegal seizure before bombs could be made.

That technical question is, of course, distinct from the question of the political possibility of successful negotiation. That is the really serious problem. One difficulty of negotiation inheres in this, that no matter what is agreed on, the Soviet Union and other states can only rely upon the good faith of the United States for disclosing what we already have. A system of operation and inspection is possible, so that we would not have to rely on the good faith of the Soviet Union at all, but the Soviet Union would always have to rely on our good faith that we had not stored away a hundred or so atomic bombs in some mine or cave which could never be discovered by any inspection. We have the job of making the Soviet people believe that we are not lying when we say we have actually given over all the atomic bombs we have to the international authority.

MR. FOX: I don't know that it is so, but I think it is quite possible, that the use of standard accounting techniques at these various

[116]

122

plants may be such that we could demonstrate even to the most suspicious that we have accounted for all the fissionable materials. I have heard rather responsible scientists, who had important policy-making positions in connection with the production of U-235 and plutonium, say that they thought that, with the opening of the books, with the showing of where the material is by not only quantitative bookkeeping but also financial bookkeeping, and by the combination, you could demonstrate that, within a handful of bombs, they were all accounted for and that you might be able to get over that hump.

But then there is another hump that I think might be even more difficult and that is that the plan has to begin by having the Soviet Union permit the world to find out whether or not they have any large uranium or thorium deposits. They know that we have adequate deposits; it does not make any difference whether any more are discovered or not; within our territory there are adequate deposits. The world does not know whether or not within Soviet territory there are adequate deposits. We ask them to make their greatest contribution first by telling us, perhaps, that they don't have anything, that they are helpless.

MR. WRIGHT: The geologists think that it would be possible to discover the opening of any new mines by periodic aerial survey. Of course, each country would have to admit the international authority to examine all existing mines.

MR. McMAHON: I am inclined to agree with Mr. Gurian and Mr. Brodie that world government is not a relevant solution to our immediate problem. The world is not ready for it today. I doubt also that the Baruch proposal would find universal acceptance. The proposal involves a sacrifice of national sovereignty. Are the Russians ready for such a sacrifice?

In addition to conflicts of nationalism today, we have conflicts of internationalism. We are not one world in the sense of having a community of ideals. The differences between Russia and the West at the political and ideological levels are serious obstacles to the formulation of a truly international order.

Should we therefore abandon support of the Baruch proposal? I do not think so, but we should not attempt to put all our eggs in one basket. We should keep other alternatives in mind, alternatives which admittedly are not so good in theory.

{ 117 }

I disagree with Mr. Gurian over the impossibility of retaliation. It seems to me that, even if cities are destroyed through atomic bombing, retaliation can be effected through installations outside of these cities. And this power of retaliation may have some weight as a deterrent to the potential aggressor.

We might effect an agreement with all other nations not to use the bomb, including the commitment to act in concert against the nation which violates the pact. This is admittedly not a perfect solution to the problem of the atomic bomb, but it is about the best possible in this era of power politics.

Mr. BRODIE: In all the remarks which have been made concerning what to do with the Lilienthal plan now that we have it, I don't think anyone would suppose for a moment that we should not try earnestly and patiently to secure its adoption. Of course, we have to analyze the minimum requirements inherent in that plan and decide what we can afford to yield without yielding the essence of the plan.

I think it is heartening, first, that the reception in this country, including the reception on the part of Congress, has been, on the whole, distinctly favorable. I think it is also heartening that thus far we have no categorical rejection on the part of the Russians; as a matter of fact, we have certain comments of positive value. But one other point arises in connection with that plan, which Professor Wright referred to briefly, and that is the denaturing process. Mr. Baruch in his speech before the Atomic Energy Commission stated that the effectiveness of denaturing has been somewhat exaggerated in the public press. I think that, if it has been exaggerated, the fault is not of the press but of government releases and of the Lilienthal report itself. I would say that the denaturing idea is basic in that report, and what we do not now know is how effective it really is. If it should turn out that the Lilienthal committee was too optimistic about it, then we should have to reconsider the question that has apparently been abandoned, namely, the question of whether the world can afford to use atomic energy at all. In other words, if denaturing is not effective, then no activity is safe. The Lilienthal plan has as its basic component the distinction between safe and dangerous activity, dangerous activity being devoted exclusively to the international authority and safe ones to private agencies.

Mr. WRIGHT: Shortly after the Lilienthal report was published the State Department put out a statement by several scientists, giving a more correct appraisal of the value of denaturing. It takes longer to

[118]

make an atom bomb from denatured material than it does to make it from pure U-235 or plutonium, but it takes less time to make an atom bomb from denatured material than from natural uranium. This report indicated that no denaturing process could be safe in an absolute sense. The material could always be "un-denatured."

WORLD UNITY

MR. MERRIAM: The discussion of the Lilienthal-Baruch report seemed to display a negative attitude, as if by some mechanisms, tricks, or skills you are going to drive war out of the world through the atomic bomb. There is another factor—certainly in line with Lilienthal's view and probably also with Baruch's—of a positive and constructive nature. That is to say, if you have control over atomic energy, which you are developing all the time, then it is also possible to consider its peacetime uses.

A world group, which knows more about atomic energy than any other group and which is disposed to favor not the destruction of fissionable material but its development, could be a tremendous agency for world government. They could become, if they had the facilities for research and were promoting peacetime uses instead of trying to eliminate nuclear energies altogether, a center of human interest, rather than expressing the negative desire to prevent the use of a destructive weapon. Everyone knows that the nuclear energies are only in the making. Here we have a group working together: it is our agency, it is a common agency, it is a common instrument through which we not only prevent war but promote human happiness and tend to elevate the standards of living. They have the knowledge, and they could be given the power through licensing authority and through other encouraging devices to build up a positive peacetime program. That would give you an element without which I don't see how you will ever get security, namely, some notion of community, of common interest, of common purpose.

I don't see how you will ever guarantee security in the world on the negative basis of getting such an elaborate system of nets that nobody can break through. There must be certain common ideals and common interests in the minds of all. You tie this all in, in an unprecedented way, first with the negative establishment of difficulties against the making of destructive war but also with the positive promotion of the welfare of man. I think perhaps that is not the common view of the Lilienthal-Baruch plan, but it is implicit in it; and it pro-

{ 119 }

vides a basis by and through which we might develop not a world government but a form of desirable common world action.

MR. WRIGHT: What are the conditions under which the people of each country will regard the world community as an "in-group"?

MR. FARIS: What is gained in the world if you say to a country going to war—and there would always be some conditions under which some country would be willing to do that—"You must not use the atomic bomb"? We have plenty of other weapons, and you can be just as dead with one weapon as with another. The United Nations, at the present moment, is like an attempt to unite the Catholic church with the Fundamentalist Baptists. You might get a paper union, but you would have no real common purpose. The motive of fear of destruction has never seemed to be very effective. It seems to me you have this much longer task of trying to get a common attitude toward the world.

MR. BRODIE: I think there would be at least one gain, and that is that under the atomic bomb, assuming reciprocal use on the part of at least two belligerents, you have a condition which you have never had before, namely, that even the victor would suffer far greater destruction and devastation than any defeated country has ever suffered in recorded history. We have just passed through the most terrible war in history, and certainly the picture of appalling destruction is very vivid in our minds. On the other hand, we know that various great nations which participated in that war were practically untouched, especially our own country; and not only is that a benefit to ourselves, but it enables us to help our less fortunate allies and even to help the defeated. I grant you, the ability does not necessarily argue that it will be done, but I think it is there and that some measure of assistance will undoubtedly be forthcoming.

With the atomic bomb you have a condition under which war becomes universally destructive. You might say that that margin of difference is not enough to give you great anxiety concerning the elimination of the bomb, but I think it is an important margin of difference.

DISARMAMENT

MR. FARIS: It seemed to me that doing away with the atomic bomb is just one rather big factor of the problem of disarmament. Why don't you talk about disarmament in general and see what the difficulties are there?

[120]

MR. BRODIE: I would fall back on the argument that, in general, and I think especially in this case, you have a greater promise of success if you press for limited objectives. Our history of the pursuit of disarmament in general has not been an especially fortunate one. It was to me very interesting to see how the idea was more or less evaded in the United Nations Charter. They speak of limitation of armaments and so on, but with nothing like the fervor that was present in the League Covenant. Some of the nations which disarmed were stung by that experience, or at least felt they were, which is the important thing.

In the case of the atomic bomb we have not only a limited objective but a new and cosmic force which we have reason to suppose will cause nations to feel differently concerning its limitation from the way they have felt concerning the limitation of more orthodox arms, and I think the reception, at least in this country, is indicative of that fact. In other words, our problem is "merely" that of making the Russians see it as we do.

MR. WRIGHT: I would go further and suggest that an effective elimination of the atomic bomb would be an elimination of war. The atomic bomb is a decisive weapon. With the knowledge of atomic weapons general, any country that starts a war by traditional methods will know that the war will probably develop into an atomic war. If the anxiety to avoid atomic war has been sufficient to achieve effective measures to prevent a sudden use of atomic weapons, it might be sufficient to induce measures adequate to prevent war altogether.

MR. BRODIE: I think that is true, and I think that what you have there is the case of being able to have your cake and eat it, too; that is, if we succeeded in eliminating the production of the atomic bomb universally, we would have that benefit, namely, the removal of immediate fear plus the benefit that the deterrent value of the bomb is still there.

MR. WRIGHT: Everybody today will recognize that any war which starts is very likely to develop into an atomic war. No one can hope to eliminate the use of atomic bombs after war has started, and that thought may have deterrent influence upon the starting of wars. One can hope to prevent a war's beginning as an atomic war. One can create that time lag so that countries are not beset with the anxiety that an atomic war will spring up overnight; and that will be, I think, a great achievement. But statesmen must examine all the conditions of peace and must create the positive conditions of co-opera-

[121]

tion which Professor Merriam referred to if they want to eliminate the danger of war. Only by success in that enterprise can atomic war be surely eliminated.

MR. PASVOLSKY: That's right; but let's emphasize that distinction you have just made. I think it is a tremendously important distinction. A war started with pitchforks can end in an atomic war. The elimination of the use of atomic energy as a weapon is not going to eliminate war. Control over the use of atomic energy as a weapon may, if the control is sufficiently drastic—and on that score I have some doubts—prevent the beginning of an atomic war, may prevent an atomic war at the outset. That distinction, I think, is terribly important and ought to be emphasized over and over again.

MR. WRIGHT: I think it is very important because if you had no control, so that there was a general fear that an atomic war might begin at any moment, that general fear would itself be a factor that would tend to begin this war. If you create such a state of anxiety in the world, then at every international tension that arises, one power or another will think: "Well, the country with which I am having a dispute is likely tomorrow morning to start bombing me. Whoever starts an atomic war has a certain advantage, and therefore I had better start it now."

I think if you relied on nothing but the fear of retaliation with no international control, the invention of the atomic bomb would have greatly increased the probability of a war's starting.

MR. PASVOLSKY: You may even have the situation which happened in Japan, when certain irresponsible elements in Japan forced the war because they thought they had something with which they could finish it quickly.

STRATEGIC INFLUENCE OF THE ATOMIC BOMB

MR. WHITE: It seems to me that the quantity, especially the time, in this matter is so important. I have seen the statement somewhere that the United States is now able to manufacture bombs at the rate of one a week at the cost of ten million dollars a bomb. If this is the case it would be some time before there would be any danger of general atomic war. I have heard scientists say that the cost of destroying a city with atomic bombs is about one-fifth what it was with T.N.T. bombs. It seems to me the whole problem is over-dramatized. Why can't we find out something about these time-and-cost questions?

[122]

DISCUSSION OF GENERAL SECURITY

Mr. Wright: General Arnold in his contribution to *One World or None* (p. 26) put the figure about one-sixth, with the high cost of the first atomic bombs. He figured that the man-hours of labor in making planes and T.N.T. "blockbusters" were about one-fiftieth of the man-hours in the enemy assets destroyed, or one-sixth of the man-hours in military assets destroyed. With the atomic bomb, those ratios would be less than one-sixth as great. In other words, with each man-hour of labor in making planes and atomic bombs you could destroy over three hundred man-hours of labor, over thirty-six man-hours of which would be of direct military importance.

I may say that prior to the T.N.T. blockbuster that ratio between the man-hours of cost and the man-hours of destruction very seldom exceeded one to one. With the decreasing cost of making atomic bombs, the figure may go up to the order of one to a thousand. That indicates the difference that the atomic bomb has brought in the relative power of the offensive and the defensive.

Mr. Brodie: Even assuming that the statement is correct, that we can make them at the rate of one a week, the United States, after all, has not devoted any great part of its industrial manpower resources to the production of those bombs. So far as I can see, the only limiting factor after raw materials, in which we have an advantage, is the amount of resources the country is willing to devote to that. The bombs can be stock-piled indefinitely, so I think one has to consider the situation which occurs at the end of, say, a twenty-year accumulation period; and then, when one considers the disparity, not so much in terms of cost as in terms of the airplanes and their trained crews necessary to do the job, I think we come out with a very different kind of answer.

As I recall, the Army Air Forces have stated that it would take something on the order of 210 B-29's to do with T.N.T. bombs what 1 B-29 did with an atomic bomb at Hiroshima. That suggests ruling out certain tactical considerations, that suggests that the 210 planes —and I think that is a very conservative figure—which would have been necessary to do that job with T.N.T. bombs, if armed with atomic bombs would be able to do that to 210 Hiroshimas in the same element of time.

Mr. Price: Plus the guided-missile possibility, instead of airplanes.

Mr. Brodie: The Bureau of Ordnance of the Navy has developed some so-called guided missiles, some of which depend on infra-red

{ 123 }

rays and some on radar, which are used for short-range bombing. It is no secret now. Hansen Baldwin had an article describing several types. Possibly that kind of technique might be devoted to very long-range rockets. And also we have to consider the fact, which I did not mention, that, with the atomic bomb, you have a premium on the development of long-range rockets such as you have never had before—and from the point of view of physics it is theoretically possible to build, even with existing fuel, a rocket capable of a few thousand miles' range.

That brings up a question that is related to what Mr. Pasvolsky was saying, though in a more direct way; that is: How much can you isolate the atomic bomb from other weapons? Mr. Baruch and Mr. Gromyko both referred also to other weapons of mass destruction; but, in terms of the atomic bomb itself, one of the distinctions we always have to bear in mind is the distinction between multilateral use and monopoly use or multilateral possession and monopoly possession. One of the factors which enter into that calculation and that distinction is not only who possesses the bombs but who possesses the best instruments for delivering them. I should imagine a nation which had, let's say, four thousand-mile rockets which had the capacity of being guided accurately would be in a somewhat better position than a nation which depended on aircraft. How much better depends on all kinds of variables.

In connection with the distinction between monopoly as against multilateral possession, it seems to me that in one case you have a clear instance not only of lack of deterrent value but also of a positive incentive to aggression; and that is something we always have to bear in mind in relation to any minimum requirements for an international system. The worst kind of system—one which would be worse than no system—would be one in which an aggressive state could by evasion gain a monopoly; and in such a case aggression would be far cheaper than it has ever been in the past, and the kind of calculation which Mr. Pasvolsky referred to on the part of the Japanese war lords would be not only much more likely to be made but also would be accurate.

I would like to say one more word on the Lilienthal report. Not only the board in its report but also various people who set themselves up as its protagonists have argued that the great merit of the plan is that it also combines with the inspection function the positive function of research and distribution of the benefits of peacetime use.

[124]

It seems to me we are justified in solacing ourselves with the fact that atomic energy does furnish promise of peacetime uses, but I think we should not deceive ourselves by it. It seems to me, if we accept the most optimistic predictions on what it will mean in welfare, in terms of combating disease as well as in producing energy, power, and heat, that the whole sum total of it is unimportant compared to the fact that we have the material of which a few pounds can blow up a whole city. I agree with Mr. Pasvolsky that we've got to consider the security angle first and the welfare angle only as it fits into it.

Mr. Wright: The economic value of atomic energy would vary greatly in different sections of the world. At present costs it is quite unlikely that atomic energy could compete against coal and hydroelectric power in the United States. There are other sections of the world, such as central Brazil and Siberia, which are lacking in coal and hydroelectric power, where it is quite possible that it could compete.

That would undoubtedly raise an important question of the balance of power, if you allowed an international authority to operate nuclear power installations only where they are most economical. These nuclear power installations are somewhat dangerous; they could be seized, and perhaps within a year or so enough material could be extracted to make atomic bombs. So the question of economic utilization of atomic energy for peaceful purposes is inevitably linked up with the security and balance-of-power situation.

[125]

THE ATOM BOMB AS POLICY MAKER

By Bernard Brodie

IT IS now three years since an explosion over Hiroshima revealed to the world that man had been given the means of destroying himself. Eight atomic bombs have now been detonated — assuming that the three "atomic weapons" tested at Eniwetok were in fact bombs — and each was in itself a sufficient warning that the promise of eventual benefits resulting from the peacetime use of atomic energy must count as nothing compared to the awful menace of the bomb itself. The good things of earth cannot be enjoyed by dead men, nor can societies which have lost the entire material fabric of their civilization survive as integrated organisms.

Yet the dilemma nevertheless faces us that the enforcement of tolerable behavior among nations will continue for an indefinite time in the future to depend at least occasionally upon coercion or the threat of it, that the instruments of coercion against Great Powers will most likely be found only in the hands of other Great Powers (who can dispense with them only by acknowledging their readiness to forfeit whatever liberties they may happen blessedly to possess), and that those instruments appear fated, largely because of those same imperfections of our society which make power necessary, to include the atomic bomb and perhaps other comparable instruments of mass destruction.

Individuals may retreat from this dilemma behind a barrage of high moral protestation, usually combined with glowing predictions of a better world to be. Such retreat is rendered doubly sweet because it is more often than not accompanied by applause, especially from the intellectual wing of our society. But the nation as a whole cannot retreat from the problem, and those who desert simply leave the others to think it through as best they can.

The impact of the atomic bomb on United States policy has thus far been evidenced most clearly in the almost frantic effort to secure the adoption of a system of international control of atomic energy. It is difficult if not impossible to find an historical precedent for the eagerness with which this nation has pursued an endeavor which, if successful, would deprive it of the advantages of monopoly possession of a decisive military weapon.

To be sure, the monopoly is bound to be temporary, but that has always been true of new weapons, the monopoly possession of which has usually been jealously guarded for as long as possible. The United States is even now behaving in the customary manner concerning all new weapons other than those based on the explosive release of atomic energy, a fact which in itself sufficiently demonstrates that the exceptional American position on atomic energy control is based on something other than national generosity. That "something other" is of course a well-warranted fear of living in a world which morally and politically is little different from the one we have known but which in addition is characterized by multilateral possession of atomic weapons.

But the fear which engendered the pursuit of international control also provoked the resolve that any control scheme must contain within itself practically watertight guarantees against evasion or violation. That was and remains a wholly reasonable resolve, but its inevitable consequence is that it greatly reduces the chance of securing the requisite agreement. Two years of work by the United Nations Atomic Energy Commission have resulted in some illumination of the problem but almost no progress towards a solution. American initiative in securing formal suspension of the activities of the Commission is a plain acknowledgment of that fact.

But where does that leave us? It leaves us, for one thing, with the unwanted bomb still in our hands, and, so far as we know, still exclusively in our hands. It leaves us also under the compulsion to go on building more bombs, and better ones if possible. We must continue our search for a workable *and secure* international control system by any corridor which reflects even a glimmer of hope of success, but we must also begin to consider somewhat more earnestly and responsibly than we have thus far what it will mean for the nation to adjust to an atomic age devoid of international controls.

The ramifications of that adjustment process are legion, but certainly they involve above all a continuing reconsideration of the effects of the bomb upon our plans for the national security. For those to whom "national security" appears too narrow a concept for an atomic age, there are at least three observations that might be made.

In the first place, as the world is now organized, and as it now operates, American security is for all practical purposes synony-

mous with world security. It is no longer a question whether our
political leaders understand that to be the case, though there is
much evidence that in the main they do so understand. It is
simply that we have reached a stage where large-scale war without American participation borders on the inconceivable. Secondly, national policy, which is perforce concerned primarily
with national security, is the only policy upon which we as
citizens can hope to exercise any direct influence, and it is our
only channel for affecting international policy. Thirdly, the
projects of policy planners are much more likely to prosper if
they conform at least occasionally to aspirations which the man
on the street fully shares and understands. To him, and to the
politician who serves him, the security of the United States is
supremely meaningful and important. World security, on the
other hand, is an abstraction which gains meaning — at least
meaning sufficient to induce him to pay a price for it — only to
the extent that he is persuaded that American security is enhanced thereby. The difference may seem superficially a semantic
one, but it is more than that. It affects very profoundly the
question of the kind and degree of risks one will accept and the
character of the price one will pay to achieve security. It certainly
affects the basic method by which we proceed to our goal.

Lest we adopt too patronizing an attitude towards the convictions of the layman or the politician, let us consider for a
moment the propositions, however dimly he may perceive them,
upon which those convictions rest. At least four such propositions
may be listed, all of which are basically unaffected by the existence of the atomic bomb.

I. International organization at its existing level of development is obviously inadequate to guarantee either world or
American security. This fact explains and partly justifies the
preoccupation of most students of international relations with
procedures for developing and improving existing bases for international coöperation. But exclusive preoccupation with such ends
leaves a large gap which it is inexcusable to ignore, and that for
a reason which provides our second proposition.

II. It is clear from any dispassionate and realistic appraisal of
the forces at work in international relations today — the kind of
appraisal which it is the first responsibility of the specialist in the
field to provide — that a highly reliable and effective mechanism
for the collective guarantee of security can hardly be deemed to

lie within the range of conditions reasonably to be expected within our time. At any rate, the degree of probability is not high. The atomic bomb makes that circumstance more tragic, but it does not otherwise alter it. However much the mechanism described deserves working for, it is certainly a matter of ordinary prudence to take heavy insurance against failure or even against too slow a rate of achievement.

III. Whatever our predictions concerning the future of international coöperation, they must take into account the following basic dilemma: The pursuit of security against war — the objective which takes precedence above all others in the modern world — is not inevitably identical with the pursuit of smoother and more intimate international coöperation, the two being especially divergent where the latter holds out little promise of significant success. Where conciliation fails, one must take steps which may make that failure more certain and more complete. Where the opponent refuses to reason, one can only appease or threaten. There are wide variations in the flexibility and subtlety with which the statesman may either appease or threaten, and the degree of skill which he brings to his task is supremely important. However, it is in the main true that appeasement tends to encourage further unreasonable or "impossible" demands; while the threat or warning, however effective at the moment, tends to wound the opponent and to stimulate in him the desire to be less vulnerable to threat in the future. Nevertheless, the statesman may at any time be faced with a choice between these two alternatives and these alone. He will do well to guarantee for himself in advance the maximum of freedom of choice *between* them.

IV. For the purpose of threat or warning, adequate national strength is indispensable. The statesman who possesses it can choose whether to appease or warn; the one who lacks it can only appease. As General Eisenhower so neatly put it, strength is required to coöperate, weakness can only beg.

II

In a world in which none of the Great Powers felt threatened by one or more of the others, we could expect to see a salutary neglect of security devices resting on the above propositions. But it is clear from the recent behavior of our Government that it feels itself exposed to a threat from the Soviet Union, and it is almost equally clear that the measures which it is pursuing in response to that feeling of exposure enjoy the broadest popular support. Moreover, some of those measures undeniably entail aggravation of the tensions between the Soviet Union and ourselves. Is it possible to look past the difficulties of the moment to see the basic reasons for that concern?

A senior American naval officer told this writer not so long ago that "American strategic calculations concerning the requirements of *great* wars must envisage the Soviet Union as the opponent, if for no other reason than that she is the only foreign Power whose defeat would require great exertions on our part."

That is a good, simple working rule for an admiral. It recalls the old doctrine of the "natural enemy." It reminds us also that there would still be a problem to concern us even if the Soviet Union were something other than what it is; and that the fact that the power system of today is a bipolar one has dominant implications of its own. The main trouble with a bipolar system, as a colleague has so tersely put it, is that the target is all too unambiguous. The admiral's statement reminds us also that concern with security is a concern with possibilities, and not necessarily with high probabilities or certainties.

Nevertheless, if the reason which the admiral gave were the only one which counted, there is no doubt that our attitudes and our efforts concerning security would be profoundly more relaxed than they are. There are special reasons residing in the character of the Soviet state (or, if one insists, in the difference between our two systems) and in the events resulting from that character (or difference in characters) which account for the special dangers and the present acute degree of tension.

There is not space here, or competence on the part of the writer, to permit any analysis of the character of the Soviet state or of Soviet-American relations during the past three years. Nor is such analysis necessary for our purpose. All we need to guide us are a few general observations which will be obvious when pointed out but which may nevertheless strike the reader as having some flavor of novelty.

First of all, one might suggest that students of international relations have perhaps muddied the waters unduly by a somewhat excessive concern with Soviet motives, particularly with the question whether the motives behind Soviet obstreperousness, and worse, are primarily defensive or aggressive. That is not to argue that motives are unimportant. Nor is it to complain that motives are always difficult if not impossible to fathom, which is certainly true. The psychoanalyst is obliged professionally to reach conclusions about motives, and it is noteworthy that his interpretations usually differ from those of the person whose behavior he is examining. What is being suggested here is simply 1, that the act may dwarf in importance, so far as counteraction is concerned, the motive from which it leaps; and 2, that a motive which stems from convictions which we cannot appreciably influence or alter by any reasonable acts on our part ceases thereby to be of much operational significance to us.

The significance of the facts that the Soviet Union is a police state and that its organizing ideology posits among other things the necessity of world revolution has been sufficiently elaborated elsewhere. But a point which is generally overlooked and which is of at least equal significance is the following: the distinctive ideology being all-pervading, it quite naturally includes a special interpretation of previously existing patterns of international relations. That fact means, among other things, that the re-assuring analogies which one can draw from western history con-cerning long periods of amicable relations between states of widely differing ideologies are of much diminished relevance. In almost all those instances we find ministers who otherwise repre-sent the most widely differing persuasions holding a common approach to the conduct of foreign affairs, a common respect for the rules of the game.

Those rules, we are often told, elevated hypocrisy to the status of a first principle. "A diplomat," as the old saw goes, "is an honest man sent abroad to lie for his country." But there is another aphorism to the effect that hypocrisy has at least the merit of giving lip service to virtue. The "hypocrisy" of western statesmen has frequently enough been self-deception. The con-stant appeal to higher principles in the instruments of diplomacy has almost always been something more than window dressing. The margin of difference between declaration and performance, though wide, nevertheless had limits which the statesman well understood and upon which he could base his expectations. It is a common pattern in all civilizations that behavior falls short of the aspirations reflected in the norms, but the norms are not thereby bereft of importance.

The Communist philosophy explicitly and systematically rejects the previously accepted norms of international conduct. The principle of expediency in the approach to the existing pattern is not simply indulged in, it is avowed and exalted.

The final and conclusive point relevant here is that the Soviet Union is a military state if not a militaristic one. Welfare, in the form of consumers goods and services, is subordinated to military requirements to a degree which also has probably never before been approximated in modern history — certainly not in Nazi Germany, which vaunted "guns before butter." While the milder kinds of Socialists have often been pacifists, no real Communist philosopher from Marx to the present has ever had the slightest use for pacifism. Marx, indeed, and Lenin too, took frequent occasion to bend their matchless scorn upon it.

The points just stated are not matters of opinion. They are the kind of conclusions which any normal intelligence operation provides, except that the factual evidence which supports them is far more abundant and incontrovertible than is usually available to the intelligence officer in his general run of problems. It is the kind of evidence upon which policy, as distinct from hope or yearning, must be based.

These conclusions do not point to the inevitability of war. They do point, however, to a policy the realization of which will at each recurrence of crisis serve to persuade the Soviet leaders that the expedient solution is the peaceful one. Such a policy would no doubt also serve to reduce the frequency of crises. For the saving grace of the Soviet philosophy so far as international relations are concerned is that, unlike the Nazi ideology, it incorporates within itself no time schedule. Hitler had to accomplish his ultimate goals not only within his lifetime but within his years of vigor. The Soviet attitude appears to be much more opportunistic. The Soviets may be unshakably convinced that ultimately there must be war between the Communist world and what they call the "capitalist" one. Since that conviction is a cardinal doctrine of their faith, we can probably do nothing within the present generation to alter it. What we can do, however, is to persuade them each time the question arises that "The time is not yet!"

III

The problem to which we now return is the problem of how to accomplish this act of persuasion in an atomic age, when the already precious objective of peace is made immeasurably more precious by the immeasurably enhanced horror of the alternative. However, since preoccupation with the horror has brought us nothing positive thus far, and offers exceedingly little promise of doing so in the future, it is time for a shift to a more sober position. There are a large number of questions pressing for an answer, and consideration of many of them requires appraisal of the atomic bomb as an instrument of war — and hence of international politics — rather than as a visitation of a wrathful deity.

No doubt the first question concerns the effect of the atomic bomb upon the basic power relationship between the United States and the Soviet Union. Postponing for a moment such qualifying considerations as stem from our present but admittedly temporary monopoly, we see at once that one of the most fundamental changes created by the atomic bomb is that it makes possible *for the first time* decisive military action between the two great centers of power.

In a brilliant study published during the recent war, Professor William T. R. Fox based much of his analysis of Great Power relationships on the proposition that a war between the Anglo-American bloc on the one side and the Soviet Union on the other would be almost inevitably bound to result in a stalemate, and that common recognition of this fact by both sides would powerfully influence (presumably for the better) relations between them. His explanation follows:

. The pressure which either the Soviet Union or the Western powers can bring to bear upon the other in its main centers of power is surely much less than is implied by the statement that the two are the strongest forces in the world. Not only are the points of direct contact few and inaccessible but the centers are widely separated. The armed power of each can be effectively carried only part of the way to the other. American control over the seaward approaches to the New World will in any foreseeable future render a transoceanic operation by the Soviet Union impossible. The massive superiority of its land army should on the other hand discourage the Western powers from attempting a large-scale amphibious operation against hostile shores controlled by the Red Army.[1]

That proposition was not only true at the time of writing, but it could also be argued that no conceivable evolution of the instruments of war then publicly known could have significantly

[1] "The Super-Powers: The United States, Britain, and The Soviet Union — Their Responsibility for Peace." New York: Harcourt, Brace, 1944, p. 102.

modified it. To be sure, strategic bombing was gradually developing in effectiveness, and the striking range of bomber aircraft was slowly but steadily increasing. However, with the experience of World War II, none but extremists could argue that strategic bombing was sufficient unto itself for winning a war against a great nation. Moreover, despite the increasing range of bomber aircraft, there were a variety of technical reasons, quite impressive in the aggregate, to support the conclusion that a comprehensive program of strategic bombing over what might be called intercontinental distances would not become practicable "in the foreseeable future." That conclusion assumed, of course, an evolutionary improvement in known types of bombs and incendiaries, roughly approximating in magnitude the developments of the preceding score of years. At any rate, it was as nearly certain as any military prediction can be that a conflict between the two major centers of power would be a prolonged one — comparable in duration to the two world wars — and not promising the same finality of decision achieved in each of those instances.

The atomic bomb has changed all that. Unless the number of atomic bombs which it is possible for any nation to make in, say, 10 years' time is far smaller than the most restrained estimates would indicate, there can no longer be any question of the "decisiveness" of a strategic bombing campaign waged primarily with atomic bombs. Also, for a variety of reasons which cannot be reviewed here but which are readily available elsewhere,[2] distance no longer presents the same kind of barrier to effective strategic bombing with atomic bombs that it does with chemical bombs. With atomic bombs, planes already in military service could effectively attack from bases within the continental United

[2] See especially "The Absolute Weapon: Atomic Power and World Order," edited by Bernard Brodie (New York: Harcourt, Brace, 1946), p. 34-40; also "The Atomic Bomb and the Armed Services," by Bernard Brodie and Eilene Galloway, Public Affairs Bulletin No. 55 (Legislative Reference Service, Library of Congress), p. 42-45. The reasons why the same plane can be effective over much greater distances with atomic bombs than with chemical bombs concern basically the intricate relationships between such factors as the amount of bombs which a plane can carry over any given distance, the total military effort expended in carrying it over that distance, and the tolerable rate of loss of attacking planes. Since the atomic bomb does enormously more damage than an equivalent load of chemical bombs, the cost per sortie which is acceptable with atomic bombs is also proportionately greater — great enough, in fact, to include 100 percent loss of planes on successful attacks. The greater acceptable cost; the fact that the plane itself need not be retrieved (whatever the arrangements made for the rescue of the crew); and the additional fact that a single atomic bomb, whatever its weight, is always a sufficient payload for any distance which the plane is capable of carrying it, will have the effect of at least doubling the maximum effective bombing range of any plane of B-29 size or greater.

States important targets in the Soviet Union, which the same planes could not do if they carried only chemical bombs. Thus, there is no absolute necessity to wage great campaigns merely to secure advanced bombing bases. Finally, it is difficult to see how the decisive phases of a war fought with substantial numbers of atomic bombs could be anything but short.

The corollary of the point made in the previous paragraph is that the atomic bomb has deprived the United States of what amounted almost to absolute security against attack upon its continental territories. Its naval supremacy was sufficient to guarantee it both against direct invasion of hostile land forces and against enemy seizure of bases close to our frontiers for large-scale bombing attack. A potential enemy might count on token raids, but nothing more. America's invulnerability was akin to that which Britain enjoyed through the centuries until the perfecting of the submarine on the eve of World War I. The language which Francis Bacon applied to superior sea power in his own time, that it might take "as much or as little of a war as it liked," still largely held for the United States, alone among nations. But with effective intercontinental bombing available to any enemy who holds in substantial numbers the tools already in our hands, that treasured position is gone. The atomic bomb has in military effect translated the United States into a European Power.

However, though Heaven is lost, not all is lost. There is still the issue of superiority to contend with. Three questions especially concern us. Is clear and conspicuous military superiority possible in an age of atomic bombs? If so, is it possible for the United States to maintain it vis-à-vis its major rival? And what will be the political consequences of an effort to maintain atomic superiority?

It is not possible in a few paragraphs to do more than outline the nature of the problem contained in each of these questions and perhaps to indicate the fallacy of certain prevalent suppositions concerning it. Let us take the third question first.

There has long been a fashion among academic specialists in international relations to deprecate as futile and worse the quest on the part of any nation for military superiority over its rivals. As the argument runs, the attempt is bound to provoke a similar pursuit on the part of the rival, the net result being an armaments race which inevitably results in war. Historical support is of course not lacking, especially if the historical instances be chosen with discrimination. The prevalence of this doctrine has had a great deal to do with our frenetic pursuit of international control of atomic energy at almost any cost, including the cost of neglecting to consider any possible alternatives.

There is of course an important element of truth in the idea. But there is also much taken for granted in it which is not true. It is not true, for example, and has not been true at least since the industrial revolution began, that the so-called Great Powers have been on an approximately equal footing in terms of their ability to compete in the production of those instruments of war that really counted. It could be said, for example, that it was the Washington Naval Treaty of 1922 which made the Pacific phase of World War II possible, for it assured to Japan something much closer to naval parity with the United States than would have been anywhere near her reach in any real building competition ensuing from the absence of such a treaty. The Treaty did avoid for a time a "costly" naval building competition. But was not the war with Japan immeasurably more costly? And would Japan have dared embark upon a war against an America boasting a naval power which was — as it easily could have been, without any untoward strain upon the American economy — two or three times her own?

General propositions should not be pushed too far, including the one just stated, but there is much cant in the field of international studies which needs to be brushed out. Those to whom armaments competition appears disastrous as well as wicked are somewhat inconsistent when they look back nostalgically on the relatively peaceful nineteenth century and on the marvelous rôle played by Great Britain in helping to preserve that peace. They will speak vaguely of Britain's invulnerability as a contributing factor, as though that invulnerability were something handed down from on high. It was indeed Britain's invulnerability at home which enabled British statesmen to play such an active and on the whole beneficent part in helping preserve the peace of Europe, but it was not simply the accident of the Channel which made Britain invulnerable. It was her clear-cut naval superiority over the Channel and adjacent seas, *the impairment of which Britain would not brook*, which gave her that enviable position.

Returning again to the atomic bomb, the issue is not whether our country ought to seek to maintain its present superiority in atomic armaments but whether it has any chance at all of succeeding in such an effort. It has been argued by some (including at one time the present writer) that it was in the very nature of atomic armaments that the kind of clear and decisive military superiority that was feasible in the past — conspicuously in the case of naval armaments — could no longer be realized. The argument was based fundamentally on two considerations: first, that there was "no defense against the atomic bomb," and second, that when a nation had enough bombs to overwhelm its opponent in one surprise attack and was willing to make such attack, it would make little difference whether its opponent had two or three times the number.

There is now reason to believe that the situation is not so simple as all that. A great deal depends on the total number of bombs which it will be possible for the various Great Powers to make in any given period of time. Clearly, a three to one superiority in numbers of bombs would mean one thing if the numbers of bombs on each side were numbered at most in the scores or hundreds, and something quite different (and much less significant) if they were numbered in the thousands. Information which would enable private citizens to make intelligent estimates concerning rate of bomb production has not been made public, but there appear to be hints in various quarters that the maximum feasible rate of bomb production is substantially less than was being generally assumed two years ago. It is also clear that the richer of the known deposits of uranium and thorium are much more accessible to the United States than to the Soviet Union.

One may also assume that the enormous technological lead which the United States has over the Soviet Union — and which shows no conclusive signs of diminishing — is bound to mean a great potential advantage for the United States in the design of the instruments for using the atomic bomb. The bomb by itself has no military utility. It must be delivered to the target in some kind of vehicle which, unless it is a free-flying rocket, is subject to various kinds of attack. Marked superiority in the vehicle or in the means of shooting down the enemy's vehicles may be no less important than superiority in numbers of bombs, especially if those numbers are something less than gigantic. If those several types of superiority are concentrated on the same side, the disparity in atomic fighting power may be sufficient to warrant comparison with outright monopoly.

The Soviet Union has been able, with the assistance of German technicians, to build several types of jet-propelled fighters, and she has also built several large bombers patterned after our B-29, some models of which were impounded by her during the war. But a few German technicians are not going to make the difference between a backward technology and an eagerly progressive one. Our lead in types of aircraft, in the ordnance of combat aviation, and in anti-aircraft matériel should, or rather *could*, be as great during the next 20 years as it was in the recent war. The only question is whether we will make the necessary effort to keep in the lead in our military technology. That the Soviet Union will spare no effort within her capabilities to overtake us goes without saying.

We are often told that our *monopoly* of the atomic bomb is a wasting asset. It is, to be sure, in the sense that some day it is bound to end and we are constantly getting closer to that day. But is our *superiority* similarly a wasting asset? In one respect, at least, we know that it is not, for our fund of bombs is increasing steadily during the period in which the Soviet Union remains without any. On the day that the Soviet Union produces its first bomb, we will have many more than we do at present. What happens thereafter depends on a large number of variables. But looking forward from the present, we may say with a good deal of assurance that our present superiority in atomic armaments will increase considerably before it begins to wane, that it may continue to increase even after the Soviet Union is producing bombs, and that it may be a long time in waning thereafter. At any rate, we know that merely to distinguish — as is usually done — between the monopoly period (in which we are safe) and the post-monopoly period (in which we are lost) is not enough.

One might incidentally point out that it is easy to be over-subtle concerning the political consequences of our present monopoly of the bomb. The duty of the intellectual to get behind the obvious too often betrays him into ignoring the obvious or even denying it. We have heard a good many references to the fact that the atomic bomb, being a weapon of mass destruction, is not really handy for diplomatic manœuvring. We have been told also that since we would never use it against cities inhabited

by friendly peoples, it would not help us one whit in stopping
Soviet armies from overrunning Western Europe. The latter observation happens not to be strategically correct, since the destruction of *Russian* cities and industries would make a great
deal of difference in the ability of the Soviet armies to overrun
Western Europe, or to maintain themselves in that area if they
got there. But the fact remains that the atomic bomb is today
our *only* means for throwing substantial power immediately
against the Soviet Union in the event of flagrant Soviet aggression. The Soviets may underestimate the power of the bomb
(as may, indeed, our own military leaders), but they cannot be
entirely oblivious of that fact. If they choose war now it will be
either because they underestimate the bomb even more grossly
than they appear to or because they would rather face the hazard
now when our bombs are few than later when they are many.

Concerning the effects of the atomic bomb upon our military
organization and strategic plans, we must recognize first of all
that, to paraphrase Clemenceau, the matter is much too important to be left to the generals — or to the politicians either
for that matter. Formulation of security policy demands anticipation of probabilities with due regard to what is politically possible
or feasible. But consideration of the latter may too easily degenerate into preoccupation with what is politically safe. Political
leaders, moreover, have neither the time nor the inclination to
preoccupy themselves with the long-term significance of changes
in military technology, and rarely the competence to make anything of it if they do. They must rely upon the advice of their
military aides, who belong to a profession long recognized as
markedly conservative — though it is easy to exaggerate the
degree and character of that conservatism — who have vested
service and personal interests which influence them consciously
or unconsciously, whose talents are not primarily dialectic, and
who are saddled with tremendous responsibility. The responsibility powerfully reinforces the conservative tendencies already
present as a result of nurture and training. We are therefore not
likely to find military leaders, or the civilian officials whom they
advise, accepting readily upon the advent of some revolutionary
military device that drastic adjustment which free and objective
inquiry may indicate as necessary or at least desirable.

It is a little startling, some three years after Hiroshima, to find
the military departments of our government still apparently un-

prepared to think in terms of what strategic effects are to be expected from the use of any given number of bombs. The national safety will of course demand close secrecy concerning conclusions reached, but in this instance there is reason for believing that "security" is concealing the absence of thinking rather than the import of the ideas derived. For example, in the paper prepared by the War Department in March 1947 on "The Effects of the Atomic Bomb on National Security," there is a reference to something called a "significant" number of bombs. The meaning of "significant" is then explained only as indicating that number of bombs which would "provide an important military capability."[3] The military profession is not the only one which habitually betrays itself with catch phrases, but when we think of the absence of logic usually inherent in such sacrosanct phrases as "balanced fleet" or "balanced force," we cannot be too optimistic about the precision of thought behind the "important military capability."

We know that one bomb will not win a war against a major Power, since it took two to produce the surrender of an already defeated Japan. The same may reasonably be held to be true of five or ten. But there appears to be little idea anywhere what number would be "significant" and even less conception of how many it takes to make the weapon "decisive." Much will of course depend on how the bombs are used, but then the significance of the whole issue is that the number available and the estimates concerning the capabilities of that number will in large part govern the way in which they are used.

It is not easy to extrapolate the strategic effectiveness of atomic bombs from the experience with strategic bombing gained in the recent war. There are too many differences, besides that of magnitude of destruction per bomb or per plane, between bombing with chemical bombs and attacking with atomic bombs. It is not even a simple matter to determine the factor of increase in power of the atomic bomb over an equivalent load of chemical bombs. But we do have enough data to provide the basis for some intensive research which might throw some light on the problem. What we need to know is: "How many bombs will do what?" And the "what" must be reckoned in over-all strategic results rather than merely in acres destroyed.

[3] The War Department Paper was published in the Public Affairs Bulletin No. 55 already cited. The specific reference above is to page 67 of the Bulletin.

The evidence is presumptive only, but nevertheless impressive, that our military planners are thinking of an atomic bomb which is an "important military capability" but nevertheless only an ancillary rather than a decisive weapon. The chief danger is that the inevitably transitory nature of the conditions presumed will not be recognized sufficiently or in time. Regardless of what the Soviet Union may accomplish in the field, our own production of atomic bombs is proceeding apace, and the justification for regarding the weapon as an ancillary one is bound to evaporate as our stockpile accumulates.

IV

If we consider national defense policy in its broader aspects, and look beyond the period of American monopoly of atomic weapons, we see that recognition of the loss of American invulnerability to overseas attack and expectation of quick decisions in the event of war will no doubt entail a violent wrench to our defense traditions. Preparedness in the old sense of the term, which meant mainly provision for great expansion of the military services and of military production after the outbreak of hostilities, will appear even less adequate than it has been charged with being in the past. What will that mean for the costs of military preparedness?

Unquestionably the costs will increase, as they have already begun to. But we should not assume that the restraints which have always operated on the growth of military budgets will become inconsequential. There have been no systematic studies of the various factors governing the size of military budgets. It is obvious that periods of international tensions generally stimulate increases in military expenditure, and historians have dwelt on the scale of the armaments races preceding the two world wars. But they have scarcely considered the significance of the fact that in each case the extent of the arming, though large in comparison with more tranquil periods, was relatively small in contrast to the expansion of the war period itself.

We are speaking here partly of ordinary human inertia, even under circumstances where war appears imminent, and in so far as that inertia can be relied upon to be both pronounced and universal it should definitely enter into our calculations. But there is more to the matter than simple inertia. Wartime economies are characteristically fat-consuming. Both the toleration of them by the public and the physical possibility of maintaining their inordinate pace depend on the fact that they are temporary and recognized to be such. If there is to be fat to consume it must first be accumulated. In other words, even from the point of view strictly of defense needs, war economies can be inaugurated too soon as well as too late. And if the relevant comments of General Eisenhower while he was Chief of Staff of the Army can be taken as representative, that fact is recognized by the military themselves.

There is also the problem of avoiding military expenditure which is improvident not only because it is too large but also because it is misdirected. We have heard much, for example, of the business of dispersing our cities as a defense against atomic attack. It is clear that such dispersion would result in a tremendous loss of fixed and sunk capital and, in all probability, in a less efficient spatial arrangement of industries than previously existed. Thus, even if one should make the wholly untenable assumption that wholesale dispersion of our cities and the losses resulting would be tolerated by the public, the project might still appear to be militarily wasteful. A great many combat airplanes could be provided with what it would cost to disperse even a relatively small city. There is no doubt a margin for the dispersion of key industries and services which would not loom large in terms of the economy as a whole but which would nevertheless have important security results. If so, the accomplishment of that objective should remain a maximum as well as a minimum goal.

These observations are of course not very reassuring to those who, like the present writer, deplore the necessity of spending on military protection even so substantial a portion of our national income as we are spending today. The limits referred to are fairly flexible and we are still far from having reached them. And what will occur in this country when the conviction settles upon it that the Soviet Union is producing atomic bombs is the big question of the future. But the error for which we are now paying was after all perpetrated some three centuries ago, when Galileo was permitted to escape burning. Our problem now is to develop the habit of living with the atomic bomb, and the very incomprehensibility of the potential catastrophe inherent in it may well make that task easier.

NEW TECHNIQUES OF WAR AND
NATIONAL POLICIES

By BERNARD BRODIE

IN CONTRAST to the titles of five other papers in this series, which contain such phrases as "international relations" or "world order," the assignment given this writer refers to the effect of new techniques of war on "national policies." It is therefore appropriate to interpret "national policies" in this context to refer to security policy whether the subjects of that policy be foreign or domestic. For the modern world it is perhaps in any case as logical to distinguish between security and welfare policies, both of which have foreign and domestic implications, as to adhere to the traditional though equally arbitrary distinction between foreign policy and domestic policy.

PRELIMINARY CONSIDERATIONS

It is important to notice at the outset that we are dealing here with two distinct but related problems. The first concerns the effects of changes in technology and in other human capacities on the techniques of waging war. One must include the "other human capacities" because, after all, total mobilization requires devices of an economic and political nature which were wholly unthought of prior to 1914 and which represent social inventions quite as ingenious and as far-reaching in their consequences as the changes in military technology. The second problem is to determine the effects of the new military techniques thus evolved upon national policies.

Speculation on the first problem demands conversance with basic strategic principles and some familiarity with things scientific and technological. The latter problem, on the other hand, demands *in addition* consideration of psychological, social, economic, and political factors upon which—in this particular context—the available data are all too sparse and nebulous. Also, the errors resulting from the former speculation become, equally with the valid judgments, the premises of the latter, and in the process they are subject to a certain multiplier action. The least, therefore, we should ask of ourselves is

[144]

some measure of humility concerning our conclusions. The number and magnitude of the variables are almost overwhelming.

As a matter of fact, the limited historical data we do have indicate that national policies have been about as often based upon erroneous judgments of the military significance of current technological trends as upon correct judgments. The error may be due to underestimation of the degree or rate of technological progress to be expected of a new development or to overestimation.[1] It may be due to a misapprehension of the strategic effect of a given technological trend even when that trend itself is more or less correctly forecast.[2] It has happened in the past that a very serious error of policy resulted from a wrong identification of the potential enemy.[3] Also, in some contexts relatively minor developments will help to stimulate or provoke panic;[4]

---

1. The overestimation has usually, but not aways, been relative, involving an underestimation of the progress to be expected of various countering weapons. Thus, the introduction of the shell gun in naval warfare in the 1830's prompted predictions that the large warship (and with it British naval supremacy) was a thing of the past. The subsequent introduction of iron armor stimulated the contrary conviction—that it was feasible to construct an "impregnable" ship. Jellicoe's handling of the British Grand Fleet at Jutland was largely governed by his fear of German torpedoes, which in fact did so little damage as to argue that the British admiral exaggerated in his mind the potentialities of the weapon as of that time. The greatly exaggerated expectations inherent in the "air supremacy" theories of General Douhet and Brigadier General "Billy" Mitchell resulted partly from an underestimation of the development to be expected of certain counterair weapons, such as antiaircraft guns, and partly from a gross overestimation of the amount of physical damage which could reasonably be expected on land and sea targets from a given weight of chemical bombs (the only kind they could consider). Another overestimation which had tremendous strategic consequences was that which the British navy and government placed upon the effectiveness of the "Asdic" (supersonic detecting device against submarines) prior to World War II.

2. Perhaps the most conspicuous historical example is the confusion which attended the introduction of the steam warship, which on both sides of the Channel was interpreted by many as favoring France at the expense of Great Britain (see my *Sea Power in the Machine Age* [2d ed.; Princeton, 1943], chap. iv).

3. Thus, the French in the late nineteenth and early twentieth centuries vigorously promoted the development of the submarine as the weapon which would destroy British naval supremacy, only to face the threat of ruin from that instrument when Great Britain became the chief ally of France against Germany.

4. The introduction of the British battleship "Dreadnought" (1906), which had an important influence on the current British-German naval race, illustrates this principle in two ways. In the first place, when measured against the innovations of the fifteen years preceding and of the eight or ten years following, it did not represent nearly so novel a departure either in design or in fighting effectiveness as contemporaries and also later historians generally assumed. Second, it was overlooked in that instance, as it has been in many others, that it usually requires numbers to make a new design of combat instrument strategically important. As one British former Admiralty official expressed it in reference to the much more radical innovation of the introduction of the ironclad: "It is deplorable that out of this expectation of novelty and progress in every newly designed vessel has grown a tendency to regard as comparatively useless all vessels of earlier date and less formidable power." If this were acceptable, he continued, "the greatest Naval Power henceforward would not be that which possessed the greatest aggregate of force, but that which possessed the most powerful ship" (Sir William White, "Our Unarmoured Ships," *Colburn's United Service Magazine*, September, 1873).

[145]

in others the most revolutionary changes will fail to disturb complacency among public and politicians. Nor can it be assumed that the context which promotes complacency is necessarily one in which friendly and pacific relations prevail with other states. Certainly the complacency which ruled in Great Britain in the mid-1930's had other bases.

The formulation of security policy is, after all, a matter of anticipation of probabilities—as qualified by considerations of what is politically possible, feasible, or safe—on the part of persons who, whether responsible by nature or not, at least have enormous responsibility thrust upon them. As politicians these persons have neither the time nor the inclination to preoccupy themselves, as some scholars or strategists may do, with the long-term significance of changes in military technology, and rarely the competence to make anything of it if they do. The Churchills, who are temperamentally disposed toward toying with strategic and tactical concepts, are rare sports among their breed. Most political leaders must rely upon the advice of their military aides, who belong to a profession long recognized as markedly conservative (though it is possible to exaggerate the character and magnitude of that conservatism), who have vested service and personal interests which influence them consciously or unconsciously, whose talents are not primarily dialectic, and who are likewise saddled with tremendous responsibility. Responsibility usually demands that one hedge one's bets, for pretty much the same reason that life insurance companies are required by law to follow a conservative investment policy. We are therefore not likely to find military leaders, or the politicians whom they advise, accepting completely, upon the advent of some revolutionary military device, that drastic adjustment which free and objective inquiry may indicate as necessary or at least desirable.

Moreover, we must concede in passing that the conservative military outlook (reflected, for example, in excessive resort to the axiom of Jomini that "methods change but principles are unchanging") has had in the past a good many opportunities of saying "I told you so." The anchor to windward, while it has often proved costly through excessive drag, has also—with sufficient frequency to be impressive—served to avoid disaster. For example, even if one concludes that the battleship is today an obsolete instrument (and whether one does so or not must depend in part on just what one means by "obsolete"), one must nevertheless acknowledge that the battleship type has been

[146]

charged with being obsolete on and off for well over one hundred years. The estimate which was proved true only after so long a delay must be deemed to have been wrong for most of the time that it was entertained.

Similarly, if one had to take part in a debate on whether Billy Mitchell or General Douhet was an accurate prophet of World War II, one could probably make as strong case for the negative in each case as for the affirmative. The question is not affected by whether or not either or both may be proved right in a third world war. The stock market usually deals severely with those speculators whose predictions are correct in character and degree but not in timing. The issues of war and of national policy are not less rigorous in their penalties for errors of timing. For the purpose of policy decisions, a short-term forecast which is correct in timing is likely to be a good deal more useful than a long-term forecast which indicates only trends.

The fact is that what looks on the surface like simple conservatism may often be due to a wider comprehension of all the factors operating in a situation than is enjoyed by the person of more visionary outlook. This is not to suggest that such is the *usual* explanation of conservatism in military matters. One must avoid giving undue credit even to those correct intuitions which are held so rigidly and uncritically as to be practically indistinguishable from prejudices. The person who is one time right for the wrong reasons may also on an equally important occasion be disastrously wrong for the very same reasons. But there are several good reasons why the person who is not swept off his feet by the advent of some new device frequently turns out at the critical moment to have been right after all.

First, it is too often overlooked that technology marches on with a broad sweep, that the development which commands attention may be in process of having its effectiveness diminished or even nullified by some concurrent development which is either too unobtrusive or unspectacular to draw attention or is being carried on in secret. One must not push that point too far. One should be especially dubious of the degree of its applicability to an innovation of such radical and far-reaching consequences as the atomic bomb. Besides, except in relative terms which permit of wide latitudes of effectiveness, it is simply not true historically (to quote a distinguished American admiral) that "there has never yet been a weapon against which man has been unable to devise a counter-weapon or defense." Neverthe-

[147]

less, the examples even in recent history when the point has been valid and significant are much too numerous to catalogue.

Second, we must remember that technology is not all that matters. In the summer of 1940 it seemed that Great Britain could not possibly stand against the odds that faced her and that conclusive defeat before the end of the year was practically a certainty. Was it bull-headedness, chauvinism, or a deeper insight which induced British leaders to reject that view? Somewhere deep in the national heritage was a trait which had survived more than a century of industrial revolution and a generation of political and social disillusionment and which was to save Britain and British liberties once again. We are speaking here of the morale factor, which Napoleon considered to have thrice the importance of the material, which may be more rather than less important in an age of atomic bombs, and which is not the only factor operating to qualify the significance of the technological factor in war.

A third point is one which would hardly have been worth considering prior to Hiroshima but which may in the future be of increasing importance. As the atomic bomb and other weapons tend under some circumstances to raise what Professor Harold Lasswell has called the "critical level of exacerbation" in international affairs, there develops the possibility that a nation which may be incapable of fighting a total war may still exercise many if not all the prerogatives and responsibilities of a great power in crises short of total war. For example, if it were concluded that the United Kingdom is hopelessly vulnerable to new forms of attack from the Continent, that conclusion might nevertheless have to be discounted even in calculations of British military-political capabilities. In a world which, however beset by antagonisms, is universally loath to pull the trigger starting a third world war, the ability to project substantial power abroad in "troubled areas" might have a significance quite separate from the issue of vulnerability at home. That is especially likely to be true if Great Britain is allied, formally or informally, to a nation like our own which is not comparably vulnerable.

We may now turn to a consideration of certain specific technological developments which appear bound to have such obvious and far-reaching effects upon techniques of waging war as to oblige political and military leaders to make substantial adjustment in their security policies. In doing so, it is impossible to avoid concentrating attention mainly upon the atomic bomb. Those other new military techniques

[148]

which are presently in process of development are likely to prove significant mainly in the extent to which they enhance and supplement the effectiveness of the atomic bomb or diminish it. For example, the very-long-range rocket (V-2 type) is important primarily in that it may ultimately become the vehicle of an atomic attack, though at present that possibility seems relatively remote. On the other hand, ground-to-air rockets and air-to-air rockets (for use against enemy aircraft) may prove most important in the degree to which they qualify the effectiveness of atomic attack. Even bacteriological warfare is likely to develop, if at all, as an adjunct to atomic war rather than as something to be used quite independently of the latter.

THE ATOMIC BOMB COMPARED WITH PREVIOUS WEAPONS

The impact of the atomic bomb on United States policy has thus far been evidenced most clearly in the almost frantic effort to secure the adoption of a system of international control of atomic energy. It is difficult if not impossible to find a historical precedent for the eagerness with which this nation has pursued an endeavor which, if successful, would deprive it of the advantages of monopoly possession of a decisive military weapon. To be sure, the monopoly is bound to be temporary, but that has always been true of new weapons, the monopoly possession of which has usually been jealously guarded for as long as possible. Indeed, the United States is even now behaving in the customary manner concerning all new weapons other than those based on the explosive release of atomic energy, a fact which in itself sufficiently demonstrates that the exceptional American position on atomic-energy control is based on something other than national generosity. That "something other" is of course a well-warranted fear of living in a world which morally and politically is little different from the one we have known but which in addition is characterized by multilateral possession of atomic armaments.

However, while the fear persists, the trend in the United States has apparently been away from panic rather than toward it. The habit of living with the bomb would itself sufficiently account for that trend, though there have also been other factors at work which will shortly be reviewed. What the situation will be when the United States acquires the knowledge or the firm suspicion that the Soviet Union too is producing atomic bombs is another matter, consideration of which we can also postpone for the moment. At any rate, our government has apparently hardened in its resolve that any international control

[149]

scheme must contain within itself practically watertight guaranties against violation and evasion. And, in so far as data are available, there is every indication that this resolve enjoys overwhelming public support.

Perhaps the most important as well as immediate consequence of this attitude is that it greatly lessens the possibility that an international control system will in fact be achieved. Indeed, American leadership in securing formal suspension of the activities of the United Nations Atomic Energy Commission is open acknowledgment of that fact. Thus, we must look forward to a period of national adjustment to the prospect of living in an atomic age devoid of effective international controls. That does not mean that efforts to secure such controls will necessarily languish. But it does mean that other forms of adjustment will receive a good deal more public attention and support than they have thus far. It will mean particularly a heightened emphasis on anticipating the character of a war fought with atomic bombs, with a view both to taking all reasonable precautions against the terrible hazards of such a conflict and to securing victory if it must come. The latter goal may appear a mockery to many sensitive minds, but it is not likely to appear such to those responsible for national policy, especially since the argument that visible strength is the best guaranty against war is not easily refuted to the public satisfaction.

We must therefore attempt to predict, first, the effects of the atomic bomb upon the military services of the future and, second, the character and extent of civilian adjustment to military needs. Among the many variables which bear upon our predictions, the most important by far is summed up by the following question: "How many bombs can one expect to find in existence any given number of years hence, and how will they be distributed among the nations?" All our conclusions depend upon the answer to that question, yet it is curious how consistently this issue has been slighted or ignored in the general debate on the destiny of the armed forces. Each view expressed usually reflects a certain presumption concerning numbers and distribution of atomic bombs, but the specific presumption being applied is rarely isolated and acknowledged. It may be said in general that those who stress the completely revolutionary character of the bomb are tacitly presuming that in the not-too-distant future it will become relatively abundant, while the conservatives tend to presume that it will remain inordinately scarce. Neither side, however, shows much evidence of being aware of the specific presumption it has made, let alone of having weighed the validity of that presumption.

In fact, with our present lack of knowledge it is difficult to say what range of numbers must be regarded as representing abundance. For example, in the paper prepared by the War Department in March, 1947, on "The Effects of the Atomic Bomb on National Security," there is a reference to something called a "significant" number of bombs. The meaning of "significant" is then explained only as indicating that number of bombs which would "provide an important military capability."[5] The Army may have specific numbers in mind when it uses such terms, but the chances are that it does not. We know that one bomb will not win a war against a major power (it took two to produce the surrender of an already defeated Japan), and the same may reasonably be held to be true of five or ten. But we have little idea what number is "significant," and even less conception of how many it takes to make the weapon "decisive." Much will, of course, depend on how the bombs are used, but then the number available will in large part govern the way in which they are employed.

We do, to be sure, have a good deal of experience with strategic bombing from the recent war, and it would appear superficially that, by merely computing the number of atomic bombs it would take (using the evidence of Hiroshima and Nagasaki) to wreak the destruction done with TNT bombs and incendiaries, we would have some measure of the number of atomic bombs necessary to achieve "significant" or "decisive" results. We have been told, for example, by excellent authority that with each plane loaded with ten tons of TNT bombs and incendiaries it would have required some 210 B-29's at Hiroshima and 120 B-29's at Nagasaki to accomplish the damage done at each of those places with one plane carrying an atomic bomb. The same source suggests that, if the more powerful Nagasaki bomb had been used at Hiroshima, the damage done to the latter city could have been equaled only by 270 B-29's loaded with ten tons each of nonatomic explosives.[6]

These figures are no doubt very useful in suggesting a means of

5. The War Department paper is included in Bernard Brodie and Eilene Galloway, *The Atomic Bomb and the Armed Services* ("Public Affairs Bulletin," No. 55 [Washington, D.C.: Legislative Reference Service, Library of Congress, May, 1947]). The specific reference cited above is on p. 67 of the bulletin.

6. The United States Strategic Bombing Survey, *The Effects of Atomic Bombs on Hiroshima and Nagasaki* (Washington, D.C.: Government Printing Office, 1946), p. 33.

{ 151 }

arriving at the factor of increase of power of the atomic bomb over the TNT bomb—a far better means unquestionably than that of merely computing the relative amounts of energy released. But the difficulty is that the two types of bombs are not really comparable in strictly quantitative terms. In some respects the atomic bomb is more destructive than the comparison given above would indicate; in other respects it is less so. Let us see why. First, it is clear that, while heat and blast effects are common to both atomic and nonatomic bombs, the element of radioactivity in the former introduces a new factor which is profoundly significant both for human casualties and for the enduring contamination of bombed areas. Second, the fact that a given amount of damage can be effected in a far shorter period of time with atomic bombs than with conventional bombs has enormous implications in terms of the ability of the target state to repair damage and to adjust its defenses to the attack. For example, by the middle of 1944 Germany was still going strong, and it could hardly be said that the strategic bombing to which she had been subject during the previous five years had yet accomplished anything like "decisive" results. For one thing, it had not been strictly cumulative. But if the same amount of destruction—or even half the amount—had been telescoped into, say, one week, it is hard to imagine how that nation could have been anything other than completely prostrate. Third, the effective bombing range with an atomic bomb of a plane like the B-29 is, for reasons which will be mentioned later in this chapter, potentially much greater than that of the same plane carrying ordinary explosives. Fourth, there is the matter of psychological impact, the terror effects of the atomic bomb, the proportions of which we can scarcely begin to predict. True, in the recent war the human animal showed himself capable of adjusting to heavy bombing raids to an astonishing degree, but at least he was given the opportunity to get adjusted through the very gradualness with which the bombing attack reached its crescendo. Moreover, the knowledge that some two or three thousand aircraft were approaching a certain city was an unmistakable signal to the inhabitants of that city to repair to air-raid shelters, and at least in part an "all-clear" signal to the inhabitants of other cities far removed—both of which characteristics are likely to be absent in a situation where individual planes carry the means of destroying whole sections of large cities.

On the other hand, there are at least two factors, apart from the issue of possible scarcity, which suggest the necessity of discounting

[152]

somewhat the "factor of increase of power" which might otherwise be attributed to the atomic bomb over the TNT bomb. First, there is the tactical question. A single plane may, as at Hiroshima, accomplish an amount of destruction comparable to that effected by 210 similar planes carrying ordinary bombs—provided it arrives over the target. But if the area is strongly defended, a force of 210 aircraft might be able to get the great majority of its planes through where a single plane would have no chance whatever. If planes bearing atomic bombs have to be attended by large numbers of decoys (perhaps armed with ordinary bombs) and fighters, the advantage of economy in logistics and operations otherwise accruing to the atomic bomb is largely lost. However, it is also true that under some conditions a single plane has a better chance of reaching its target than a large force. Second, since the atomic bomb in its minimum efficient size is necessarily of "city-buster" destructiveness, there are relatively few targets on which its full destructive power can be utilized. Even Nagasaki, because of its configuration, suffered much less damage than Hiroshima, despite the fact that the Nagasaki bomb was more powerful. When we say that a plane carrying an atomic bomb can do the same amount of damage as two hundred or three hundred planes carrying conventional bombs, we are speaking of an exceptionally favorable target. We must therefore consider the effectiveness of a bomb partly at least in terms of the target. It happens, of course, that the most appropriate of indicated targets—that is, the large city—is an extraordinarily important one. It may be used on other targets if it is plentiful enough, but on most other targets its relative advantage over TNT bombs will not be nearly so great. On the other hand, we must ask ourselves whether it would ever have to be used on "other targets" after the main cities of a nation were destroyed.

These are only the more outstanding of the considerations which affect the question of how many bombs are "significant" and how many could be considered a "decisive" force. It can readily be seen that the magnitude of the terror created might well make a rather small number decisive, and then again it might not, depending largely on the preparation of the target population, psychological and otherwise, and on their degree of awareness or ignorance of what is going on (in this case ignorance might be an asset). In any case, there is a large problem area here demanding a great deal of intensive investigation. The essential question to be answered is: "How many

{ 153 }

bombs will do what?" And the "what" must be reckoned in over-all strategic results rather than merely in acres destroyed.

However, if our present knowledge is closely confined, our ignorance also has its limits. For the best of political reasons we are not being told the current rate of United States production of atomic bombs, but even the most conservative guess would lead us to conclude that the number which will have accumulated after, say, ten years of production will certainly be "significant." And we know also that for purposes of planning ten years is not a long time. It is less than half the normal life-expectancy of a cruiser. Thus, there is no time like the present to begin to think of how wars will be fought when the atomic bombs available to one or both belligerents will be numbered at least in scores and possibly in hundreds.

THE FOUR CONDITIONS OF ATOMIC-WAR STRATEGY

As we project into the future the effects of the atomic bomb upon the armed services, we must distinguish between at least four different phases or conditions: (1) American monopoly expressed in a small number of bombs; (2) American monopoly with a relatively large number of bombs; (3) the end of American monopoly but with the United States still enjoying a large margin of superiority over its major rival both in atomic bombs and in the means of delivering them; and (4) the end not only of monopoly but of significant American superiority.

Here again we are using terms like "small" and "relatively large" without any effort at precision, but for the reasons already given we are obliged to do so and will continue to be obliged to do so until we have more knowledge than yet possessed by any one person. Nevertheless, these rough distinctions have value in organizing our thoughts. They indicate, at the very minimum, that to distinguish merely between the monopoly period and the post-monopoly period —as is usually done—is not enough. Thus, the position described under (3) above, while probably not so favorable as that described under (2), is nevertheless not an adverse one, and it may last much longer. It may even be a more favorable position than that described under (1). And it is apparent that each situation requires a distinctive strategy.

The situation described under (1), "American monopoly with a small number of bombs," is certainly that situation in which we found ourselves immediately following the end of the war. It may be

[154]

the situation we are in at this writing, depending on (*a*) our current rate of production and (*b*) the old question of how many bombs is a "small" number.

Although we must know the answers to these questions to determine just how long this situation will last, if it is still with us, we do know that it is bound to be very limited in time. For example, even if our present rate of production of atomic bombs should be as low as two a month (a wholly random figure), the continuation of that rate would result in ten years' time in the accumulation of the materials for some 240 atomic bombs, which could hardly be called a "small" number.

Situation (2), "American monopoly with a relatively large number of bombs," would, of course, not occur at all if our monopoly should be broken by a rival state in the very near future. But if the more optimistic predictions (from our point of view) concerning Russian capabilities to produce the bomb are true, this situation might last from five to ten years, possibly longer. The military strategy dictated by this situation is distinctly and perhaps drastically different from that indicated under situation (1).

The situation mentioned under (3) above suggests that the end of monopoly need not and probably will not spell the immediate end of decisive superiority, especially when we remember that what counts is not the atomic bomb alone but also the vehicles and devices connected with its use. It is too generally forgotten that our position vis-à-vis the Soviet Union in atomic warfare will be much better on the day the Russians produce their first bomb than it is at present, for the simple reason that we will then have many more bombs, perhaps several times as many, as we do now. It may be true that our *monopoly* is a "wasting asset," since it is bound soon or later to run out, and we are always getting closer to the day it does so. But our *superiority* will increase considerably before it begins to wane; it may continue to increase even after the Soviet Union is producing bombs; and it may be a long time in waning thereafter. If the raw materials available in the world for the production of atomic bombs are as limited as some seem to think, this situation may be a permanent one, that is, it may not in our time give way to situation (4).

Situation (4), "the end not only of monopoly but also of significant American superiority," envisages the two-way war with atomic bombs which is most discussed even though most remote in time. How remote in time it is must remain for the time being a huge question mark. Certainly we must include it in our thinking as a possibility to be reckoned with even within the next ten years. But within such a time period it is hardly the most likely contingency and, at any rate, is not the one for which our policy-makers will plan exclusively.

It is, of course, very difficult to define in simple terms what superiority or the lack of it must involve. For example, a three-to-one margin of superiority might be very significant if the total number of bombs in existence was reckoned in scores or even hundreds, but would be much less significant if the number was reckoned in thousands, since in the latter case the side with the smaller number might nevertheless have enough to win decisive results in a surprise attack. Similarly, as already indicated, the side which has the best means of delivering the bomb has an advantage which may either implement a superiority in numbers of bombs or offset an inferiority in numbers. And the "means of delivery" definitely must include "sabotage" devices as well as aircraft or rockets, though one must not regard as easy the laying of bombs by secret means.

We may now take up these situations one by one and attempt to see what each of them means for the strategy of war. We must confine ourselves to broad outlines, because we are likely enough to be in error even if we do so, and we are bound to be in error if we attempt to construct the details as well. We must also isolate out the possibility of revolutionary developments comparable to the atomic bomb, such as might occur in bacteriology, though we must, of course, reckon with pronounced evolutionary advances in the weapons we now know.

AMERICAN WAR STRATEGY UNDER CONDITIONS OF MONOPOLY

Situation (1): American monopoly expressed in a small number of bombs.—The strategy of this situation must obviously conform closely to the strategy followed before the advent of the atomic bomb. In other words, the role and general composition of each of the existing services remains pretty much unchanged. The two questions of chief importance are (*a*) how the relatively few atomic bombs available should be used if war should occur during this period and (*b*) to what extent and in what way the services should begin to remodel themselves in anticipation of succeeding phases.

This is the period during which we may accept as presumably valid the dictum of General H. H. Arnold that "the great unit cost of the

[156]

atomic bomb means that as nearly as possible every one must be delivered to its intended target."[7] To make the statement strictly correct, one must substitute the word "scarcity" for the words "unit cost." Once the shooting begins, the unit cost paid at some date in the past is of no consequence whatever, but the existing scarcity, which may have been in part dictated by that cost, does make it necessary to seek maximum effectiveness of each of the bombs in hand.

General Arnold, in amplifying the statement quoted above, goes on to state that the very heavy bomber (i.e., B-29 or larger) is as yet the only way to deliver the atomic bomb, and he adds that delivery with such a vehicle can be "certain of success only when the user has air superiority." Since air superiority presumably depends largely upon vigorous fighter-plane support of attacking bombers, and since fighters are inevitably of much lesser range than large bombers, the implication is that bombers operating from distant bases are not *by themselves* a sufficiently reliable means of delivering atomic bombs. They or at least their supporting fighters must have bases close enough to the enemy so that the latter can operate over the targets. To be sure, one must consider the likelihood of the independent use of very high-speed jet-propelled bombers, but these types, too, are for the present of substantially shorter range than conventional propeller-driven aircraft of like size.

Thus, a probable basic requirement for the effective use of atomic bombs under the conditions here envisaged would be the acquisition and development of air bases relatively close to the enemy targets. With types of aircraft now in service that would mean at least as close as Iwo Jima is to Japan. Presumably, too, the scarcity of the bombs would militate against their all being expended in one brief bombing campaign. Thus, the advanced bases would, if held from the outset, have to be made secure. And, if not so held, they would have to be won and developed. In each case not only time is required but also the services of large sea, land, and air forces, roughly comparable in character to those of the last war. To be sure, if it proves feasible to launch atomic-bomb-carrying planes from aircraft carriers, the initial use of atomic bombs could come quite early in the war even if we did not already possess bases close to the enemy.

The conventional land, sea, and air forces would have to be brought into play not only to acquire the means of effectively launching atomic bombs, but—since we are postulating a relatively small num-

7. See his *Third Report to the Secretary of War, November 12, 1946*, p. 68 (printed ed.).

ber of bombs—to win the war. By definition, bombs which are "scarce" are insufficient in number to be decisive. One can therefore not expect that the major lines of strategy will be drawn with the use of atomic bombs primarily in mind. The atomic bomb will instead be considered a weapon of opportunity, to be used when circumstances indicate its use, and not something which dictates primary preoccupation with creating suitable circumstances.

It should incidentally be observed that if the atomic bomb is used as an ancillary weapon rather than a primary one, one of the chief military advantages ordinarily attributed to it is lost. From the point of view of logistics and of mobilization of war potential, the important thing about the atomic bomb is not that one bomb can destroy a city but that *one plane* can destroy a city. But if it is so scarce that it can be used "only when the user has air superiority," that is, only when the situation has been well prepared in advance and when the plane carrying the atomic bomb is attended on its mission by a large number of other planes, then one must conclude that it will make strategic bombing more effective without essentially changing the gigantic character of the effort from that which had to go into the strategic bombing campaigns of World War II.

Whether or not the strategy here described would really be applicable to a war fought in the near future, the fact is that our military leaders appear to be accepting it as applicable. If that be so, it is possible that they are underestimating the strategic effects to be gained from a bolder use of even a small number of atomic bombs. The stipulation that so far as possible each one must be delivered to its intended target has implications which conceivably might diminish rather than enhance the military effectiveness of the bombs available.

Situation (2): American monopoly with a large number of bombs.— To avoid reviving the question—which remains to be answered satisfactorily—of what is a "large" number of bombs, let us assume arbitrarily that by "large number" we mean one measured in three figures. Thus, if our present rate of production were two bombs per month and were to continue unchanged, our accumulation of atomic bombs (or rather the materials for assembling them) would be entering the "large numbers" category about four or five years hence.

There are at least two criteria separating this situation from the one described previously in terms of the method of using the bomb. First, the atomic bomb is now the primary weapon of strategic bombing, which is itself the decisive instrument of attack. Second, the possession of a large number of bombs indicates the acceptance of substantial wastage in their use. As is true of every missile fired in war, it is still *desirable* that every bomb reach its intended target. But since, as we have seen, the rigid stipulation that it do so is bound severely to limit and circumscribe its use, insistence upon it must frustrate full realization of the gigantic offensive potentialities of this new weapon.

All that is suggested here is the application to the atomic bomb of principles which govern the use of all other implements of warfare. The atomic bomb provides, potentially at least, the cheapest way of destroying enemy cities, but, paradoxically, that cheapness can be realized only if the user pushes out of his mind consideration of unit cost of the individual bomb. Only if he does so can he conceive of those bold uses of the bomb which will result in the maximum damage to the enemy in the briefest possible time.

Since we are assuming a situation in which we feel fairly confident the enemy has no atomic bombs, there is little reason why we should hesitate to expend the bulk of the bombs early in the war, before enemy defenses are alerted or at least before they reach their optimum organization. The surprise and shock value of a devastating raid early in the hostilities is bound to be far greater than one of equal magnitude later on. What do these postulates suggest for the strategy of attack?

In the first place, so long as we had long-range bombers capable of delivering the bombs from bases already in our possession, it would be foolish and wasteful to withhold our bombs until we had reached bases closer to the enemy. Closer bases would no doubt enable us to give strong fighter support to our invading bombers and would thus provide both greater security for those bombers and a great percentage of hits with our bombs. But offsetting those advantages would be the time and cost spent in acquiring and developing the advanced bases and the adjustments which that time would permit the enemy. Or perhaps some compromise scheme would be preferable, such as that of using perhaps half the bombs in an initial long-range blow to disorganize the enemy and then using the important advantage gained to seize the advanced bases (which should now be much easier to accomplish) for the more methodical use of the remaining bombs. But what seems on the face of it *not* to be indicated

[159]

is a concern from first to last with getting every atomic bomb on its intended target.

Now is it feasible to launch an atomic-bomb attack upon a distant great power such as the Soviet Union from bases already in our possession or likely to be available to us within a very few years? On the basis of technical performance even of types of aircraft now in service the answer would seem to be "Yes," and it should certainly be in the affirmative with new types of aircraft already existing in experimental models.

It must always be remembered that, from the point of view of military economics, a plane which has delivered an atomic bomb has paid for itself many times over, and upon making the sortie the plane must therefore be regarded as being at least as expendable as is the bomb itself. This freedom from the necessity of retrieving the aircraft means in effect a one-way flight, and therefore an approximate doubling of what is usually regarded as the "effective bombing range" of the plane. The crew (if there be one) is another matter. Strictly from the point of view of military bookkeeping, it too could be regarded as expendable. Other considerations will, however, influence the enterprise and perhaps prevail; but in any case it is not necessary that the crew members return to their jumping-off point in the same plane in which they departed. All sorts of possibilities will arise for their rendezvous with friendly submarines or other aircraft or for their landing and internment in neutral territory. So long as the principle is established that the plane itself need not be salvaged, an enormous extension of range results, and that extension need not be greatly affected by plans for the rescue of the crew. One must add that there are also other possibilities which may be developed for extending the range of existing aircraft, as, for example, by refueling in flight.

With these considerations in mind, we may contemplate the facts that a B-29 has made a nonstop flight of 8,200 statute miles, that bombers of considerably greater carrying capacity are far beyond the blueprint stage, and that Moscow is only 4,300 miles from the nearest United States air base in Maine. Certainly intercontinental warfare, at least as concerns strategic bombing, is not merely a possibility for the future. The seizure of advanced bases close to enemy territory may still present advantages for the successful use of the atomic bomb, but it is no longer an indispensable prerequisite to such use. And, depending upon its costs in men, resources, and especially time,

[160]

the attempt to seize such bases as a preliminary to the use of the bomb may well prove a strategy of waste.

The character of the adaptation required of the military services generally under the situation we are postulating is governed, first, by the fact that the atomic bomb and the system for delivering it are indisputably the major or "decisive" arm and, second, by the absence of any grave threat of an atomic counterblow. The first of these factors will demand not only that the mechanics of atomic attack will receive overriding priority in development and resources but also that the services not directly concerned with those mechanics nevertheless be oriented toward a strategy which recognizes the atomic bomb as the decisive weapon. Such orientation would involve, among other things, great emphasis on mobility of troops, in order that advantages gained by initial use of the atomic bomb may be promptly exploited. The second factor, in so far as it can be relied upon as a reality (which would depend mostly on the character of our intelligence), would give our services the freedom of action necessary for their proper orientation. That freedom can never be complete, since, whatever the excellence of our intelligence, we would never be justified in proceeding exclusively on the assumption that the enemy had no atomic bombs or means of delivering them.

A strategy which gives first place to offensive use of the atomic bomb implies an implementing but by no means inferior role for the navy and ground forces. For one thing, the amount of resources which the system of atomic attack can absorb will always be ruled by the number of atomic bombs in hand. Then there is the matter of diminishing returns in the use of any one weapon however powerful, and the atomic bomb might by its very successes quickly put itself into a subordinate role. That is exactly what happened to the American submarine in the latter stages of the Pacific war, when the lack of ship targets as a result largely of our previous submarine successes caused us to cut back our submarine-building program. Finally, the fact that a weapon is deemed decisive does not in military parlance mean that it is necessarily conclusive. The enemy may continue to resist though his cities be devastated, and, if a final conclusion to the business is desired, his territory may have to be invaded and occupied. Or his armies may have to be driven out of countries which they have occupied. In any case, large ground, sea, and air operations extending over months or even years of time might have to be undertaken.

[161]

A word should be added about the use of very-long-range rockets as vehicles for the atomic bomb. Some scientists and engineers in the field of guided missiles insist that, before we can have an accurately guided rocket of two or three thousand miles' range, such revolutionary developments are necessary that it is safe to presume that the event is at least twenty-five years away. Others among their colleagues argue that the length of time required depends largely upon the effort put into the job and that a fraction of the amount of effort that went into the Manhattan District Project would bring the result much sooner. Certainly the atomic bomb is a powerful enough weapon to warrant a good deal of research and development upon special vehicles for its conveyance. But those special vehicles need not take the form of rockets. Jet-propelled bombers, perhaps reaching supersonic speeds, would be difficult enough for any defense to cope with, and they are certainly much closer in time and would probably be much more reliable than three-thousand-mile rockets of the V-2 type.

Moreover, it must be remembered that the V-2 in our hands in 1944–45 would not have been nearly so useful to us as it was to the Germans. To us, with our overwhelming air superiority, it would have been a rather wasteful means of adding to our air bombardment strength. To the Germans at the time it was almost the only means of hitting back. The fact that it had certain advantages over aircraft is by no means unimportant, but it would be wrong to conclude, as some senior officers have concluded, that the effective use of atomic bombs must await a development in rockets which happens to be comfortably far off.[8]

Another question which arises is whether we would use the atomic bomb at all in another war if we were confident that we had a monopoly. To be sure, monopoly conditions would give us a certain freedom of choice in this matter which would probably be absent if the enemy too had a substantial number of atomic bombs. But, apart from the historical fact that we used the bombs against Japan when we had only two in hand and when we recognized that Japan was already defeated, there is another factor bearing on this question.

8. On this point see the paper entitled "U.S. Navy Thinking on the Atomic Bomb," in the already cited "Public Affairs Bulletin," No. 55, pp. 30–33; see also the relevant comments in the "Compiler's Critique on U.S. Navy Views," in the same bulletin, pp. 42–48. Some senior naval officers interviewed appeared to believe that the bombing plane was too "unreliable" a vehicle for the atomic bomb and that the development of a very-long-range rocket capable of carrying it lay in the distant future. The *reductio ad absurdum* of this argument is too obvious.

[162]

So long as the number of atomic bombs in our arsenal is small, their existence has relatively little influence on the composition and strategy of our armed services. In that case we can choose whether or not to use them in the event of war. But the latitude of choice tends to narrow as the number grows. For if the possession of a large number of bombs demands that all our armed services orient themselves toward an atomic offensive strategy, they must either carry out that orientation (in which case they would not be well prepared to fight a great nonatomic war) or pay heavy forfeit in the effectiveness of the bombs available. In other words, we cannot forever go on planning for two drastically different kinds of large-scale war. Considerations of economy and of getting the most possible fighting strength out of our military resources will dictate that we make up our minds at an early date whether or not we will use the bombs in war and adjust accordingly. There is not much doubt about what that decision will be, especially since the general expectation is that—failing the setting-up of an effective international control system—our major rival will begin to make atomic bombs within the next ten to twenty years.

AMERICAN SUPERIORITY UNDER POSTMONOPOLY CONDITIONS

Situation (3): the end of American monopoly, but with the United States still enjoying a large margin of superiority over its major rival both in atomic bombs and in the means of delivering them.—This situation has been virtually ignored in the debate on the strategic implications of the atomic bomb, yet it is one which will almost certainly endure for a long time after the Soviet Union produces its first bomb. There are several factors supporting this estimate.

First, there is some reason to believe that the amount of uranium and thorium available in the world for the manufacture of atomic bombs is much more limited than was being assumed two years ago, and the deposits available are much more accessible to the United States than to the Soviet Union. Hanson Baldwin was probably reflecting informed and heretofore confidential opinion when he made the following observations in the *New York Times* for November 9, 1947: "Responsible Government authorities have made a reassessment of atomic possibilities, short-term and long-term, in the past two years and a dramatic change in attitude toward the short-term future has resulted. Two years ago atomic scientists were talking glibly of 10,000 atomic bombs as if they were an accomplished fact; we were assured repeatedly that Russia could catch up and overtake

[163]

the United States in short order. . . . Today more sober judgment has intervened. . . . We know, too, that atomic bomb production is not a rapid and easy process, and that for a very long time to come the numbers available to us will be limited, and they will be far more limited to the Russians." Earlier in the same article Baldwin makes the following statement: "But it seems probable that the U.S.S.R. does not now have—although she may be able to find and develop at some future time—sufficient quantities of uranium to build many bombs. Unless she can get access to more uranium she probably will not be able to turn out bombs at a production rate in any way comparable to our own. In other words, we seemingly have almost a monopoly today on the *known* important sources of uranium." Thus, even apart from the matter of the important head start which we have, and which is likely to grow much greater before the Soviet Union produces its first bomb, the ultimate maximum production in that country is by no means likely to compare with our own ultimate maximum production.

We need only remember that the three most important known deposits of uranium lie in Canada, the Belgian Congo, and the United States, and that the fourth major deposit—in Czechoslovakia—is far less rich than any of the other three, to get a conception of the relative accessibility of uranium as between the United States and the Soviet Union. In thorium the situation is not far different, the two major known deposits being in Brazil and in India.

Second, the enormous technological lead which the United States has over the Soviet Union and which shows no immediate signs of diminishing is bound to mean a great potential advantage for the United States in the design of the instruments for using the atomic bomb. The atomic bomb by itself has no military utility. It must be delivered to the target in some kind of vehicle which, unless it is a free-flying rocket, is subject to various kinds of attack. Marked superiority in the vehicle or in the means of shooting down the enemy's vehicles may be no less important than superiority in numbers of bombs. Especially if those several types of superiority are concentrated on the same side, the disparity in atomic fighting power may be sufficient to warrant comparison with outright monopoly.

The Soviet Union has been able, with the assistance of German technicians, to build several types of jet-propelled fighters, and she has also built several large bombers patterned after our B-29, some models of which were impounded by her during the war. But a few

German technicians are not going to make the difference between a backward technology and an eagerly progressive one. Our lead in types of aircraft, in the ordnance of combat aviation, and in anti-aircraft material should, or rather *could*, be as great during the next twenty years as it was in the recent war. The only question is whether we will make the necessary effort to keep in the lead in our military technology. That the Soviet Union will spare no effort within her capabilities to overtake us goes without saying.

How do the military characteristics of situation (3) differ from those of the situation described in the immediately preceding pages? We must first acknowledge that situation (3) covers a wide range of possibilities, shading from near-monopoly position, on the one hand, to insignificant superiority, on the other. But so long as we are stipulating an *important* superiority both in bombs and in the instruments for using them, our problem is much simplified.

As concerns the offensive use of the atomic bomb itself, the same considerations which operated in situation (2) will tend to prevail here as well. The fact that the enemy possesses *some* atomic bombs may, on the one hand, put a greater urgency upon our using those we have in order to anticipate his attack and to weaken the potential strength of that attack; or it may, on the other hand, cause us to hold our bombs as a threat to induce him to withhold his. The latter procedure would, of course, nullify the offensive significance of our superiority unless our plan was to withhold our bombs only until the enemy was no longer in a position to use his effectively.

The fact that the enemy has some bombs will, however, greatly affect the offensive use of our forces other than those directly concerned with atomic warfare. The most obvious example is to be found in the case of the amphibious operation. It has been often enough observed that the Germans would not have needed very many atomic bombs utterly to disrupt and frustrate our Normandy landing in 1944. Our offensive strategy will have to be careful to avoid tactical concentrations of force in markedly exposed places. That is much more easily said than done, since the essence of offensive power has always been assumed to lie in the concentration of superior force at the appropriate place. In fact, the orthodox textbooks on strategy have usually elevated the idea of concentration to the status of a basic principle and have spoken of the "principle of concentration" as a corollary to the "principle of the offensive." The solution to this dilemma, and some solution will no doubt be found under any given

set of circumstances, will probably emphasize the distinction between tactical and strategic concentration. A force can be strategically concentrated while dispersed over a considerable amount of
space, so long as its components can work together to effect a common end and can achieve temporary tactical concentrations if need
be. There is still the dilemma that tactical concentrations may on
occasion be necessary, as they have been in the past, but no doubt
some ways can be found of achieving the degree of concentration
necessary to a tactical end while minimizing the vulnerability of that
concentration to atomic-bomb attack. These are problems to be
worked out in the future, and they can usually be worked out satisfactorily only with a given set of circumstances pertaining to a particular campaign at a given point of time. On the other hand, it is
by no means too early to begin thinking about some of the basic issues involved. It is not too early, for example, for our strategists to
start rethinking the campaigns of the recent war with the assumption
that the enemy had had a few atomic bombs to use at critical places.
Some very important conclusions would no doubt follow from such
exercises.

It is on the defensive side that the most significant changes take
place. The most important statement in this respect is to be found in
the War Department paper previously cited: "The atomic bomb,
primarily an offensive weapon, serves to emphasize the principle that
only by offensive action can victory be attained. However, the development of the atomic bomb by other nations requires that the U.S.
adopt a principle of strategy in seeming conflict with the fundamental importance of offensive effort. *We must devote a higher percentage
of our national resources than ever before to the measures we take for
defense.* We must do this in order to insure that we retain the
capability of delivering effective offensive effort."[9]

This statement is contained in a paper which declares at the outset
that it is considering in the main a situation in the future when other
nations besides the United States possess "significant quantities" of
atomic bombs. However, it applies at least as cogently in a situation
where the enemy has only a very small number of bombs, for two
reasons: (1) even a very few bombs—fewer than twenty, for example—could accomplish demoralization and perhaps fatal disruption in an America quite unprepared to cope with them, and (2) the
kind of defenses described in the War Department paper make more

9. *Op. cit.*, pp. 77–78.

[166]

sense, in terms of probable accomplishment, against an attack confined to a very limited number of bombs than they would against an attack involving hundreds of bombs.

The kind of defenses alluded to by the War Department paper might be summarized as comprising the following: defense against the vehicles of atomic attack (i.e., aircraft or guided missiles) through a development of devices comparable to those used against air attack in the recent war (air-fighter interception plus antiaircraft missiles plus radar detection); defense against the air-borne and sea-borne invasion forces which might seek to capitalize on the disruption caused by the attack (hardly a likely contingency where we are positing great atomic superiority on our side); readiness for instant retaliation; and a very modest amount of selective dispersion of vital industries (the paper is quite explicit and emphatic on the point that any wholesale dispersion of American cities is wholly out of the question).

THE SECURITY PROBLEM IN THE EVENT OF LOSS OF ATOMIC SUPERIORITY

Situation (4): the end not only of monopoly but also of significant American superiority.—This is the "all-out" atomic war upon which most of the prognosticators have been concentrating their attention. It might also be called the "impossible war," especially if a large number of atomic bombs were presupposed on both sides. It would be impossible to fight by any traditional use of traditional arms, and the cost even to the victor would be greater than that paid by any vanquished country in history. Yet the "impossible" war might have to be fought, partly because real threat of instant retaliation is the most important single defense under a situation of bilateral or multilateral distribution of large numbers of bombs, and partly because there is no precedent in history for supposing that large and proud nations will go on yielding forever to a rival whose strength, while terrible, is not overwhelmingly superior. The burdens on diplomacy for avoiding war under the conditions we are postulating are unimaginable, but the task is incomparably important. But the only thing that will keep diplomacy from breaking down ultimately is the conviction *on all sides* that war is far too horrible even to be contemplated. And the great dilemma is that that conviction can be sustained only by our making every possible effort to prepare for war and thus to engage in it if need be.

[167]

TECHNOLOGY AND INTERNATIONAL RELATIONS

The condition of no-monopoly–no-superiority requires the least discussion, not only because it is most remote in time (and perhaps probability), but also because most of the meaningful ideas on the subject thus far expressed have already been gathered together in two or three quite brief and easily accessible pieces.[10]

To make a brief exposition even briefer, these ideas seem to the present writer to boil down to the following basic conclusions.

First, since the chief "defense"—in the sense that it is the chief hope of avoiding war under the postulated conditions—lies in the threat of instant retaliation in kind in case of atomic attack, the provision of such means of instant retaliation must have complete and overriding priority. That means, among other things, that the organization responsible for such retaliation must be as far as possible isolated not only from the rest of the national community but also from the rest of the armed forces. It must be insulated from the effects of the catastrophe and horror which the enemy's initial attack will have visited upon our cities. In short, it must have as much freedom as it is humanly possible to provide for it to carry out its appointed task.

Second, not only must mobilization be complete or nearly so at the very outset of hostilities, but the means of fighting too must be stock-piled in a finished state. The situation will demand not a stock-piling of raw materials—for the processing of which there will be neither time nor facilities—but a stock-piling of finished commodities. There is little room under these conditions for planning which presumes a great expansion of war production after hostilities or projects campaigns involving heavy and continuing reliance upon a large and well-integrated industry, because the basis of such reliance will have quickly dissolved into thin but radioactive air. Great navies will not roam the seas in the absence of an industrial base to keep them at sea, nor will great armies take the field. The fighting will be done by small but mobile forces operating from autonomous and previously provided sources of supply.

Third, every *feasible* means of dispersion of populations and of industry will have to be carried out in advance. Admittedly the maxi-

10. See especially my two chapters, entitled "War in the Atomic Age" and "Implications for Military Policy," in *The Absolute Weapon, Atomic Power and World Order*, ed. Bernard Brodie (New York: Harcourt, Brace & Co., 1946); also the already cited "Public Affairs Bulletin," No. 55, especially the War Department paper contained in it; see also Ansley Coale, *The Problem of Reducing Vulnerability to Atomic Bombs* (Princeton, 1947).

[168]

174

mum feasible amount is not likely to mean a wholesale dispersion of our cities.

Fourth, it goes without saying that the provision of a system for detecting and attacking the enemy vehicles of atomic attack has a priority second only to that of providing means of retaliation. It fails to have first priority only because it is not presently conceivable that a defense against the air vehicles of the future carrying large numbers of atomic bombs will be so successful as to prevent the large-scale destruction of our cities. If it becomes conceivable through new developments, then clearly the system of defense has priority over everything, and offensive forces will then be able to operate from a hinterland representing something other than complete ruin. But under those circumstances we would really be postulating situation (3), already described, rather than situation (4). While it is improbable that the most advanced form of defense will be adequate to cope with the most advanced form of offense, it may be less improbable over the next twenty years that American methods of defense will be adequate to cope with Soviet offense.

To be sure, the no-monopoly–no-superiority condition might be expressed with a small number of bombs on both sides, in which case the situation is closest to that described under (1)—but that condition could arise only if a previously effective international control scheme suddenly collapsed. On the other hand, if we go on building bombs, and if the Russians later overtake us, it is not likely that at that time the number in the hands of either party will be small.

For logical completeness we should add another situation, that is, No. 3 in reverse: the Soviet Union enjoying a large margin of superiority both in atomic bombs and in the means of delivering them. It is not squeamishness but simply a disinclination to deal with futility on which we base our refusal to be logically complete.

What adjustments do the propositions suggested above indicate for our over-all national policy? We have, first of all, to consider the consequences of the fact that in a world armed with substantial numbers of atomic bombs the decisive phase of a war between great powers is bound to be short. That will mean an accent, which at least for the United States will be unprecedented, not merely upon preparedness in the old sense of the term—which involved mainly provision for great expansion of the military services and of military production after the outbreak of hostilities—but upon having a military establishment ready to shift to a war footing on very short notice.

[169]

We are already witnessing the stirrings of that recognition in the measures recently adopted to institute a peacetime draft and to build up our air force to seventy groups. These measures have been, to be sure, markedly stimulated by our current difficulties with the Soviet Union, but those difficulties have probably served merely to hasten an adjustment which was inevitable in any case. When and if we enter a happy period of relatively easy relations between the Soviets and ourselves, we can count upon our military leaders to carry out their unquestioned duty of reminding us that we are after all living in an age of atomic bombs.

This country has long been accustomed to the policy of having at least one branch of the armed services, the navy, ready at least in theory to assume a war footing in short notice. The fact that the emphasis now shifts to the air forces—in fact, the atomic bomb threatens to deprive the navy of most of its historic functions—makes a great deal of difference in the degree of effort necessary to maintain what is loosely termed "preparedness." In the first place, the rate of obsolescence of the basic equipment of the navy—that is, the warships themselves—has for the last forty years been far lower than the recent and current rate of obsolescence of aircraft. That, of course, gives some indication of mounting costs. Coupled with that, and more important, is the fact that the atomic bomb has for the first time destroyed the invulnerability of the United States to direct air attack from the Eurasian continent. To be sure, there were bombs before the atomic bomb and aircraft which were steadily increasing in potential range, but no reasonably conceivable development of aircraft, at least along principles now known, would have made such attack a practical proposition on a sustained basis so long as one had to use chemical bombs. It requires only a brief digression to indicate why.

The problem of very-long-range bombing has never been simply that of getting a few bombs delivered to the maximum possible distance. Except for purely demonstration purposes (such as the Doolittle raid on Tokyo and our first B-29 raid on the same city from bases in China), it has meant carrying *enough* bombs per sortie to make militarily worth while the cost of the sortie. And since costs tend to rise with distance by something comparable to a geometrical progression, the barrier to extreme-range bombing has been that the necessity for carrying large payloads (of chemical bombs) mounts most rapidly just as the physical feasibility of doing so drops drastically. With an atomic bomb, however, there is little question of the

[170]

sortie paying for itself at whatever distance it is physically possible to deliver it. Moreover, whatever developments the bomb may undergo, there is no necessity for its ever weighing more than either the Hiroshima or the Nagasaki bomb. Thus, any improvement in the weight-carrying capacity of aircraft can be devoted entirely to the carriage of more fuel for either greater range or speed or both. There is no necessity for proportionately increasing the bomb load. Besides, as we have already noted, the fact that much larger costs can be accepted for sorties with atomic bombs than for sorties with chemical bombs means that in the former case the aircraft need not be retrieved, while in the latter case there must be a high percentage of recovery.

What do these new factors indicate concerning the future costs of military preparedness? Oddly enough, there is little direct correlation historically between the rate of innovation in weapons and the size of military budgets. For example, between 1808 and 1893, at a time when the character of the warship was changing at a fantastic rate—when ships were actually becoming obsolete before they were completed relative to new ships already under construction—the naval budget for Great Britain remained practically stationary at a figure of about eleven million pounds. If that figure is related to the rising national income during that time, we see that the proportion of the national wealth spent on naval security for Britain was rapidly diminishing—and that during the period when the cost of the individual ship was expanding most rapidly. What are the reasons for that? Of course the times were relatively pacific, but it was also true that the changes then ensuing were not fundamentally altering the basic premises of degree of national security and of the duration of wars. As long as Britain retained superiority on the seas against other powers, which she could do with the new weapons as well as with the old, she did not have to worry about being overwhelmed in the first days or weeks of war.

The atomic bomb, on the contrary, is bound to result, as it already has, in increased costs of military security. That is something to be perturbed about, unquestionably, but we should not assume that there is no roof to those increased costs. There are certain important restraining factors. We have already noticed in Congress, during the recent debate on the increase of the armed forces, a very decided reluctance to appropriate sums which threatened to cause a deficit in the national budget. Congress quite properly feels that deficit financing is not appropriate for times of boom. Thus, while Congress approved by overwhelming vote the principle of a seventy-group air force, it rejected the contention of Secretary Forrestal that an increase in air groups required also a proportionate increase in the army and navy involving a total additional cost of fifteen or sixteen billion dollars.

Historians have dwelt on the scale of the armament races preceding the two world wars, usually without observing that the scale is partly a question of the point of view. In each case the extent of the arming turned out with most the belligerents to be relatively small in comparison to the expansion of the war period itself. We observe, in other words, a certain pronounced and effective reluctance to strain the national economy overmuch even when war appears imminent. It is characteristic of wartime economies that many kinds of production for civilian consumption are deferred and that expenditures creating huge inflationary pressures are made as a matter of course. In both cases the abnormality is accepted largely because it is deemed by the population to be temporary. Dictatorships and democracies differ only in degree but not fundamentally in kind in the limits of toleration accorded to advances in the permanent level of military budgets. Despite the recent great rise in the United States military appropriations, the American people have not yet in their entire history accepted in peacetime any increase that could be deemed to have a clear and immediate depressing effect upon their standard of living. That does not argue that they will never do so in the future. But it does suggest the existence of powerful inhibiting forces acting to limit the rate of growth of military expenditures.

In that connection we have heard much of the business of dispersing our cities—a matter which has already been alluded to in the foregoing pages. Such dispersion would have to be accomplished within the next twenty years at most if it is to keep pace with the development of the need. Within such a period a wholesale dispersion of our industries and populations would be physically if not economically impossible. Much of the wealth of this country exists in the form of fixed and sunk capital and therefore, by definition, not subject to removal. Second, one might venture to estimate that such dispersion would probably be militarily improvident even if it were possible. A great many fighter planes could be provided with what it would cost to disperse one moderate-sized city. Third, if our intuitions about how people feel about those things are anywhere near correct,

[172]

it would in any case be vigorously resisted. There is a good margin for dispersion which would be minor in scale but probably important in quality, and commitment to such dispersion is about as far as one can expect our government will ever go, if indeed it goes that far.

In venturing such a prediction, one must make due allowance for the excitement which will prevail in this country when the conviction settles upon it that the Soviet Union is producing atomic bombs. Measures not otherwise imaginable might then become entirely feasible. The main question is whether the outlet for the perturbation will take the form of extravagance in defense (including wholesale dispersion) or a will to aggression. In that connection we must bear in mind the observation made above that on the day the Soviet Union makes its first atomic bomb the United States will have many more than it does now. Depending upon when that situation occurs, the promptness with which the realization of it is communicated to the American people, and the current state of relations with the Soviet Union, the psychology of "preventive war" might become a much more difficult one to suppress than it appears to be at present. On the other hand, it is equally conceivable that the capacity of the human animal for inertia in the face of clear and present danger will again be demonstrated. The very incomprehensibility of the potential catastrophe inherent in the atomic bomb may well make easier the development of the habit of living with it.

[173]

PROFESSOR BLACKETT AND
THE BOMB

In *Fear, War and the Bomb*,[1] Professor Blackett, British Nobel Laureate in Physics, presents a new evaluation of the military and political consequences of atomic energy. He dissents vigorously from the view that nuclear fission has revolutionized warfare, on the grounds that the atom bomb is just one more powerful addition to the large and varied stock of weapons. The political consequences of atomic energy, therefore, flow not from the unique military position which the (temporary) monopoly of production and stocks of bombs gives the United States, but rather from the attempt of the United States and the other western powers to exploit for political purposes in the international power struggle the legend of the bomb as an "absolute weapon."

I

Blackett's argument is briefly as follows. That the military importance of air power has been exaggerated by the United States is shown by the United States Strategic Bombing Survey of strategic bombing in World War II, especially in Germany. Moreover, a consideration of the nature of the A-bomb and of the potentialities of air delivery versus those of air defense suggests that any changes in the future are likely to diminish rather than increase the military significance of strategic bombardment. Thus any war between major powers in the foreseeable future will be a war of all arms, fought on a grand scale; and, in particular, any war in which the United States and western Europe would fight the Soviet Union and eastern Europe would be waged on land in Europe, as were the last two world wars. Furthermore, a war between the United States and Russia, in which Europe would be occupied by Russian forces, would be essentially impossible, unless the United States could launch an invasion of Europe from American bases, for bombardment alone could have no decisive effect.

Along with the deliberate overvaluation of the military importance of nuclear fission by the United States, Mr. Blackett continues, there is an equally deliberate undervaluation of its economic significance, especially in terms of electric power generation. This undervalua-

[1] P. M. S. Blackett. *Fear, War and the Bomb.* New York: Whittlesey House. 1949. vii+244 pp. $3.50.

tion is motivated by the desire to hinder the economic development of the USSR, since the United States, already possessed of large power generation facilities, has much less need of additional power generated in novel ways than does the power-poor Soviet Union. Thus, the United States-sponsored program for the international control of atomic energy (the Baruch Plan) emphasizes a fictitious military security at the expense of economic benefits. By providing for international ownership and control of all "dangerous" nuclear reactors (which includes those used in power generation) and their allocation among nations on considerations of "strategic balance," the Baruch Plan would prevent the USSR from building nuclear generation stations in the number needed for rapid economic growth. That such is the intention of the United States is made clear by American insistence on the abolition of the veto in the proposed international control authority, thus making the internal development of Russian economy subject to control by the western-bloc majority in the United Nations.

Nor is this the only defect in the Baruch Plan, according to Blackett. The problem of time stages in the application of controls bristles with difficulties from the Russian point of view. Much of the United States position on the control of atomic energy and on the functioning of the Security Council in the UN rests on the idea that the monopoly possession of atomic bombs (by either the United States or the future international authority) makes possible the swift and effective punishment of any violator of UN rulings without a major war, even if the violator be a great power. This view is false, in the light of a true understanding of the military significance of the A-bomb. The way out of the present international impasse, therefore, is to abandon such notions and related notions of preventive atomic wars to force the USSR to conform to the wishes of the West, and to consider the A-bomb as only part of the wider problem of general disarmament which must be discussed as such in the United States.

So much for the general structure of Blackett's argument. It is our intention here to examine in some detail the two pillars of the argument: the relative economic importance to the USSR and the United States of electric power generated by nuclear reactors, and the probable military significance of strategic bombardment with atomic weapons. Blackett's political conclusions rest essentially on his specific contentions and will therefore not be examined independently.

II

Blackett begins his analysis of the comparative significance to the United States and the Soviet Union of electric power from atomic energy with an examination of the relation between total energy production per capita and wealth per capita among the nations of the world. He repeats the observation, familiar to economic historians, that there is a close correlation between energy production, industrialization, and wealth. From this, it follows that one of the great needs of the USSR in its drive toward industrialization and increased output is increased power production; this inference is buttressed by quotations from Soviet sources on the key role of electrification in the achievement of Soviet industrial goals. In contrast, the United States is already rich in energy supplies, producing 25 percent of the world's coal power, 60 percent of its oil power, 100 percent of natural gas power, and 40 percent of water power, with only 7 percent of the world's population. The need for additional power generation in the USSR is thus clearly much more pressing than it is in the United States.

The need established, Blackett moves to identify nuclear energy as the fulfillment of the need. Average production costs of power generated from coal in the United States, Great Britain, and Argentina are compared with estimated generating costs from nuclear reactors: the former range from 0.6 cents per kwh at the mines in the United States to 1.8 cents per kwh in inland regions of Argentina; the latter range from 0.4 cents per kwh to 1 cent per kwh. An analogy is drawn between conditions in Argentina and those in the USSR in respect to the low level of existing power supplies, and sparsity of the railway network, and thus it is implied that atomic power will be of the highest importance to the USSR. This chain of inference is bolstered by the following direct argument (p. 109): "Even if atomic power proves no cheaper in money costs than coal-produced power, it may prove appreciably cheaper in manpower. For atomic power will bring a large expansion of the highly skilled engineering and chemical engineering trade, whereas coal power demands a very large population of miners and heavy-transport workers. Such a shift in the demand for labor could only benefit the general economy of a country."

The whole fabric of this argument is shot through with errors, both logical and factual. In the first place, the comparison of total costs between coal-generated and nuclear-generated power should not be made indiscriminately across national boundaries. At least part of the reason why coal power costs in, say, Argentina, are higher than those in the United States lies in the higher cost of capital in the former, which would be reflected in the cost of nuclear power as well. Even within one country, the approximate costs of coal power to use in such a comparison are those of the newest steam plants, not overall average costs which include costs of plants built fifty years ago and operating with technically inferior methods or in very unfavorable sites. New steam generating stations in the United States produce power for as little as 0.4 to 0.46 cents per kwh. Moreover, the figures for costs of nuclear power quoted by Blackett (p. 108) appear optimistic, in the light of the most recent researches on this problem. The latest estimates give costs ranging from 0.94 cents to 1.45 cents per kwh, for respective load factors of 50 and 80 percent.[2] Thus it seems doubtful that power from nuclear sources will be competitive with coal power in general, except in special locations, where the transportation cost of coal is very high. In the USSR, as in other industrial countries, the major industrial consumers of coal and power are located near coal fields: the great heavy industries of the Ukraine, the Donbas, and the Urals all draw on nearby supplies of coal, the existence of which was, of course, a primary factor in the establishment of industry in those particular regions.

The fundamental fallacy of Blackett's argument lies deeper, however, than the errors in estimated relative costs of coal and nuclear power. The real difficulty is the failure to appreciate the economic character of the substitution of nuclear for coal power as a substitution of a relatively capital-intensive method of power production for a more labor-intensive method. The actual generating equipment of both nuclear and coal power plants would be much the same: the chief differences between the two processes lie in the substitution of an atomic pile, with its associated chemical and metallurgical plants, for a coal mine and the transportation facilities required to bring the coal to the power plant. About three quarters of the estimated costs of a pile and the associated equipment are capital costs, while approximately three fifths of the costs of coal at the power station in the United States are labor costs. This difference can be stated in another way: while the fuel expenses of a nuclear plant are of course much lower than those of a coal plant, the capital investment per kw capacity is almost three times as great for a

2 See article by W. Isard and J. Lansing, scheduled to appear in *Review of Economics and Statistics* (August 1949).

nuclear plant as for a coal plant.[3] Now the USSR is in an economic position in which, relative to the United States, labor is cheap and capital is dear. The USSR has a large, young, rapidly growing population, the greater part of which is still engaged in agriculture, an industry of low productivity. Her industry is young, and the rate of industrial growth tremendous, creating great demands for new plant, buildings, and equipment. Consumer durable goods, including housing, are in very short supply. Thus, so long as adequate reserves of coal exist, it would be a strange economy for the USSR to attempt to expand power production by the most, instead of the least, capital-using methods available in order to gain small, if any, savings in current costs. If nuclear power is uneconomical power in the United States, a mature industrial country with relatively plentiful capital supplies, it must a fortiori be uneconomical in the USSR. This is not to argue that there may not be special regions of the USSR, such as the Siberian Arctic, in which nuclear power would be highly useful, but to assert that it is altogether implausible that the USSR should, in the near and middle future, place its reliance on atomic energy as the main source of power development for industrial expansion. Consequently, Blackett's claim that United States policy is motivated by the intention to choke off Soviet industrial development appears groundless.

III

An evaluation of Professor Blackett's conclusions on the military importance of atomic energy is a more difficult task than the relatively elementary exercise in economic analysis presented above, and the reviewer presents the following discussion with some diffidence. In part, this difficulty stems from the allusive and inexplicit character of Blackett's reasoning. More important, however, is the fact that much of the argument must be frankly speculative in nature, since the knowledge required for more factual discussion is either as yet unattained or lies veiled in military secrecy.

To support his conclusion that the atomic bomb is only "another weapon" which will change decisively neither the techniques of warfare nor the relative military potentials of the major powers, Blackett examines in turn the effects of strategic bombing on Germany in World War II, the effects of strategic bombing on Japan, the nature of the atomic bomb as a weapon, the probable future

[3] *Ibid.*, and J. R. Menke, "Nuclear Fission as a Source of Power," in *Econometrica*, vol. 15, no. 4 (October 1947) pp. 314-34.

technical developments in the means of air warfare, and the probable scale of atomic attack required to inflict major damage on a large nation.

The examination of the role of strategic bombing in the European war leads Blackett to the conclusion that such bombing played no decisive role in winning the war, and further, that its total contribution, outside of the essentially tactical achievement of helping to win air superiority for the Allies, was small. Whatever success bombing finally did achieve in reducing Germany's ability to wage war was attained in the context of a two-front struggle on land, which imposed a continuing drain on German manpower and economic resources.

Turning to Japan, Blackett finds that the USAAF attack on Japanese cities in the last part of the war was the first fairly successful campaign of mass destruction by air attack in history. This success was due to the existence of certain special conditions: great productive superiority of the United States over Japan, which permitted an air offensive on an increasing scale; complete air supremacy over the target area and security of United States air bases; and finally, previous "decisive" defeat in naval and amphibious battles, and successful naval and air blockade which had seriously impaired the Japanese island economy.

Blackett's examination of the nature of the atomic weapon starts from the effects of the bombs dropped on Hiroshima and Nagasaki. His own and others' calculations suggest that the damage done by an atomic bomb is equivalent to that done by about 2,000 tons of ordinary bombs (mixed high-explosive and incendiaries) appropriately distributed over the target. This is recognized as a probable understatement of the casualty-producing power of the atomic bomb. Calculations then follow as to the relative effectiveness of "unit attacks" with atom bombs and conventional bombs, on the assumption that tactical considerations require that the unit force consist of a minimum of 50 bombers (B-29's). If all 50 bombers carried atomic bombs, only a city of some 400 square miles (London, New York, or Los Angeles) would furnish an appropriately large target, since each A-bomb causes serious damage over an area of some eight square miles. Thus if the target were a "normal" city of say, ten square miles, only one A-bomb would be required, and the other 49 aircraft would carry 490 tons of ordinary bombs. Since the same 50 aircraft could deliver 500 tons of conventional bombs, using them to carry one A-bomb plus 490 tons of conventional bombs would multiply the destructive power of the unit force by only five. A similar argument with respect to a large industrial target, occupying, say, one square mile, shows that the unit force with one A-bomb would be no more effective than the same unit force carrying conventional bombs. Thus the atom bomb could be used effectively only against very large cities, for area bombing.

An appraisal of probable developments in the near future, that is, the next five to ten years, constitutes the next point in Blackett's case. He assumes that improvements in atomic weapons within that period will produce an A-bomb equivalent to some 3,000 tons of ordinary bombs. He rules out rockets and other "unstoppable" missiles as methods of delivery in this period, on the grounds that it will not be possible in so short a time to achieve the angular accuracy necessary to hit targets at long range, that is, 1,500 miles or more. The major part of the appraisal is concerned with the relative changes to be expected in the power of air offense (bombers) and air defense (fighters) in the near future. It is concluded that the balance of advantage probably lies with the defense, especially in respect to long-range bombing attacks, carried out from bases 1,500 or 2,000 miles distant from the target area. In the case of short-range attacks, however, it is recognized that the advantage may well rest with the attacker.

Finally, Blackett comments briefly on the scale of atomic attack required to do serious damage to a major nation. First he calculates that about 400 (future) atomic bombs would have been required to produce the damage done in Germany by the 1.35 million tons of conventional bombs dropped on her during World War II. The peak attack rate on Germany was the equivalent of 50 A-bombs per month. And, of course, as was previously noted, this amount of damage was hardly enough to be an important, much less a decisive, factor in the defeat of Germany. A qualitative judgment on the same score is made by noting the huge losses of territory and industrial capacity contained therein that Germany inflicted on the USSR, despite which the Russians defeated and drove out the German armies. "A huge number" of atomic bombs would be required to inflict equivalent damage on the USSR by bombing.

IV

What can be said about this line of argument? First, a general qualification must be made with regard to Blackett's interpretation of the lessons of strategic bombing in the last war, which is, in essence, a projection into the future of the *average* results achieved in Germany. Such an average conceals the great changes in the techniques of bombing during the course of the war, the differences in effectiveness of American day-bombing and British night-bombing methods, the varying degrees of wisdom in the choice of targets, and the wide differences in the success of attacks on different kinds of targets. A more logical, if more difficult, procedure would have attempted to analyze the influence of all these changing factors, and so produce some estimate of the *best* level of performance attainable over a sustained bombing campaign, taking into account the failures and mistakes of the actual bombing campaign of 1941–45. Thus, for instance, the great inaccuracy and small weight of the early night-bombing attacks on German cities means that the period 1941–43 might well be left entirely out of account in estimating the possible future effects of bombing from the German experience. Also, the relative failure of attacks against submarine pens and building yards as compared with the relative success of attacks against large synthetic oil plants makes dubious any projection based on an analysis which lumps the two types of targets together.

Further, there is too ready an identification, both for Germany and Japan, of strategic bombing with the area raids on large cities, and too little attention is paid to the results of attacks on industrial installations. Of course, such an identification is justified by the argument which seeks to show that an atomic attack can have only a large city as a target, but that conclusion rests on a rather questionable assumption to be discussed later. Broadly, it can be said for Germany that each ton dropped on at least certain industrial targets was many times more effective in reducing German military potential than each ton dropped in area attacks on large cities.

Certain propositions which Blackett emphasizes as limiting conditions on the effectiveness of strategic bombing have positive as well as negative implications, and these Blackett fails to bring out. For example, the limited results of the combined bomber offensive against Germany are examined in relation to the now, well-known undermobilization of the German war economy before 1944, and the conclusion drawn that the effect of a strategic bombing campaign depends on the degree to which the target nation's economy is already strained by a major war effort on land. This is indeed an important point, but it must be observed that an economy may be strained in more ways than by a major war effort on land. A country, such as Russia, in which the standard of living is low, where industrialization is proceeding at a rapid rate, and where women form a substantial part of the peacetime labor force, is under economic strain even in peacetime. This is especially true in relative terms, when comparison is made with an economy such as that of pre-1939 Germany, in which the standard of consumption was high, almost no women worked, and much income was devoted to luxury capital-formation in the form of *Autobahnen* and *Sports-paläste*. Similarly, there is repeated emphasis on tactical control of the air as a prerequisite to successful strategic bombing. This emphasis is entirely correct; but in Blackett's argument it appears in the context of an analysis of air tactics which suggests (but does not state) that such control will be impossible to achieve.

More important in the structure of the argument under examination than the evaluation of bombing in World War II are the propositions on the nature of the atomic bomb as a weapon, which enable Blackett to analyze possible future strategic bombing campaigns as merely larger varieties of the same species as those of the last war, and therefore to discuss the tactics of future bombing in terms of those of the past. Blackett's procedure of treating 3,000 tons of ordinary bombs as equivalent to one atomic bomb, chiefly on the basis of the amount of structural damage produced, and of substituting the former for the latter in calculations, involves a number of fundamental difficulties. At least one is recognized by Blackett himself, in his admission that the lethal effect of an atomic bomb is probably considerably greater than the lethal effect of its calculated equivalent in ordinary bombs. But the importance of this difference is overlooked, in part because of mistaken notions on the effectiveness of shelters. In the bombing attacks of the past, the number of civilian casualties was too small to have any substantial effect, through either economic loss or psychological and political repercussions. Yet it is clear that *some* rate of civilian casualties will have both economic and political effects of the greatest importance. Horrible as it is, the possibility that mass killing of civilians in sufficient magnitude in air raids can add a new dimension to the effectiveness of bombing must be examined. Nor can this possibility be dismissed on the grounds that even light shelters offer protection against the flash burns and radiations associated with the detonation of the bomb. The problem of long-lasting secondary radioactivity produced in the target area by the explosion of the bomb, as, for example, on the target ships at Bikini, must be examined in relation to casualties. The bombs exploded at Hiroshima and

Nagasaki were so fused that there was apparently little or no long-lasting radiation, but in any case Blackett discusses this question and the whole issue of radioactivity only very cursorily.

The likelihood of lingering radioactivity under appropriate conditions is important with respect to material installations as well as casualties. The equivalence formula between atomic and conventional weapons reached by Blackett depends largely, as observed above, on a comparison of the area of structural damage produced by each. But damage also has a time dimension—its duration in the face of repair efforts—which is as important as its space dimension in an extended bombing campaign. One of the major counteractives to even the most successful attacks on German industrial targets was the rapid rate of repair and recovery of production. This was vividly demonstrated by the Germans' ability to restore even heavily damaged synthetic oil plants to partial production in periods as short as six weeks. It is now known that special repair brigades of up to 10,000 workers were set to work on damaged oil plants immediately after a raid. Thus, repeated attacks on the same installation were required to keep it out of production; examples of once-and-for-all destruction were rare. The significance of the need for repeated attacks was increased, in the tactical situation of the last war, by the fact that reattack of a reconstructed plant at the appropriate time was not always possible, since accurate bombing of industrial targets required favorable weather conditions.

The potentiality of an atomic attack for producing long-lasting radiation in the target area, which would prevent even the initiation of repair efforts for many weeks or months, could therefore multiply the effectiveness of an attack on an industrial target several times. This property in itself might be sufficient to negate Blackett's contention that industrial targets are "too small" to be worth attacking with atom bombs.

To the extent that area attacks on cities were aimed at the destruction of housing and the disruption of urban transportation and utility services, a similar increase in the time dimension of effectiveness of the attacks could arise from lingering radioactivity. Indeed, the relative increase on this account would be greater for area than for industrial attacks. Blast and fragmentation damage to utilities and transportation right of ways is typically easy to repair, and even a badly ruined house will contain a room or two and a cellar which can be made habitable after an attack. But lingering radiation might make whole areas of a city uninhabitable and impassable for long periods. Thus the reduction of an atomic bomb to an equivalent number of conventional bombs, by ignoring the characteristic features in which explosive nuclear fission differs from chemical explosions, greatly falsifies the relative potency of the atomic weapon.

Another difficulty in the equivalence-formula approach to the understanding of the atom bomb lies in its failure to take account of the intimate connection between the concrete tactical conditions under which bombs are delivered, and the damage they do. This is obvious enough in respect to matters like the relation of weather, altitude, and enemy opposition to the accuracy of aim. Blackett indeed stresses repeatedly the importance of the amount of opposition in determining the effectiveness of bombing. Yet the relation between bombing effectiveness and the number of aircraft required to deliver a certain amount of explosive, or its equivalent in A-bombs, or the number of separate missiles in which this explosive is contained, is entirely ignored in Blackett's argument. One of the great tactical problems of the air attack on Germany was presented by the situation that a very large number of aircraft were required to deliver a weight of bombs sufficient to inflict major damage on a large target; that the limited availability of fighter escorts required that the bombers form a compact stream in the air which could be guarded as a whole by the fighters, rather than breaking up into separate groups and following each other after substantial intervals of time; and that the aiming accuracy of all but the first group of bombers over a target was greatly reduced by the smoke, dust, and flames obscuring the target area after the bombs of the first group had exploded. The whole tactical employment of the bomber force was conditioned by the need to use large numbers of planes per target and the limitations on the number of escort fighters. The atom bomb, by giving one plane the striking power possessed by, say, 1,000 in the offensive against Germany would make possible a new tactical employment of bombers. Even the small increase in striking power which the B-29, carrying ten tons of bombs, had over the B-17, carrying three tons, contributed to the greatly increased efficiency of bombing in Japan. (This difference, incidentally, vitiates Blackett's direct application to the German campaign of calculations of equivalence between atom bombs and conventional bombs based on damage done in Japan. As does also, of course, the greater vulnerability of Japanese cities to fire and conflagration from the effects of ordinary incendiaries.) The new tactics could involve several radical changes. There might be a much higher ratio of fighters to bombers. A great incentive would exist for the development of fairly large, long-range fighters, with somewhat the same relationship to bombers that cruisers and battleships have to aircraft carriers, so that a typical attacking force would contain only a few bombers and a much larger number of fighters of several varieties.   Moreover, with reductions in required numbers, the proficiency of the aircrews could be greatly increased by more selectivity in recruitment and more intensive training.   That great improvements in bombing accuracy and in the ability to find and hit difficult targets can be expected from the employment of such selected crews is shown by the experience of certain specially trained groups of the RAF, which maintained a standard of performance far above the average of both American and British air forces in Europe.

The assumption of 50-bomber minimum striking force units, used to justify the conclusion that only very large targets can be economically attacked by atom bombs, is again rooted in the tactical situation of the last war.   With tactics appropriate to the new weapons, much smaller striking forces may be possible.   For instance, under the conditions of the last war, diversionary efforts, designed to draw enemy fighter defenses away from a certain target, or aimed at distracting radar detection organizations, had to be of substantial magnitude. The enemy, knowing that a few planes could do no serious damage, made no serious effort to oppose small incursions.   With atomic bombs, one or two planes could constitute a major threat; the possibility of all kinds of diversionary operations, such as the disorganization of radar defenses by the use of single fast planes, is therefore much greater.   It is hardly necessary to demonstrate in greater detail that arguments based on tactical considerations appropriate to the last war are not necessarily relevant to the use of the new weapons.

With the abandonment of the assumption of 50-bomber minimum striking units for each target, and the recognition of the great potential importance of radioactivity in extending the time dimension of damage, the basis for Blackett's identification of strategic bombing with area bombing and his rejection of industrial installations as targets vanishes.   There exist certain kinds of industrial targets, such as steel mills, which could not be successfully attacked during the last war owing to their great size, relative invulnerability of installations in them to damage from ordinary bombs, and the large number of individual targets included in the whole system. Such targets could be very suitably attacked with atomic bombs. Further, the great area of damage of an atomic bomb makes feasible a combination of area and precision attack, through the use of industrial installations in cities as the aiming points for area raids on the cities.

If Blackett's evaluation of the relative future strengths of offense and defense in air warfare is correct, the great power of the atomic bomb may be of no significance, because of the difficulty of delivering even a relatively small number of bombs to their targets. The great advantage of the defense is seen in the speed advantage of the short-range fighter over the long-range bomber, the limitations on range of escort fighters, and the continuing improvement of anti-aircraft weapons and warning systems. Some of these arguments already seem obsolete in the light of Air Force announcements of the achievements of B-36's; and in view of the possibilities of bombers relying on piston engines for range and on jets for speed over defended areas. More important than these specific counterarguments is a general weakness in Blackett's analysis of offense versus defense in future air campaigns. This weakness is the implicit assumption, underlying the whole discussion, that the technologies of attacker and defender will be on a par. Or specifically, in the context of the book, that the USSR will match the United States in technological development with respect to aircraft, aircraft armaments, radar, proximity fuses, guided missiles, and so forth. This is a bold assumption, which appears to contravene the obvious facts. The large margin of superiority in technical achievement of United States industry over that of the USSR is well known. The fact that research in air weapons is very expensive, requiring wind tunnels and other large items of capital equipment, and that development expenses of new aircraft are also costly reinforces the expectation that a rich United States can lead a poor USSR in a deliberate race for technical superiority. Finally, the United States has had a large headstart in the race. The technical level of the Russian air force in World War II was very low relative to that of the western allies. No better evidence of this can be given than that the Germans concentrated all their newest and best air force equipment on the western front; aircraft which were obsolete in the west in 1942 were being used on the Russian front until the end of the war.

The last point of Blackett's argument is the contention that very large numbers of atom bombs would be required to do serious enough damage to a country to have any military effects. The basis for this estimate of about 400 atom bombs as the number required to do the damage done in Germany has already been questioned. It should be further added that, of the 1.35 million tons of bombs dropped on Germany on targets of all kinds, only about 0.6 million tons hit the kinds of urban targets Blackett is considering. The rest went astray, or were aimed at targets irrelevant to the argument. And, of course, the whole argument ignores entirely the time dimension of damage, both in duration and impact. If all the damage done to Germany from the air had been inflicted in the course of a single month, its effects would undoubtedly have been different, and they might conceivably have been great enough to push Germany over the edge into surrender. The comparison implied by the citation of the USSR's loss of territory to the invading Germans is also beside the mark. It ignores the important economic contribution made by lend-lease, the ability of the Russians to evacuate a part of the productive installations eastward before retreating, and the fact that the necessity to feed and supply the population in captured territories vanishes with the territories.

The emphasis Blackett puts on the "large" number of bombs required to do serious damage (where a large number is one between 100 and 1,000) is somewhat hard to understand. As a counter-argument to what may be called the "one-or-two-bombs-and-it's-all-over" school of military analysts, who seem to dominate the editorial pages of many American newspapers, it is quite useful. But, as an aid to a serious examination of the military situation, the weight of this argument can rest only on the implicit assumption that the stocks of atomic bombs available to the United States in case of war are really small—some 10 to 50 bombs, let us say—and production rates appropriately low. There is no explicit reference to an estimate of this sort in the book, although it is clearly crucial to the kind of argument Blackett presents. The purest speculation, without any factual basis, suggests that in the three years since Hiroshima, the United States stock of bombs may easily have reached 200 in number, if it is assumed that two bombs were initially produced in the month between the test detonation at Los Alamos and the attacks on Hiroshima and Nagasaki, and that this initial production rate has grown in the fashion which is customary in many new industrial processes. A "large" number of atom bombs may be required to decide a war; and a "large" number may be available for use!

The evaluation of the military potentialities of atomic energy can be best summarized in terms of the possible grand strategies of a future war. Enough of Blackett's discussion survives the criticisms made above to leave much force in his rejection of the "easy-war" possibility: namely, that the United States could defeat the USSR in a war of one or two months' duration or even less, merely by dropping a small number of atomic bombs on the larger Russian cities. Only if a convincing demonstration can be given that the Soviet regime is on the verge of internal collapse, does this possibility appear important. The other extreme possibility—that the atomic bomb will make no great change in the character of warfare, and that any war in the near future between the USSR and the western powers will be fought out primarily on land in Europe, which is the view put forward in *Fear, War and the Bomb*—appears equally improbable in the light of the foregoing analysis. What appears most likely is that a war between the East and the West might well have two phases. The first might be a struggle for definite air supremacy on the part of the West, which would probably involve attempts to hold at least parts of western Europe and other territories contiguous to the USSR for use as bases, especially fighter bases. Atomic bombs might well be used in this phase, partly for the sort of tactical purposes Blackett discusses, but strategic bombing would be subordinate to the establishment of air superiority. This part of a war would certainly be what Blackett calls a struggle of all arms. Land areas such as the Scandinavian peninsula and Turkey, which do not present to the USSR terrain suitable for ground army attacks on a broad front, might become especially important. But once air superiority is achieved, there would seem to be no valid military reason why the main effort of the West should not be turned to strategic bombing, in an effort to make the USSR surrender by destroying its basic industries, making uninhabitable its great cities, and killing large numbers of its citizens. Provided a sufficient measure of air superiority is gained by the West, this program cannot be ruled out as impossible. The greater the technological superiority of the West in the production of air armaments, the sooner will a future war enter into this phase.

There is what might be called a metamilitary argument against the validity of this strategic picture, which is hinted at, though not elaborated, by Blackett. This is the contention that the postwar political and economic problems created by atom-bombing the USSR and possibly other areas in Europe occupied by the USSR, would be so great as to preclude the use of the atom bomb by a "responsible" government. While the prospect of the horrors of strategic air war on a massive scale may well be (and certainly should be) a deterrent to the starting of a war by a "responsible" government, the view that, once the war has started, military considerations will be subordinated to ideal political goals of this sort seems naïve. The more so, if, as Blackett contends, the position of the two antagonists in a war would be such that strategic bombing would present the United States with its only substantial chance of winning. The examples of the past, from the Thirty Years War to World War II, hardly bear out the idea of a "rational" subordination of military policy to political views on desirable postwar situations.

Despite the deficiencies of *Fear, War and the Bomb*, detailed in the preceding pages, the book deserves wide reading. For one thing, it is a useful antidote to notions of an easy "preventive" war. Its criticism of the popular American view on the veto in the UN and its recognition of the problems created by the American proposals for international control of atomic energy are worth thinking about, and cannot be dismissed as mere Soviet-inspired propaganda. Continued discussion of these issues, as well as of the military and economic implications of nuclear fission, is an essential condition for the achievement of a coherent, long-range foreign policy, of which military policy forms an integral part.

CARL KAYSEN

Society of Fellows,
Harvard University

STRATEGY, ECONOMICS, AND THE BOMB

JOSEPH E. LOFTUS

Formerly economic adviser at the Office of Economic Stabilization and at the Office of War Mobilization and Reconversion, Mr. Loftus is now Director of the Teaching Institute of Economics at the American University, Washington, D. C. During the past year, the Institute has concentrated its resources on an extended examination of the economic aspects of atomic energy utilization. This paper is one of a series of studies developed in the course of the Institute's work.

THE publication of Professor Blackett's book *The Military and Political Consequences of Atomic Energy* last October in London, and the subsequent American "translation" under the title *Fear, War, and the Bomb,* has elicited wide attention and comment. The volume of book reviews in the past few months has been so large that a reviewer, at this late date, can quite safely assume that his readers have at least read enough reviews—if not the book itself—to be quite familiar with the general thesis of the book, its method of analysis, the main evidential materials of the analysis, and the general conclusions.

Accordingly, this review will not spend limited space on another summarization of the contents of the book. Nor will it concern itself with an analysis of its political arguments, or the general conclusions and recommendations of Professor Blackett. Rather, this review will limit itself to a detailed examination of three themes which, on the one hand, are fundamental to Blackett's position, and which, on the other hand, have not been scrutinized too critically or carefully in the reviews published thus far. These three themes are: (1) the emphasis on the employment of "numerical or statistical" analysis in military and economic problems, (2) the imputed importance to Russia of atomic energy as a source of electric power, and (3) the effort to deflate, in the light of World War II experience with large-scale aerial bombardment, the generally held opinions on the tactical and strategic consequences of the A-bomb.

ON QUANTITATIVE ANALYSIS

In the introduction to his subject matter, Professor Blackett emphasizes the importance of "numerical or statistical" reasoning as opposed to "qualitative" reasoning in considering the military and political consequences of atomic energy.

He summarizes his own predilections in this respect with a quotation from Charles Babbage: "Nor let it be feared that erroneous deductions be made from such facts; the errors which arise from the absence of facts are more numerous and more durable than those which result from unsound reasoning respecting true facts." It is not just a flippant digression to point out that this opinion of Babbage's was not arrived at by a numerical or statistical comparison of the number and durability of errors obtained by the one method as against the other! It is purely and simply a qualitative value judgment of precisely the sort that Professor Blackett is in principle complaining against.

To the extent that Professor Blackett, in this emphasis on quantitative reasoning, means simply that what is required today in the conduct of human affairs is less hysterical and emotional thinking and more—much more—realistic and sober thinking, one must thoroughly agree with him. To the extent, however, that he means that there is an intellectual process called "numerical or statistical" analysis as opposed to, and distinct from, "qualitative" reasoning, one must vigorously disagree with him. One must disagree even more vigorously if he means also that there is something objective and conclusive per se about what he calls "numerical" reasoning. The blunt fact of the matter is that in dealing with social science and military science data, quantitative and qualitative are inseparable. The manipulation of quantitative data requires not less but more exercise of the highest order of qualitative reasoning from beginning to end, from the initial determination of the statistical categories into which the data will be sorted to the final interpretation of the numerical results.

This point cannot be emphasized enough in view of the fact that there prevails in our age an unhappy inclination to identify facts and figures

310

with objectivity. Professor Blackett's convincingly written discourse on method in the preface, coupled with his impressive use of facts and figures throughout the book, may lead the unwary into believing that subjective and qualitative considerations are at a minimum, when really they are not.

Lest this appear to be quibbling over a methodological nicety, one somewhat extended illustration is worth while exploring.

All of Professor Blackett's analysis of the effectiveness of the atomic bomb, in terms of the experience of the bombing offensive against Germany, hinges upon the proposition that there is a rough rule-of-thumb damage equivalence between the atomic bomb and ordinary high-explosive bombs. The equivalence is of this order: 2,000 tons of ordinary bombs equal one Nagasaki-model atomic bomb; 3,000 tons of ordinary bombs probably equal one improved-model atomic bomb. Now in the technical discussion (pp. 44–46), Professor Blackett correctly, but quietly, states that this equivalence holds true providing the ordinary bombs are *properly distributed over the target*. Nowhere does he examine the problem of what are the real difficulties, the real probabilities, in an actual bombing situation of obtaining this sort of "proper distribution." Even more important is the fact that in all other parts of the book where this rough principle of damage equivalence is applied, not a single reference is made to the "proper-distribution" assumption.

That this is most important can be demonstrated from just two typical case studies from the USSBS reports. Monograph Number 71 in the European Theatre Series of the USSBS studies[1] describes in some detail the bombing effort that was made to eliminate the Hermann Goering Werke steel plant near Hallendorf. The buildings and equipment of the plant were generously spaced over a 1,200-acre plot, although the main installations (i.e., the coke plant, the blast furnaces, the steelworks, the rolling mills, and the 360,000-KVA powerhouse which supplied not only the steel plant but also a substantial amount of power to the industrial economy of this area of Germany) were located in the center of the site, covering an area less than two thirds the size of the total site area.

During the course of the war, this plant was raided twice in 1941, twice in 1943, fifteen times in 1944, and twice in 1945. Accurate bomb tonnage figures were available for only four of these raids; but since this plant was never a priority target it can safely be assumed that through the end of 1944 the tonnages would have been so light as to have caused no significant damage. That this is a prudent assumption is indicated by the fact that the tonnage dropped on December 17, 1944, was only six tons! Accordingly, it is not unreasonable to assume that the bulk of the damage that was done to the plants was done during the 478-ton raid of January 14, 1945, and the 253-ton raid of March 29, 1945.

Although it would be interesting to discuss in detail the nature of the damage done, the important point to be emphasized is that despite the fact that both these raids were conducted in midafternoon at a time when the air forces had complete control of the air, no "proper distribution" of the ordinary bombs was achieved. For example, in the big January raid, out of some 3,190 high-explosive bombs dropped (mainly 500-pound bombs), only 1,200—much less than half—fell within the total plant area, and the bombs that did fall within the plant area were neither spread evenly and symmetrically over the whole area nor concentrated at the main vulnerable points. What was in fact obtained was a random scattering of bombs all over the site. The powerhouse, coke plant, and the ore preparation plants, which offered "the greatest opportunity for disrupting operations with the smallest direct bomb effort," were not severely damaged.

Picture the results in the same 1,200-acre plot if an atomic bomb were dropped anywhere in the center of the large triangle formed by the powerhouse, the steelworks, and the second battery of blast furnaces—or, for that matter dropped, within limits, outside the periphery of the 1,200-acre plot. It is a significant point, though not mentioned at all by Professor Blackett, that the A-bomb when used in precision bombing of key industrial and military targets has greatly extended the destructive range of "near-misses." The atomic bomb literally provides a new connotation for the old boyhood taunt, "A miss is as good as a mile"!

The second case study that illustrates the unreality of an easy assumption of "proper distribution" of ordinary bombs is taken from Monograph Number 185[2] of the USSBS series on the European Theatre. This monograph describes in detail the bombing offensive against the Synthetic Oil Plant at Meerbeck-Hamburg, Germany. The plant was one of the largest Fischer-Tropsch process plants in Germany, and, although it accounted for only 1.7 percent of Germany's synthetic oil production, was an important producer of mixed and light Diesel oil, *Triebgas*, and gasoline.

As a target, this plant was located on an even smaller land area than the Hermann Goering plant at Hallendorf. All the buildings were concentrated close together on a trapezoidal area covering but 100.8 acres. Despite the relative smallness of the land area of the target, it was found necessary, during the war, to drop a total of 7,403 tons of high explosives on the target. Of this total, 6,343 tons were dropped during the intensive attack period, July 20, 1944, to November 20, 1944.

The plant, of course, was completely destroyed by the end of the intensive attack period. The significant point is, however, that of the 7,403 tons dropped, the USSBS was able to find evidence of only 116 tons of bomb hits in the plant area. Or, stated another way, of 19,126 bombs dropped, only 328 fell within the plant area. Only a vigorous effort finally obtained the distribution of bombs over the target area that was required to render it inoperative.

With the plant located in such a small area (100.8 acres), one atomic bomb dropped anywhere in the area, or anywhere outside the area for a considerable distance beyond the periphery, would have accomplished the same physical destruction with considerably less total effort.

Detailed examination of the bomb plots and the analyses of air raid damage contained in the USSBS individual monograph studies of sixteen German cities subjected to heavy area bombing eloquently testify that it is a most difficult task to obtain a "proper distribution" of ordinary bombs.[3]

To summarize, Professor Blackett has based a substantial part of his elaborate "numerical" analysis of the number of atomic bombs required to accomplish the same amount of damage inflicted on Germany by ordinary bombs on the principle of equivalence that one new-style atomic bomb equals 3,000 tons of high explosives properly distributed over the target. His failure to adjust his "numerical" application of the equivalence principle to take account of the fact that one of the reasons that such great amounts of high-explosive bombs were required was the enormous difficulty of obtaining a proper distribution of bombs, represents on his part a qualitative judgment (or lack of it!) that raises some serious questions as to the validity of the conclusions of some of his extended quantitative analyses.

Other and more important instances of the same sort of thing will become apparent in the subsequent discussion of Professor Blackett's analysis of the economic and military implications of the atomic bomb. The caution to be emphasized,

for the moment, is that in reading Blackett one must ever be on the alert to avoid mistaking statistical arguments for objective arguments. It must be recognized that the making of significant qualitative assumptions is inescapable in the process of assembling and interpreting numerical data. It is these qualitative judgments that ultimately determine the validity and the significance of the numerical results.

THE ECONOMICS OF THE BOMB

In a somewhat brief chapter entitled Power From Atomic Energy, Professor Blackett attempts to establish the argument that one of the significant contributory causes for the breakdown of negotiations for an international agreement on the control of atomic energy has been—and will continue to be—the disparate importance of atomic energy as a source of electric power in the USA, a power-rich country, and in the USSR, a relatively power-poor country.

The argument, cleansed of the exaggerated—and unnecessary—digressions on the motives of certain people and groups in the USA, can be summarized as follows:

1. The industrial strength of any modern nation (and thus, also, its standard of living and its military potential) depends on the availability of electric power;
2. But historically there has been a wide disparity in the levels of energy production and consumption in the USA and the USSR—the former in 1935 consuming six times as much energy as the latter;
3. Now, atomic energy shows bright promise of providing a new source of electric energy, with unique and attractive physical and cost characteristics.
4. In a world without international regulation of atomic energy, therefore, the USSR would in all probability exploit the development of atomic energy for industrial purposes at a faster rate and in greater magnitude than the USA because she has a much greater incentive to do so.
5. But, in a world with international regulation of atomic energy (a la Baruch), the USSR would be prevented from exploiting atomic energy for industrial purposes at the speed and to the extent that she otherwise would in an unregulated world. This, Blackett contends, would hold true regardless of whether in the international regulation arrangements the allocation of primary generating plants were done by an initial binding treaty or by a series of ad hoc decisions by an international regulatory commission. If the former, the treaty would have to allocate primary plants according to a formula that would preserve the "strategic balance" among the great powers, thus perpetuating the existing energy disparities as between USA and USSR. If the latter method were adopted, the USSR would always be a minority member of such a commission. As such, she would always have to fear discrimination by the majority; the best she could hope for would be the sort of automatic treatment resulting from a decision of the committee scrupulously to pursue a policy of preserving the "strategic balance."

At first glance, the argument sounds most plausible and convincing. Upon close scrutiny, the argument can neither be substantiated nor refuted. Too many unknown factors are involved. The strongest statement that can be made is that this is a *hypothesis,* not an argument, that merits much more analysis and *quantitative* study. As the life of the world's economies unfolds in the future, the hypothesis may eventuate to have been correct; but there is no governing consideration for accepting it now. If anything, the very meager evidence available now suggests either rejecting the hypothesis or initiating in the UNAEC an extended quantitative inquiry on the problem— the sort of inquiry that Professor Blackett pleads for in his introductory chapter but does not provide in this chapter!

Despite the present paucity of good evidence, certain relevant observations can be made that will be useful in assessing the merits of Blackett's economic argument. The first set of observations concerns the differences in the national incentives of the USA and the USSR to develop and assimilate atomic energy into their economies.

In general, it may be stated that Professor Blackett tends to underestimate not only the incentives of the USA, but also, peculiarly enough, the incentives of the USSR. With respect to the latter, it is true that Russian energy consumption is roughly one sixth of American levels. Much more important, however, is the fact that in terms of estimated per capita energy potentials, the USSR has only about 60 percent as much potential energy from conventional sources as this country. Most important is the fact that, even though in the aggregate the USSR has sufficient potential energy to provide her people with a per capita consumption equivalent to current USA levels, certain economically important regions of the USSR have inadequate and uneconomical power resources. A few conspicuous illustrations of this are pertinent.

In the southern Urals, Sverdlovsk, Chelyabinsk, and Magnitogorsk (the Russian Pittsburgh) constitute an industrial triangle tha represents one of the key areas in the Russian economy. Within this triangle are located rich supplies of iron ore, copper, nickel, cobalt, bauxite, potassium, and salt, but poor and inadequate supplies of fuel and power. Coal, the *sine qua non* for development of the rich industrial resources of the region, has to be transported over seven hundred miles from Karaganda and Kuznets. Clearly, in such a resource context, atomic energy electricity, if cheap enough, would be a boon.

In the northern Urals, Bogoslavsk has rich bauxite deposits and is currently the heaviest aluminum-producing region in the USSR. This same region, however, is lacking in adequate power resources. The nearest hydro stations are beyond the range of economical transmission of power and, worse still, are located in a temperature zone where the rivers freeze over in winter. Necessarily, then, bauxite is reduced to aluminum by coal. In such a situation, a completely integrated aluminum operation based on cheap atomic power would be highly desirable.

The situation in industrial Leningrad is much the same. Leningrad has a large supply of peat but inadequate supplies of other fuels. Thus it is necessary for Leningrad to import coal distances of over a thousand miles. Clearly, atomic power, if cheap enough, could greatly benefit such an area.[4]

There can be little question, therefore, about Professor Blackett's assertion that the incentives for pressing forward the development of atomic power are strong in Russia. In fact, the incentives, considered by themselves, are stronger than he indicates. Offsetting these incentives, however, are several other important factors which would have to be taken into account by the USSR in making any final determination to press forward with the development and assimilation of atomic power into its economy.

The first such factor is an important military consideration. If, because of the absence of international regulation of atomic energy, the USSR were successful in quickly developing atomic energy as a cheap source of electric power, she would be early confronted with the problem of making a difficult decision between the economic advantages and the military disadvantages of locating atomic energy power plants in the industrial areas where it would be most needed. In the case of important industrial areas like Leningrad, Bogoslavsk, and the Chelyabinsk-Sverdlovsk-Magnitogorsk triangle, cheap atomic power would be a tremendous economic advantage. But for at least two reasons it would constitute a sizable military disadvantage. In the first place, it is clear that, with or without atomic power, the critical objective of attack in any future war will be the atomic energy industry of the enemy. The destruction of an enemy atomic energy installation would constitute an important reduction in the enemy's capacity to produce atomic weapons. The target, of course, would be doubly attractive if the atomic installation, in addition to making weapons material, were also the base supplier of energy to such strategic industries as steel, aluminum, etc. For this reason, in a bipolar world ungoverned by atomic energy controls, the USSR would have to be extremely cautious in increasing its economic and military vulnerability by gearing its power-poor industrial areas to an atomic energy power base.

Quite apart from the problem of vulnerability would be the additional risk of having plutonium supplies for an atomic power station curtailed in time of war. Until such time as plutonium is in extremely long supply, the USSR will always have to face the possibility during a war of allocating all its plutonium supplies to weapons, even if this should entail closing down its atomic power plants. In view of this, the USSR will have to be extremely cautious in adapting its important industrial areas to a power base that it might not be able to supply without interruption.

A second factor that might tend to restrain the rate at which the USSR would develop atomic power would be the cost of the effort in terms of the other projects which have a high priority in their development effort, and in terms of what burdens the economy can stand at a given point in time. Measured in units of skilled manpower, or in units of critical materials, any rapid and extensive development of atomic power by the USSR alone would be an extremely costly proposition.

When these limiting factors are combined with the positive incentives the USSR has for developing atomic power, no clear picture emerges. At best, the Soviet Union will have to make a difficult decision between the economic advantages of cheap power and the military disadvantages. It is not inconceivable that it is the recognition of these limiting factors that prompts the USSR to make less of an issue at UN of the power implications of atomic energy than does Professor Blackett. For, Blackett's analysis notwithstanding, the curious fact is that in general the USSR delegation has been congenial to the idea of using quotas in controlling peaceful atomic activities.[5]

With respect to the USA, Professor Blackett again underestimates the incentives. In the first place, although this country is now at a uniquely high level of per capita energy consumption, there is evident no clear indication that the persistent historical surge toward higher and higher levels of per capita consumption will die down. The trend toward greater utilization of electricity-consuming equipment in the home, on the farm, and in the factory continues strong.

Second, the USA per capita annual consumption of energy is beginning to press upon its estimated per capita annual potential energy output. Currently, the USA is consuming, on a per capita basis, roughly 30 percent of the energy it could produce if its potential annual per capita output were completely exploited. The corresponding figure for the USSR—unadjusted upwards for recent territorial changes—is in the neighborhood of only 10 percent. Although even a figure of 30 percent at first glance looks so low that there need be no concern for seeking new sources of electric power, the fact of the matter is that, when you take out of the potential figure all the high-cost and locationally unattractive potential energy sources, the 30 percent figure becomes significantly higher. In short, for the long view, even taking into account the effect of a declining population, but assuming the continuance of the tendency to consume ever-increasing amounts of power, the USA has a considerable long-run incentive to develop atomic power as a significant supplementary source of energy.

In this connection, Professor Blackett might argue that even if this were true this is something for the future, and that since the USA is not accustomed or capable of taking the long view, such a future prospect would not constitute an effective incentive to the early and quick development of atomic power by the USA. Such, certainly, is the implication of his discourse on the disposition of the USSR to take the "long view" (p. 110), and the intent of his several references to the pressure groups within the USA that are hostile to the development of atomic power. It may be that Professor Blackett's opinion will prove to have been a sound appraisal of the American scene. Sadly enough, the fragmentary evidence there is suggests that he may be right; happily, however, it is not conclusive. There are sufficient forces at work in the economy for one to be hopeful that this country will take the long view as it has in other contexts in the past.

A third consideration respecting USA incentives that Professor Blackett completely neglects is the impact of atomic power on the American economy in the absence of any substantial international regulation of atomic energy. Let us suppose that the present impasse between the USA and the USSR should continue. Suppose further that the impasse should continue to be characterized as it now is by: (a) chronic war scares, (b) high armament expenditures, and (c) an effort on the part of both countries to achieve and maintain a supremacy in atomic weapons. If such a situation persisted long, it is not unreasonable to conjecture that the American people, burdened on the one hand by a heavy tax rate, and impressed on the other hand by the use of atomic energy as a source of electric power, might insist on the conversion and distribution of atomic power as a means of somewhat reducing the net cost of the high national military budget. If such eventuated, the USSR—doing the same thing—would gain in its absolute level of energy utilization but would not gain in reducing the existing disparity between the levels of utilization in the two countries.

On the whole question of incentives, then, little of a really conclusive nature can be said. The USSR clearly has sizable incentives, but these incentives are circumscribed by serious limiting considerations. The USA may have less compelling incentives, but what incentives she has are less diluted by limiting factors.

Even assuming, however, that somehow or other the USSR should have more intense incentives, in the final analysis the extent to which the one economy or the other will or will not embrace atomic power will depend on the cost of such power in a given situation relative to the cost of obtaining power by alternative means.

In commenting on some opinions that have been expressed on the possible economic gains of atomic power in different countries, Professor Blackett wisely asserts that

The sounder way of estimating the potential gain to any country from increased power supplies is to calculate the total social cost, not of replacing its existing power supplies by atomic power, but of raising them to the level found necessary for the attainment of an adequate living standard. . . .

This is correct but incomplete. The sound way of estimating the potential gain to any country is to calculate not only the cost of its marginal supply of power, but also the comparative cost of obtaining that additional increment from all other energy sources. Thus for a given new addition to the power supply of a country it is necessary to calculate and contrast the probable cost of that increment if produced by atomic power, if produced by the most efficient hydro plants, if produced by the most efficient steam plants, and so forth. Atomic power, say, twenty years from now, will be adopted in any particular economic locality only if the net cost of so producing power is equal to, or less than, the cost of producing power in that same area by the then most efficient style steam stations or hydro stations or any other process for producing power.

The figures which Professor Blackett cites from Mr. Schurr's study are of little help in making such a calculation. Indeed, as they are used by

Blackett, they tend to be misleading. For example, even if the Thomas estimate of 8 mills for atomic power should eventually prove to be correct, there is no reason to think that this figure would be the same in all countries of the world. This is a most plausible conjecture to make if one assumes that atomic power will be developed outside the framework of an International Development Authority. Because of the fact that atomic power will involve large capital costs, the unit cost of power from atomic energy in any country is going to be seriously influenced by the cost of money in that country. Other factors, such as differences in salary scales for skilled technicians, differences in construction costs, and variations in the demand for electricity, will tend to produce variations in the total unit cost of atomic power in different countries. For example, in the case of Argentina, it would not be impossible that because of factors such as these the cost of atomic power there would be 19 mills as contrasted to an 8-mill atomic power cost in the United States. In such a situation, Argentina would make her decision to construct atomic plants on a comparison of the 19-mill figure with the cost of producing power from the then existing most efficient alternative methods of generating power.

If the figures on atomic power costs as used by Professor Blackett are unintentionally misleading, his use of the figures on generating costs for Argentina, Great Britain, and the USA is surprisingly careless. Despite the fact that Mr. Schurr, in his article, took pains to point out that these cost data are not actual generating costs, but rather are costs estimated from the cost of fuel in various regions, Professor Blackett in quoting them states that they are "actual average cost[s] of electricity" (p. 108, Table 3).

This, by way of digression, is a good illustration of the importance of recognizing always the qualitative foundations of a quantitative analysis that was referred to in the earlier paragraphs of this paper. Mr. Schurr chose to use estimated costs rather than actual average costs for a quite sound reason. Had he used average actual costs, his final cost figure would have had an upward bias because the average figure would reflect the costs not only of the latest and most efficient plants but also the costs of the old, obsolete, and inefficient plants. Since reliable figures on costs of the most efficient plants were not available, he adjusted the costs of a modern 100,000-kilowatt plant as described in the December 2, 1939, issue of the *Electrical World* to reflect variations in the cost of fuel in different areas. To the extent that there have been technological improvements resulting in cost reductions since 1939, the figures overstate the costs of generating electricity in the several countries. To the extent that there have been changes in the net cost of coal, the generating costs have an upward or downward bias depending on the direction of the movement of coal and transportation prices.

What Mr. Schurr has done is ingenious, yet legitimate. It must be recognized, however, by anyone using the figures to demonstrate a given point that the validity of the figures is necessarily limited to the validity of the qualitative assumptions that went into their original composition. This Professor Blackett has neglected to do.

Much more could be said on the question of the comparative costs of atomic and conventional power. The main points to be stressed here, however, are simply these two. First, the studies so far available are too fragmentary, too conjectural, to be used for reaching firm policy opinions that atomic power would be more economical in one region than in another. Second, it is of the utmost importance that economists exert a more vigorous and extended inquiry into the power aspects of atomic energy. The work of Schurr[6] and Isard[7] is a sizable contribution; but measured against the amount of knowledge that is required if wise policy decisions are to be made, it is insignificant.

One last word on Professor Blackett's analysis of the power implications of atomic energy is in order. Although he describes in some detail the power poverty of India, China, and other backward economic areas, he fails to consider how in fact such countries would benefit by atomic power in a world without an International Development Authority. At best, he implies that by some mysterious process, power-poor countries possessing indigenous supplies of uranium and thorium would produce atomic power.

But such is not the testimony of history. Kuwait, with her rich petroleum deposits, has always been a power-poor country; so also Alaska, despite of her extensive coal deposits; and so also the Belgian Congo, despite its abundant hydro potential. Less dramatically, countries like most of those in the Latin-American bloc have not significantly exploited their limited energy potentials.

In all probability, availability of fuel resources is a relatively unimportant factor in national economic development. Availability of capital, climatic conditions, political stability, the cultural texture of the inhabitants—all these and many other factors influence the rate of economic development in a given country. Left to themselves, the backward economies of the world will probably have

their relative energy positions worsened rather that bettered by atomic power.

This, however, would not have to be the case if atomic power were developed on a cooperative international basis. In the financial resources and in the technical knowledge of an International Atomic Energy Development Authority resides a real hope for the backward areas of the world. The same holds true for the more developed areas which lack adequate power resources and capital: France, Italy, Japan, and even England.

It is an unfortunate thing that thus far this aspect of international control of atomic energy has not been sufficiently emphasized. Too much emphasis has been placed on the necessity of international control as a mutual protection against atomic warfare; too little attention has been given to the great positive possibilities for improving the standards of living of the countries of the world that are inherent in an International Atomic Energy Development Authority. It is to be hoped that the current discussions at UNAEC on such questions as the use of quotas and the financing of an international authority will bring out in clear light this important point.

In this connection, it is not easy to appreciate Professor Blackett's low estimate of the "generosity" of the Baruch proposal. Considering the preponderant financial, technical, and personnel contribution that this country would have to make to an International Development Authority, Professor Blackett does not establish too convincing a case that the American proposal is ungenerous.

THE MILITARY ASPECTS OF THE BOMB

The backbone of Professor Blackett's book, of course, is the analysis of the strategic and tactical consequences of the atomic bomb. Starting from the prudent position that in order to assess the effects of atomic bombs in future wars, one must begin with as sound and detailed knowledge as possible of the effect of atomic bombs and weapons of comparable destructiveness in the past, he proceeds to an extended review and appraisal of the performance record of aerial bombing efforts during World War II. Since there is available only the wartime experience with two atomic bombs, released under quite exceptional circumstances, the bulk of experience analyzed is in terms of the enormous conventional bombing effort over Germany and Japan.

In studying the analyses of the air offensives against Germany and Japan, as contained in the five summary volumes of the USSBS, Professor Blackett observes that the significant fact is that a huge weight of bombs dropped on Germany did not lead to a failure of either production or civilian morale. From this observation, he makes two important deductions: (1) since 3 million tons of bombs were dropped by the Anglo-American air forces on German and Japanese targets without decisive effect, it is certain that a very large number of bombs would be needed to defeat a great nation by bombing alone; and (2) in any future war between the USA and the USSR, the conflict would not be decided by atomic bombing alone, or in a short period of time. On the contrary, he contends, there would ensue a protracted, bitter struggle spread over much of Europe and Asia, involving million-strong land armies, huge military casualties, and widespread civil war.

Earlier in this review, the point was stressed that quantitative analysis necessarily involves the making of significant qualitative judgments. Professor Blackett's extended numerical treatment of the Anglo-American bombing offensive against Germany is another sad illustration of how qualitative judgments, however hidden they may be, determine the whole numerical outcome. For reasons known only to himself, Professor Blackett has chosen to evaluate the effectiveness of strategic bombing in terms of the total tonnage dropped from 1940 to 1945 considered as an aggregate, rather than as a series of periods in which strategic bombing as an instrument of warfare was being progressively perfected. Given this qualitative decision, it was inevitable that he should arrive at his conclusion that the Anglo-American air forces received a relatively small dividend in return for their investment of over a million and a third bomb tons dropped on Germany. Thus, also, the inevitability of his conclusion that over four hundred improved atomic bombs would be required to inflict comparable damage.

The fact of the matter is, however, that so important were the lessons learned in the course of five years that any substantive similarity between the strategic bombing of 1940–43 and the strategic bombing of 1944–45 is of only a nominal nature. The developments were not simply in the nature of improved planes, bombsights, long-range fighter bombers, navigational aids, and photographic interpretation; fundamentally, the most important development was a realization of the strategic character of strategic bombing.

The basic resources of an economy are its industrial capital equipment, its industrial manpower, and its supply of raw materials. For strategic bombing to have a decisive effect, it is essential that the bombing be directed at the most

vulnerable points in these basic resources. Largely out of desperation, but partly out of bad judgment, the British Air Command chose in the early years of the war to attack that German basic resource which was the least vulnerable but the most accessible, namely, German urban manpower.

The choice was unwise for at least two reasons. In the first place, Germany at the beginning of the war through to at least mid-1944 had more than ample manpower reserves. A large native labor supply, supplemented by sizable increments of foreign labor, provided the German economy with adequate insurance against almost any conceivable high casualty rate from area bombing. In the second place, the labor supply that was concentrated in the cities subjected to area bombardment did not contribute greatly either to total Reich production or to total Reich war production. For example, Augsburg, Bochum, Leipzig, Hagen, Dortmund, Oberhausen, Schweinfurt, and Bremen—cities that were the targets for severe area attacks—contributed to total Reich industrial production in very small percentages. In the order named, the contributions of these cities were: 0.3 percent, 0.9 percent, 1.7 percent, 0.3 percent, 0.9 percent, 0.5 percent, 0.2 percent, and 1.2 percent.[3] With the exception of the iron and steelworks at Dortmund, and the aircraft plants at Bremen and Leipzig, none of these cities were significant producers of war material.

A later choice by the Air Command to attack aircraft production centers was as imprudent a decision as that to attack urban centers. Aircraft production in Germany was a highly decentralized and deconcentrated operation. Planes were produced in many plants spread throughout the land—plants that were of modern type, well camouflaged, and constructed with a view to minimizing the damage effect of bombs. As a direct target for air bombardment, it was a highly invulnerable sector of the German war economy.

Despite the fact that because of its resource base Germany was not an easy target, there were at least three points of great vulnerability: her power system, her synthetic oil industry, and her transportation system.

The first-mentioned vulnerable point, much to the wartime surprise and the postwar delight of the Germans, was never a high-priority target. The tightness of power supplies, on the one hand, and the frangible nature of most power-generating and -transmitting equipment, on the other hand, were never adequately understood by Allied air intelligence. Hence, this crucial target was unfortunately overlooked. Had it not been, much greater returns could have been achieved by the air offensive for an infinitesimally smaller investment. For example, officials of the Berliner Staedische Elektrizitaetswerke A. G. have stated

that if the power plants of Klingenberg and West had been destroyed by bombing, the industrial life of Berlin would have come to a complete standstill. Not even the outside national networks could have supplied sufficient power without seriously curtailing the consumption in other parts of Germany.[3]

The significant fact is that 50,412 tons of bombs dropped on the city as a whole never achieved the industrial paralysis that a few hundred tons dropped on two electrical plants would have. By Professor Blackett's calculus at least sixteen improved atomic bombs would have been required to obtain the same limited industrial paralysis of Berlin that was in fact obtained. The more significant calculus is that two atomic bombs placed anywhere within a wide near-miss radius of the two power stations would have brought the industrial life of Berlin to a complete standstill. The weapon assumes an even more formidable appearance if one considers the radioactive effect of an atomic bomb detonated much closer to ground zero than was done at Nagasaki.

Because of her lack of indigenous supplies of petroleum, Germany was precariously dependent upon her synthetic oil production. Despite her invulnerable capacity to produce planes and tanks in large numbers, the final determinant of how many she could effectively put into battle rested with her synthetic oil industry. The complete destruction of her synthetic oil capacity, after allowing a time lag to account for the exhaustion of accumulated reserve stocks of processed oils, spelled the end of the German war machine. An investment of less than two dozen atomic bombs well placed could have rendered the German war machine inoperative after the expiration of the short time in which it would have used up its reserve stocks.

In this connection, Professor Blackett erroneously attributes the late mounting of the air offensive against the synthetic oil industry to the necessity of the Allied command waiting until it had advanced German bases and air superiority. Actually, a good part of the delay was caused by the long time it took the Air Command to learn the decisive strategic importance of oil in the German war economy.

The third soft spot in the German economy was her transportation system. Since coal was the key to German industrial production, war production of tanks, munitions, and so forth could have been as effectively stopped by the interdiction

of the transport system as by a much, much larger effort at destroying all the individual plants producing finished goods. Once this was realized by the Air Command, extensive raids on concentration yards, bridges, tunnels, and rail bottlenecks were launched. Eventually, this effort was successful in so reducing coal shipments that industrial production came to a standstill in many areas.[8]

It is difficult to speculate on the effectiveness of atomic bombs on the transportation system of a country. The USSBS study of Hiroshima and Nagasaki is anything but informative. From the meager evidence available it would appear that atomic bombs might be quite effective against concentration yards; their effect on tunnels, and especially bridges, would seem to be negligible.[9] This is not merely of academic concern for at least two reasons: (1) experience in Germany suggests that the destruction of bridges was the most effective single way of disrupting rail movements for significant periods;[8] and (2) in both the USA and the USSR the transport systems are highly vulnerable points of the economy. This is especially true of the USSR.

The experience with mass bombing in the European and Pacific theatres has several important lessons that can be briefly summarized. In the first place, for strategic bombing to be strategic in the literal sense of the word, and effective in terms of military consequences, it needs must be directed at those points in the economy of the enemy that are most vulnerable, those points that if destroyed would bring about disproportionately larger disruptions of the economy and war machine as a whole. What those vulnerable points will be for a given country depends upon the structural specifics of that economy. For example, in the USSR, considering her industrial dependence on coal and the large distances that coal would have to be moved over inadequate transport facilities, a high-priority target in a rational strategic plan would be the interdiction of her rail network. Like Germany, the USSR has a highly invulnerable aircraft- and tank-production capacity; thus, only a larger bombing effort than makes sense would be required to reduce such production. Somewhat like this country, USSR steel production tends to be concentrated in one area—Magnitogorsk—thus providing a highly attractive target for strategic bombing.

A second and more important lesson is to be derived from the World War II experiences. It seems fairly clear that urban area mass bombing would be employed in a future war in three different contexts: (1) as a "what-else," desperation effort to achieve decisive effects at the outset of a war; (2) as a by-product result of the precision bombing of a key industrial installation located within or near the periphery of a city; and (3) as an effort to hasten the conclusion of a war after the industrial capacity of the enemy to continue the war has been destroyed. This was the rationale of the urban attacks on Japan by conventional bombs and atomic bombs in the closing months of the war.

With respect to the first context, one must agree with Professor Blackett that this sort of effort would in all probability not be made in a future war. Recognizing the passive defense opportunities available, the absence of the surprise element of Hiroshima and Nagasaki, the futility of manpower annihilation against a nation with substantial manpower reserves, it is difficult to conceive of the generalship of either side of a conflict wanting to engage in such a grim, futile business at the beginning of a war.

Allowing, however, as Professor Blackett does not, for the facts: (*a*) that generalship is not always rational, and (*b*) that the radiation effects of atomic bombing are not sufficiently known for one to have firm judgments, one must admit there is more than just a slim possibility that such an endeavor would be made by one side or both. If such were the case, the USA would be at a disadvantage because of its greater urban population concentration and its lesser total manpower reserves.

It should be pointed out, however, that Professor Blackett tends to underestimate the degree of population concentration and urbanization in the USSR. For example, in discussing Dr. Oppenheimer's statement that it is not inconceivable that United States air squadrons could eradicate 40 million people, Professor Blackett asserts that to do this "many of the targets would be quite small cities with many less than 40,000 people in them" (p. 72). In other places he speaks of Russian "towns"—the clear implication being that there is relatively little urbanization in the USSR in the American sense of the word.

Such, however, is not the case. In 1939, somewhat over 34 million people lived in Russian cities of over 50,000 inhabitants. Eleven cities, with an average population of 1.1 millions had populations of over 500,000 inhabitants; 71 cities, with an average population of 200,000 people, had populations between 100,000 and 500,000; and 92 cities, with an average population of 73,000, had

between 50,000 and 100,000 inhabitants. Or, stated another way, 172 cities with an average population of 198,000 had populations of over 50,000 inhabitants.[10] The comparable figures for the USA are: 197 cities with an average population of 230,000 had populations of over 50,000.[11]

Taking into account the changes brought by the war, the relocation of cities and population, and the increase in population, it is most probable that the degree of population concentration in the USSR is greater than before the war. The rapid rate of industrialization since 1939 would almost necessarily bring about a greater rather than a lesser urbanization.

Although Professor Blackett has established a convincing case that another war in the foreseeable future would not be a push-button war decided decisively in a short period of time, one cannot accept as convincing his conjecture that the next war would be fought by million-strong land armies over much of Europe and Asia. That Professor Blackett can accept this conjecture in view of his own recogniton of the tactical uses of atomic bombs is hard to understand.

A much more plausible forecast is that initially another war would be a struggle for bases, followed by an unprecedented use of air power to cripple the industrial potential of the opponent, and concluded with a bloody annihilation of cities to accelerate the recognition by the enemy that his warmaking capacity had been destroyed.

It should be clearly understood that the reviewer has the same intense feelings as Professor Blackett on the futility and inhumanity of a preventative war. The difference between the two writers is that this one is convinced that a persuading case against a preventative war cannot be made on the grounds that militarily such a war would be difficult, bloody, and of long duration, if not impossible to win. Nations simply do not behave in such a coldly rational fashion. If a preventative war *can* be prevented, it will be because of the recognition by the nations of the world of some governing moral principles, or the unification of the nations of the world around some positive program that promises overriding attractive benefits for all involved.

This rather lengthy review has narrowly limited itself to the military and economic aspects of Professor Blackett's thesis. His political analyses and conclusions, others have and will continue to discuss. When all is said and done, however, one contribution of the book will stand out to its lasting credit. Like no other book on the subject matter, Professor Blackett's *Fear, War, and the Bomb* has brought clearly to a large number of people the realization of the importance of a wide popular consideration of the politics of atomic energy. In the last analysis, it is the people generally who can and must make the decisions concerning the uses to which this strange force is put. If nothing else, this book has taught many people that without being physicists they can comprehend the political and economic issues of atomic energy.

REFERENCES

1. *U. S. Strategic Bombing Survey.* Reichswerke Hermann Goering A. G., Hallendorf, Germany.
2. *U. S. Strategic Bombing Survey.* Synthetic Oil Plant Meerbeck-Hamburg, Germany.
3. *U. S. Strategic Bombing Survey.* Detailed Study of Effects of Area Bombing on Hamburg; Detailed Study of Effects of Area Bombing on Wuppertal; Detailed Study of Effects of Area Bombing on Dusseldorf; Detailed Study of Effects of Area Bombing on Solingen; Detailed Study of Effects of Area Bombing on Remscheid; Detailed Study of Effects of Area Bombing on Darmstadt; Detailed Study of Effects of Area Bombing on Lubeck; Brief Study of Effects of Area Bombing on Berlin, Augsburg, Bochum, Leipzig, Hagen, Dortmund, Oberhausen, Schweinfurt and Bremen.
4. GWIAZDZINSKI, J. The Power Resource Structure of the Soviet Economy. Unpublished research paper, Teaching Inst. of Economics, American Univ., 1949.
5. CAVERS, D. F. New Life for the UNAEC. *Bull. of the Atomic Scientists,* 1948, **4**, (12), 355–56.
6. SCHURR, S. H. Economic Aspects of Atomic Energy as a Source of Power. *Amer. Econ. Rev.,* 1947, 37, (2), 98–108.
7. ISARD, W. Some Economic Implications of Atomic Energy. *Quart. J. of Econ.,* 1948, 62, (1), 202–208. ISARD, W., and LANSING, J. B. Comparison of Power Costs for Atomic and Conventional Steam Stations. *Rev. of Econ. Stat.,* 1949, 31 (forthcoming).
8. *U. S. Strategic Bombing Survey.* The Effects of Strategic Bombing on German Transportation.
9. *U. S. Strategic Bombing Survey.* The Effects of the Atomic Bomb on Hiroshima and Nagasaki.
10. LORIMER, F. K. The Population Statistics of the Soviet Union: History and Prospects. Geneva, 1946; Sotsialisticheskoye Stroitelstvo. Statisticheskiy Yezhegodnik. Moscow, 1939.
11. *Statistical Abstract of the U. S.* Washington: U. S. Dept. of Commerce, 1948.

STRATEGY AS A SCIENCE

By BERNARD BRODIE

THE recent resignations from posts of high civil authority or ceremonial rank of former military officers will no doubt allay somewhat the suspicions current a year or more ago that the military were "moving in" where they did not belong. Although the original appointment to civil posts of such men as Generals George C. Marshall and Walter B. Smith was hardly due to design on the part of the armed services, being quite easily and plausibly explained on other and quite innocuous grounds, the military departments unquestionably do have a greater influence upon high policy decisions than was true before the recent war. It is therefore time to express concern not so much that that military will move in where they do not belong, but rather that in the process of moving in where in part, at least, they do belong, their advice will reflect their imperfections not as diplomatists but as soldiers.

That concern, besides receiving its immortal expression in the famous apothegm of Clemenceau that war was too important to be left to the generals, has often been expressed by soldiers themselves.[1] It is not simply that the waging of war or the preparation for it requires many skills to which the soldier makes no pretentions. It is that the skill which is peculiarly his own is in all but the rarest instances incomplete with respect to one of its fundamentals—a genuine understanding of military strategy.

That is hardly surprising, since the understanding would have to follow the development of a theoretical framework which as yet can scarcely be said to exist. Creating the mere foundations of such a framework would require a huge enterprise of scholarship, and the military profession is not a scholarly call-

---

[1] One of the more recent instances is contained in the illuminating book *Operation Victory* (New York, Scribner's, 1947), by Major General Sir Francis de Guingand, former Chief of Staff to Marshal Montgomery. This author points out again and again that the World War II experiences of the British Army reflected a lack of training in high strategy on the part of the British armed services, which have in fact devoted at least as much attention to the subject as their American counterparts.

ing—as its members would be the first to insist. Nor, for various reasons, including good ones, does it wish to become so. The scholar who on rare occasions appears within its ranks can expect but scant reward for the special talents he demonstrates. It is for quite different accomplishments that the silver stars which are the final accolade of success are bestowed.

The soldier's rejection of the contemplative life would be of no concern to him or to us if the universally enduring maxims of war—the so-called "classical principles of strategy"—which are quite simply elucidated and easily understood, really did provide an adequate foundation upon which to erect precise strategic plans. The soldier has been trained to believe that they do. I shall try to demonstrate that on the contrary the theory contained in those maxims is far too insubstantial to enable one even to begin organizing the pressing problems in the field, that the bare core of theory which they do embody is capable of and demands meaningful elaboration, and that that elaboration and the mastery of it by military practitioners must require intensive, rigorous, and therefore prolonged intellectual application. If I succeed in doing that, there will be no difficulty in demonstrating that strategy is not receiving the scientific treatment it deserves either in the armed services or, certainly, outside of them. And it will also be quite easy to show that our failure to train our military leaders in the scientific study of strategy has been costly in war, and is therefore presumptively—perhaps even demonstrably—being costly also in our present security efforts.

There are, to be sure, certain basic ideas about fighting a war which over the centuries have been proved valid. These ideas have been exalted by various writers to the status of "principles," and have been distinguished from other elements in the art of generalship chiefly by their presumptive character of being unchanging. "Methods change, but principles are unchanging" is the often-quoted dictum of Jomini. These principles, while not often apparent to the uninitiated, are certainly not esoteric. They have the characteristic of being obvious at least when pointed out, and many generals, from Napoleon to Eisenhower, have stressed their essential simplicity.

However, it is also true that as generally presented, these

"principles" are skeletal in the extreme. They not only contain within themselves no hints on how they may be implemented in practice, but their very expression is usually in terms which are either ambiguous or question-begging in their implications—a trait which has grown more marked since Jomini's day under the effort to preserve for them the characteristic of being unchanging. For example, in a recent list of ten "Principles of War" adopted by the Canadian Chiefs of Staff Committee for the use and guidance of the Canadian Armed Forces, we find "Economy of Effort" (traditionally called "Economy of Force") listed as No. 7, with the following explanation:

7. ECONOMY OF EFFORT

Economy of effort implies a *balanced* employment of forces, and a *judicious* expenditure of all resources with the object of achieving an *effective* concentration at the *decisive* time and place.[2]

The four words I have italicized are obviously the points at issue. To give them genuine meaning in a way that would convert them to tools useful in the planning process would clearly require in each case a large amount of analytical elaboration. One must note, of course, that even as stated the principle is not without meaning. It argues that military resources should not be wasted either through failing to use them at all or through dispersing them among ill-chosen or ill-coordinated objectives.[3] Although the idea is thus reduced to a truism, the fact remains that its violation has often been advocated during war and sometimes practiced, and is also clear historically that in the main (though with conspicuous exceptions) the military leader

[2] Reprinted from an article in the *Canadian Army Journal* for December 1947 by *Military Review*, vol. 28, no. 7 (October, 1948), pp. 88f. The Canadian list of principles, which I am selecting only because it happens to be one of the most recent official pronouncements on the subject, appears to be a somewhat revised version of an article published under the title "Principles of Modern Warfare" in the *Royal Air Force Quarterly* (Great Britain), January, 1948.

[3] To the purist it must be acknowledged that this interpretation and indeed the original Canadian statement quoted somewhat scramble at least two of the traditional principles. As usually stated, the principle of "Economy of Force" confines itself to the dictum that all forces available should be effectively utilized. The rest of the statement belongs to the doctrine usually called the "Principle of Concentration." There is also more than a redolence of that fine old thought called the "Principle of the Aim." In that connection it is noteworthy that the Canadian list cited does give place to the latter two principles, as Nos. 6 and 1 respectively, and the authors seem to be unaware that in No. 7 they were largely repeating themselves. All of which may conceivably reflect the barrenness of the concepts.

has been somewhat less prone to reject or ignore the principle
than the civilian leader who sometimes urges strategic views
upon him. The soldier's indoctrination is thus not without value,
since it tends to fix in the front of his mind a rule which might
otherwise slip out of that place, but it amounts to little more
than a pointed injunction to use common sense.

There have been a number of books—extraordinarily few in
any one generation—which have attempted to add flesh to the
bare bones of the orthodox principles by presenting historical
examples both of their conspicuous violation and of their ideal
observance.[4] These have been exceedingly useful contributions,
and it would be a good thing if more professional soldiers read
them. In a day when the techniques of war changed but little
from one generation to the next, they were more than adequate.
Napoleon, who often mentioned the simplicity of the principles
by which he was guided, nevertheless admonished those who
would emulate him: "Read over and over again the campaigns
of Alexander, Hannibal, Caesar, Gustavus, Turenne, Eugene,
and Frederick. Make them your models. This is the only way to
become a great general and to master the secrets of war." It is
still a good rule. It tempts one to indulge the fantasy that if
Admiral Halsey had read over and over again the campaigns
of Nelson and his colleagues in the wars of 1793-1815 (quite
accessible in Mahan and elsewhere), he might have been a good
deal more skeptical of the "Don't divide the fleet" doctrine that
betrayed him at Leyte Gulf.

In the present day, with the techniques of war changing radically not only from generation to generation but from decade
to decade, a list of theorems inherited almost intact from the
early nineteenth century, however much embroidered by examples even from recent military history, can hardly serve the
function generally reposed upon it. The modern officer account-
able for strategic planning and decisions has a burden of which
his counterpart of a century or more ago was quite free. Nelson

---

[4] One of the best modern examples is Major-General Sir Frederick Maurice's *Principles
of Strategy*, New York, R. R. Smith, 1930. On the naval side we have, besides the works
of Mahan, the excellent volume by Julian S. Corbett, *Some Principles of Maritime Strategy*,
London, 1911. Corbett, incidentally, was a civilian and a professional historian, and
the chief works of Mahan likewise are essentially and predominantly histories with only
occasional analytical interjections.

could spend his lifetime learning and perfecting the art of the admiral without any need to fear that the fundamental postulates of that art would change under his feet. His flagship at Trafalgar was then forty years old, but in no wise inferior in fighting potentialities to the majority of the ships engaged. The modern admiral or general has no such assurance. Changes, even marginal ones, in the inherent potentialities or limitations of the machines with which war is waged may affect not merely the handling of those machines but a whole strategic concept. Principles may still survive those changes intact, but if they do it will be because they have little applicability or meaning for the questions that really matter. The rules fathered by Jomini and Clausewitz may still be fundamental, but they will not tell one how to prepare for or fight a war.

That the "enduring principles" have endured so long as a substitution for a body of live and flexible theory is due mainly to their exceptional convenience. Because they lend themselves so readily to "indoctrination," they are peculiarly well adapted to the traditional patterns of military education. They can be quickly learned as part of a brief course in a war college. And since the graduates of that college may then be presumed to have a common denominator of strategic knowledge, that knowledge can be disregarded in considering candidates for promotion to top rank. Moreover, the common denominator permits the assumption that in the crisis of battle the subordinate commander will readily understand and perhaps on occasion anticipate the intentions of his supreme commander. That it is desirable to achieve such rapport is beyond doubt; the only question is the price paid for it.

Closely related to the "principle" in inherent character, and often derived from it, is the aphorism or slogan which provides the premises for policy decisions. The military profession is by no means alone in its frequent recourse to the slogan as a substitute for analysis—certain scholarly disciplines, not excluding political science, have been more than a little untidy in this regard—but among the military we find some extreme examples of its ultimate development. The slogan may originate in fact or in fancy, it may have but a brief vogue or it may endure apparently forever, it may enthrall a particular service or the entire profession of arms, but in any case it provides in the area and in the moment of its ascendancy the key to the basic decisions. "The ram is the most formidable of all the weapons of the ship" was a dictum never genuinely substantiated in battle and basically untrue, but it dominated naval architecture for almost half a century.[5] "He will win who has the resolution to advance" was the maxim of du Picq which inspired the pre-World War I French school of the *offensive à outrance*. It might have better survived the battles of 1914 had not those battles inspired a slogan even more terse and homely: "Fire kills." Those latter two words, trenchant enough but scarcely incisive, had more to do with determining· Allied strategy in World War I than any number of volumes could possibly have had.

The maxim may indeed be the supreme distillate of profound thought, but only at its first use—that is, when it is still an apt expression and not yet a slogan. No sooner does it become currency than it is counterfeit. The function of a slogan is to induce rigidity of thought and behavior in a particular direction, which in art may mean the development of a school having its own distinctive value. If the conduct of war is an art rather than a science, as is often alleged, at least it is not art for art's sake. The progress of strategy as a science will be roughly measurable by the degree to which it frees itself from addiction to the slogan.

Of late the armed services have, to be sure, devoted some care to analyzing the "lessons" of their campaigns. General Eisenhower, for example, shortly after V-E Day set up a commission under General L. T. Gerow to study the lessons of the European theatre in World War II. Despite the pre-occupation of such studies with tactics and especially administration, their value for stimulating strategic insights is potentially great. But unless the analysts are properly equipped intellectually to exploit such values, the net result of the studies is likely to be that of intensifying the military propensity to "prepare for the last war." With their traditional reverence for what they term the "practical," the military are inclined to dignify by the name of "battle experience" what is in fact an excessively narrow pragmatism.

[5] See my *Sea Power in the Machine Age*, Princeton, Princeton University Press, 2nd ed., 1943, pp. 85-8, 237. This idea and its origin provide an interesting case study in the deriving of tactical "lessons" from the experience of battle.

There is of course no substitute for the test of battle or experience in war, but there are at least three reasons why such experience is of limited usefulness and may even be positively misleading.

First, since great changes occur from one war to the next, military planners are obliged to make far-reaching decisions on issues concerning which there is little or no directly applicable experience. We certainly have no experience today with the mass use of atomic bombs. There is a good deal of experience which is in some manner relevant, but it must be sought out and applied with subtlety and discrimination and with constant concern for the qualifications enjoined by the elements of dissimilarity.[6] The incredible and sometimes disastrous lag of tactical and strategic conceptions behind developments in materiel, which Mahan regretfully regarded as inevitable in view of the ancient "conservatism" of the military profession, is due less to conservatism than to the absence of the habit of scientific thinking.

Secondly, the larger decisions of any war, or of the preparation for that war, cast the mold for the experience which ensues, so that the results often fail to provide a basis for judgment upon those decisions. The experience may be fortunate or unfortunate; but since the enemy's responses have a good deal to do with its being one or the other, and since his capacity for error may be no less than one's own, one cannot rely upon success or failure to provide the whole answer. Was a decision which turned out well rather than ill a good decision? From the pragmatic point of view, clearly yes! But the analyst who wishes to derive general lessons applicable to the future, who is anxious to find the solution which will minimize the appalling human

[6] Professor P. M. S. Blackett has demonstrated that even a person trained as a scientist may conspicuously fail to demonstrate proper discrimination in applying analogous experience to the military problem of the atomic bomb. See his *Fear, War, and the Bomb*, New York, Whittlesey, 1949. The only safeguard against such error, as in any field of scientific endeavor, lies in expanding the number of persons with similar competence. In this instance, Dean Louis Ridenour, among others, was able promptly to expose some of the fallacies in Blackett's analysis. See his review article in *Scientific American*, vol. 180, no. 3 (March, 1949), pp. 16-19 (reprinted in *World Politics*, vol. I, no. 3, under the title of "The Bomb and Blackett"). In the military profession the problem of criticism is greatly compounded by the institution of rank, with its extravagant rigidities not only of obedience but also deference. Through the process of promotion the individual is accorded, by fiat, wisdom as well as authority, the stage of infallibility being attained at approximately the fourth star.

costs of war, may not be so easily persuaded. He will be obliged to go beyond history—*i.e.*, beyond experience—to explore the feebly lit realm of "what might have been."

Thirdly, even within the scope of what our experience does illuminate, the lessons it affords are rarely obvious in the sense of being self-evident. Too many "analyses" of World War II experience remind one of the seven blind men who touched different parts of the elephant. The evidence which relates to a question is generally massive and many sided. Its examination requires not only thoroughness but also imagination. The examiner must be on the alert for rigidities of thought and action in the actors which vitiated the results of even repeated experiment.[7] He must look for the hidden jokers in a situation, the vagaries of circumstance which profoundly affected the outcome, and must clearly distinguish between the unique and the representative. In short, he must engage in a refined analytical operation involving a large element of disciplined speculation. The task requires a mind trained for analysis and for the rigorous scrutiny of evidence.

The strategist of the American armed forces has often in the past stressed the difficulty of his problems as compared with his opposite number of European military establishments. The latter has always been much less in doubt concerning the identity of the probable adversary and the probable theaters of operations. Although the Soviet Union has very conveniently narrowed the problem for us, the sets of circumstances which might govern a conflict with that country still cover an extraordinarily broad range. It is all the more necessary, therefore, that we

[7] The Battle for Leyte Gulf furnishes some interesting illustrations of the rigidities to which I refer, of which I shall here mention only one. Because it had been so in every previous major action in the Pacific War, Admiral Halsey erroneously assumed that in this instance too the enemy's principal force had to be where his carriers were. His conviction that battleships could only play a supporting role caused him to confine his own battleships to such a role. By keeping them with the fleet which he threw against a decoy force he deprived them of any chance of affecting the outcome. If his six modern battleships had been left off the mouth of San Bernardino Strait they would almost certainly have sunk the major force of the Japanese Fleet. An interesting question poses itself: had that happened, what would have been the popular (and professional) attitude today on the value of the battleship type? It might not have been a wiser attitude than the presently prevailing one—Leyte Gulf was after all a special case—but it would surely have been different. Since I am making several references to Leyte Gulf, I might refer the reader to my review article on the subject, "The Battle for Leyte Gulf," *Virginia Quarterly Review*, vol. 23, No. 3 (Summer, 1947), pp. 455-60.

develop a conceptual framework adequate not only as a base of departure for specific strategic plans but also as a means of weighing one plan against another. The planning operation goes on apace. There are divisions of the Military Establishment set up for that purpose which manage to keep themselves earnestly employed. All sorts of new paraphernalia, including electronic computer machines for solving logistics and mobilization problems, are brought into use. All that is lacking is a conceptual basis for determining whether the plan in hand is a good one— whether it is better than some conceivable alternative. It is an old military dogma that any decision is better than none; the same apparently holds true for strategic plans.

That strategic theory is reducible to a few common-sense propositions does not distinguish it from other social sciences, including the science of economics, which has undoubtedly enjoyed the most systematic and intensive development among the social sciences and which, as I shall shortly point out, bears other and more significant parallels to strategy. One of our leading economists, Professor Frank Knight, has characterized his discipline as follows: "Economic thought runs almost entirely in terms of the obvious and the commonplace . . . The most interesting feature of economic theory is that its larger and more important questions are generally self-answering when explicitly and correctly stated—in so far as they can be answered at all. Indeed, the problem of social action, from the economic standpoint, is chiefly that of getting people . . . to act in accord with principles which when stated in simple and set terms are trite even to the man on the street."[8]

Whether or not other economists would entirely agree—and any process of reducing a large body of knowledge to a few simple propositions necessarily involves arbitrariness—the fact remains that one distinguished economist was able to see his field in that light and could presumably have produced the phrases necessary to implement his assertion. That he did not feel especially obligated to do so is itself revealing. Save for the purpose of persuading busy or simple people to a desired course of action, there is no profit in such an enterprise. The profit is all in the opposite direction, in refinement and retesting of

[8] Frank H. Knight, *Freedom and Reform*, New York, Harper, 1947, p. 130.

one's conceptual tools in order that analysis of a particular problem may be more precise, that is, more correct. At any rate, in the effort to explore the ramifications or specific application of those questions which "are generally self-answering when explicitly and correctly stated," the economics profession has produced a tremendous body of literature of impressive quality. The far older profession of arms, content with mere reiteration of its wholly elementary postulates, which change not with the changing years, has yet to round out a five-foot book-shelf of significant works on strategy. The purpose of soldiers is obviously not to produce books, but one must assume that any real ferment of thought could not have so completely avoided breaking into print.[9]

The comparison drawn above between economics and strategy is especially telling in view of the similarity of objectives between the two fields. Although the economist sometimes disclaims responsibility for those community values which determine economic objectives, it is quite clear that historically he has been devoted mainly to discovering how the resources of a nation, material and human, can be developed and utilized for the end of maximizing the total real wealth of the nation. Even where somewhat different objectives are stressed, such as the maintenance of full employment, the character of his task is affected only marginally, because that task is fundamentally a study in efficiency. It is the study of the efficient allocation of the national (or other community) resources for the economic ends set down by the community, and the lists of ends presented will differ from one community to another and from one generation to the next more in the nominal priorities accorded specific items than in general content or basic structure.

Strategy, by comparison, is devoted to discovering how the resources of the nation, material and human, can be developed and utilized for the end of maximizing the total effectiveness of the nation in war. The end thus stated is of course also subject to various qualifications. During peacetime we are more interested in avoiding war than in winning one when it comes, and

[9] I am trying desperately here to restrain the bias of the academician that the effort of writing is an almost indispensable catalyst to the production of original thoughts. On the other hand, too many people have found that it is so to enable us quite to reject the idea.

our military preparations will be affected thereby not only quantitatively but qualitatively as well. Also, we wish to minimize, both in peace and in war, the burden which our security efforts impose upon our pursuit of other values and objectives. Security is, after all, a derivative value, being meaningful only in so far as it promotes and maintains other values which have been or are being realized and are thought worth securing, though in proportion to the magnitude of the threat it may displace all others in primacy. For that reason there is a vast difference between peace and war in the proportion of the national resources made available for security purposes. But in any case we are dealing primarily with problems of efficiency in the allocation of limited resources and with measuring means against policies and vice versa.

In the narrower military sense, strategy deals only with mobilized resources and is concentrated upon achieving victory over a specific enemy under a specific set of political and geographic circumstances. But strategy must also anticipate the trials of war, and by anticipation to seek where possible to increase one's advantage without unduly jeopardizing the maintenance of peace or the pursuit of other values. This broader enterprise, which might be called "security policy,"[10] can be construed to cover the total preparation for war as well as the waging of it. It would thus deal—though with clearly defined and limited objectives—with political, social, and economic as well as military matters in both domestic and foreign contexts.

Security policy so defined can hardly be the province primarily of the soldier, though he should be able to offer pertinent advice concerning it based on his mastery of the military problem. A large number of other skills are more directly related. In matters concerning industrial mobilization, for example, the function of the military specialist is or should be confined to specifying the items needed and their respective orders of priority. The handling of the business must devolve upon the politician, the industrialist or the factory manager, and the

---

[10] The temptation to use the finer-sounding phrase "grand strategy" must be suppressed in deference to historic usage, though that term has sometimes been used to cover what I mean by "security policy." In traditional usage, "grand strategy" refers to the basic but all-embracing features of a plan of war, as distinct from either the details of a war plan or the strategy of a particular campaign.

social scientist. Similarly, in problems involving political relations with other states, the soldier's function is confined to pointing out the military advantage or disadvantage which might be expected to follow from a specific course of action. The question of offsetting costs, political and otherwise, and the consequent determination of net profit or loss in a proposed policy is not only a question of civilian responsibility but actually involves skills with which the soldier is normally not equipped, though it is desirable that he appreciate the limitations in freedom of maneuver which beset the politician and the diplomatist. Even in the matter of determining the overall size of the defense budget, the soldier has relatively little to contribute. He should be able to provide us with a rational plan for the allocation of whatever sums are accorded him, but the determination of how large those sums should be must depend upon consideration of a wide range of factors, many of which lie entirely outside his usual realm of discourse.[11] One can go still closer to the heart of the military problem—and point out that the strategy of strategic bombing is very largely a matter of target selection, where the economist (possibly also the psychologist) has at least as much to offer as the military specialist.

In any case, whether we are discussing security policy in the broad sense or more specifically military strategy—or even tactics—we are discussing problems involving economy of means, i.e., the most efficient utilization of potential and available resources to the end of enhancing our security. One might expect to find, therefore, that a substantial part of classical economic theory is directly applicable to the analysis of problems in military strategy. One might further expect that if the highly developed conceptual framework which lies ready at hand in the field of economics were in fact so applied, or at least examined for the suggestive analogies which it offers, some very positive results would follow.

A good example is to be found in the military concept of the "balanced force," in the name of which all sorts of aggressions

[11] All will agree that concerning military appropriations the soldier is not well situated to tell us what we can afford. But what is equally important, he lacks any objective criteria for telling us what he needs. Under pressure from Congress, he is accustomed to presenting his "minimum essential requirements" in quite precise terms; but if he were under equal pressure to be honest, he would admit the wholly illusory character of that precision. I am developing this point in another paper to be published shortly.

against good sense have been perpetrated. The concept has been applied to all levels of military organization, tactical and strategic, and has long been familiar in its distinctively naval form of the "balanced fleet." Almost too obvious to be worth recording, but nevertheless basic and all-too-often forgotten, is the point that "balance" can mean little or nothing except in relation to predictions or expectations concerning circumstances of future combat, including those circumstances created by one's own strategic plans. A force which is well "balanced" with respect to one set of circumstances is likely to be wholly unbalanced with respect to another, except in so far as the balance sought represents a compromise between different sets of possible or probable circumstances.[12]

Once this point were firmly grasped, and the effort made to establish orders of probability and of risk[13] for various sets of circumstances—in strategy we are always dealing with multiple-contingency analysis—we would have a context for resolving the issues of balance according to the well-known concept of *marginal utility*. That is, a balanced force could be defined

[12] In a penetrating essay written during his imprisonment, Grand Admiral Karl Doenitz has analyzed Germany's failure on the seas in World War II. He argues convincingly that if Germany had concentrated her pre-war naval expenditures mainly or exclusively on the submarine arm—instead of dispersing her naval resources on a "symmetrically balanced" fleet—she would have been able to defeat Great Britain within a few months of the opening of hostilities. The error in judgment stemmed from Hitler's conviction that they would not have to fight the British and that a surface fleet would be useful for dominating the Baltic against the Soviet Union. Through Doenitz does not make the point, what he is in effect arguing is that a balanced fleet for a war against the Soviet Union alone was a wholly unbalanced one for a war against Britain, and that proper balance for the latter task would have entailed almost exclusive reliance on the submarine.

[13] Clearly applicable in this connection is an idea which an economist in a high policy-making post in the government has called "the principle of the least harm," and which might be expressed as follows: Other things being equal, that policy should be selected which will do the least damage in case the prediction upon which it is based turns out to be wrong. Or, in other words, different sets of circumstances envisaged as possible for the future must be weighted for policy purposes not alone according to their presumed orders of probability but also according to the degree of risk inherent in the policy which each suggests. One can of course point to numerous instances in the military field where this principle has been more or less consciously followed. The only admonition necessary is that the "order of probability," while it must be qualified by considerations of risk, should not be lost sight of. Otherwise, the "principle of the least harm" will no doubt serve to incur the most harm. For those interested in mathematical systematization of this and related problems, the work of Professors John von Neumann and Oskar Morgenstern on the theory of games would be illuminating. See their *Theory of Games and Economic Behavior*, Princeton, Princeton University Press, 1947. However, for various reasons I do not share their conviction that their theory could be directly and profitably applied to problems of military strategy.

as one in which the marginal utilities, tactically and strategically considered, of the last increments to each of the existing components were approximately equalized. To gauge marginal utilities among those components would be anything but easy, but at least the conceptual basis of balance would be clarified in a way that helped to indicate the scope and the direction of the analysis necessary to provide the answers. In that respect the situation would be immeasurably superior to reliance upon such tradition-charged abstractions as "homogeneous" and "symmetrical," to mention two adjectives frequently found in consort with "balanced force." In short, what we are discussing is the difference between thought and dogma.

It might of course be aesthetically abhorrent to discover gallant admirals and airmen discussing their common problems, or the occasional amiable debates between them, in terms like "marginal utility," "diminishing returns," or "opportunity costs." It happens, incidentally, to be quite abhorrent to this writer to find himself inadvertently pleading for a jargon in any discipline, though in this instance there is no danger of corrupting the pure; the military already have a quite substantial jargon of their own. But the advantage of using symbols which are tied to well-thought-out formulations has at least two advantages besides the obvious one of providing a short-hand for intra-discipline communication: first, it may help to assure that the fundamentals of a problem will not be overlooked, and secondly, it may offer economies in the process of thinking the problem through.

To persuade oneself that the fundamentals *can* be overlooked in a strategic problem dealing with the composition or balancing of forces, one need only study the arguments propounded by both sides in the recent inter-service controversy over the super-aircraft-carrier, the *United States*. Secretary Louis Johnson's decision of April 23, 1949 to abandon construction of the vessel seems to have been based on considerations of dubious relevancy, to say the least. It could scarcely have been otherwise, inasmuch as the issue was quite openly a jurisdictional dispute. The Air Force was exercised over an attempted invasion by another service of what it regarded as its exclusive domain, strategic bombing. Such a consideration is of course a basic irrelevancy, out of which all the others were bound to proceed.

For example, the Air Force argument that aircraft carriers were "vulnerable" and the Navy reply that "not a single large aircraft carrier was lost in the last three years of World War II" had in common the characteristic of conveying little illumination. We all know that any ship afloat can be sunk and any aircraft can be downed. We also know that both types of craft have had great utility in war in the past. The real issue is utility, and since every military unit or weapon is expendable in war, the question of relative vulnerability is significant only because it affects utility. This is another of those truistic assertions which somehow need to be repeated. What we need to know is the circumstances under which aircraft carriers have succeeded in their missions in the past and those under which they have failed, either through their own destruction or otherwise. We also need to know how current trends, technological and otherwise, are affecting those circumstances. And in so far as we are considering a carrier capable of launching large bombers as well as the types of planes traditionally carried by such vessels, we should have to investigate thoroughly the distinctive ways in which the performance of the ship-plane team would compare with or differ from the performance of long-range land-based bombers. In such a comparison the question of relative cost for the two types of operation would obviously be important,[14] but costs can be compared only where functions are comparable. To the extent that the carrier was discovered to have distinctive functions and performance characteristics—the Navy insists it would need the large carrier even for strictly naval use—the real issue would be the importance of those distinctive functions and characteristics as weighed against their cost. In all this we would obviously be obliged to tie our analysis to a specific enemy and to sets of conditions which have at least the quality of being conceivable.

We can already see the extent of the research and analysis involved, but the marginal utility concept warns us also against static comparisons. The value of the proposed carrier in com-

---

[14] And exceedingly difficult to work out. The issue is confused by all sorts of differentials in related fixed and sunk capital, in rates of obsolescence, in multiple-use characteristics, and in operating as distinct from initial costs.

parison with its rough equivalent (performance-wise) of long-range, land-based aircraft must vary with the number of such aircraft and of such carriers already in hand or planned for procurement. As numbers were added to either type (*e.g.*, B-36s), the onset of diminishing returns in further additions to that type would involve an increase in the relative value of the favorable qualities distinctive to the other type (carrier-aircraft team). At what point, if ever, that increase would be sufficient to cause us to shift production resources from the former type to the latter would be a question for which our research would seek answers. But to ask such questions is to put the issues of balanced force generally, and of B-36s *versus* large carriers in particular, on a rational and meaningful plane —which is to say an entirely different plane from the one on which such issues have thus far been fought out.

One thing is certain—that the cost of conducting such a research would amount to considerably less than the cost of one B-36, let alone one carrier. Whether the armed services have within their own ranks personnel who are equipped to ask the proper questions and to direct the relevant research is another matter. Of two things this writer is convinced: that they can have persons so equipped if they want to, and that they should want to.

We do, to be sure, find the services under the pressure of events acting as though they intuitively perceived the considerations involved in the principle of marginal utility. That is to be expected, since the principle reflects only a relatively modest refinement of common sense. For example, during 1944 the Navy severely cut back its production of submarines not because those in service in the Pacific had failed but because they had been too successful. They had sunk so many Japanese ships that they were having difficulties finding new targets. The situation for submarines was described as one of "saturation." But the trouble with intuitive perception *in lieu of* conceptual understanding is that it is likely to be tardy and incomplete. Prior to our entry into World War II, the rough rule of thumb method of thinking implied by the word "saturation" was applied quite disastrously to another problem: how much antiaircraft armament should be installed on our combatant ships? The reasoning was entirely in terms of the minimum number of guns necessary to "cover" with defensive fire each of the ship's quadrants. The governing dogma was that offensive strength should not be sacrificed for greater defensive strength. The result was that our battleships on the day of Pearl Harbor were virtually naked with respect to antiaircraft defenses.[15] And it was not until more than a year after that attack that the principle was finally adopted that the amount of antiaircraft armament to be installed on an existing ship was to be limited only by the amount it was physically capable of carrying and servicing, and in order to raise that level a good deal of top hamper was removed. What was belatedly discovered, in other words, was that long after the four quadrants of the ship were "covered," the marginal utility of another antiaircraft gun remained much higher than the marginal utility of many other items of comparable weight or space consumption (including empty space itself) to be found on the decks of our warships.

There is of course a great hurdle between clear understanding of the principles applicable to a problem and the practical resolution of that problem. The antiaircraft problem just discussed might not have been solved any better on the basis of marginal utility theory—if the valuation applied to each antiaircraft gun had remained inordinately low—than it actually was in the absence of such theory. And we do frequently encounter that intuitive perception which effectively replaces conceptual understanding. But so frequently we do not. Besides, there is a great practical difference between that rule of thumb which is recognized to be the optimum feasible realization of correct theory and that much more common species of rule of thumb which simply replaces the effort of theorizing.

Moreover, one cannot forbear to add that some of the more glaring errors of our recent military history could not have been perpetrated by intelligent men who were equipped with even a

[15] The explanation frequently offered by Navy spokesmen during and since the war, that our gross deficiencies in naval antiaircraft armament at the time in question was due chiefly to the unwillingness of Congress to appropriate sufficient funds to the purpose, seems not to withstand the test of the record. I can find little evidence that the Navy as a whole—and particularly the Bureau of Ships—came anywhere near predicting the needs of the war in that category of weapons, or that any concerted effort was made to persuade Congress of the urgency of the problem. Certainly one can find little to indicate that the Navy was eager to sacrifice other, less necessary things accorded it by Congress in order to remedy this glaring deficiency.

modicum of theory. To tarry a moment longer with our "marginal utility" concept but to shift now to an operational example already alluded to above: could Admiral Halsey possibly have followed the "Don't divide the fleet doctrine" to the preposterous length of hurling ninety ships against sixteen at Leyte Gulf (the Japanese sixteen also being greatly inferior individually to their American counterparts) if he had had any inkling at all of marginal utility thinking? He had other and pressing tasks in hand besides the pursuit of the northernmost Japanese force, and surely many of those ninety ships, especially the new battleships, would have had a far greater utility on those other tasks—which were in fact completely ignored—than they could possibly have on that pursuit. We know that Halsey applied the doctrines he had been taught. It was not that he had failed his teachers but that they had failed to teach him much that could genuinely assist him.

But examples could be piled on indefinitely. Nor can one permit the inference that a single concept borrowed from economics could magically resolve the strategic problems which confront us. It does happen to be the conviction of this writer that a substantial part of economic theory could be very profitably adapted to strategic analysis, including analysis of operational plans, and that those responsible for such analysis would do well to acquaint themselves with that theory—but even that is not the essential issue. Whether this or that concept can be applied with profit is something which interests us only in passing. It is in the field of methodology that a science like economics has most to contribute, and the point which it is the whole purpose of this article to bring home is that what is needed in the approach to strategic problems is *genuine analytical method*. Formerly the need for it was not great, but, apart from the rapidly increasing complexity of the problem, the magnitude of disaster which might result from military error today bears no relation to situations of the past.

For evidence of the primitive development of strategic theory, it is not necessary to compose an ideal model of what can be as a contrast to what is. Historically, we have the case of Mahan as Exhibit A. The tremendous impact (furthered, it should be noticed, by the active interest of various highly placed civilians) of Mahan's writings upon the naval branch of the calling can be explained only, as the French strategist Admiral Castex explained it, by the fact that those writings filled "a vacuum." And since Mahan's theories were almost without exception gleaned from studious observation of the practice (and to some extent the writings) of the great naval leaders of a hundred years and more before his time, there is a rather persistent vacuum to account for. Mahan was, as a matter of fact, in some essential respects behind his own times.[16] Certainly he could not be called systematic. But he stood before his colleagues as one who seemed to know the purpose for which warships were built, and he carried all before him. Nor is it altogether irrelevant to point out that Mahan in his maturity felt obliged to regard himself as a misfit in the naval profession, and that the service in which he found himself put itself to few pains to encourage the development of his exceptional and indeed anomalous talents.[17]

Moreover, Mahan has remained, for the United States Navy at least, an isolated phenomenon. The groundwork which he laid for what might have become a science of naval strategy was never systematically developed by the profession. In the thirty-five years since his death—years of overwhelming technological and political change—the service from which he sprang has not produced his successor. Mahan's endowment was a high and rare one, to be sure, but his genius was hardly so resplendent as to paralyze any incipient will to emulate. There can be no doubt that the failure to develop what was so auspiciously begun

[16] For example, his dogmatic insistence that the *guerre de course* (commerce raiding) could not be "by itself alone decisive of great issues" clearly contributed to the almost universal failure prior to World War I to anticipate the strategic significance of the submarine as a commerce destroyer. The submarine had become before Mahan's death in all essential respects the instrument it is today, but in any case his assertion was illogical on the face of it. Whether commerce destruction against a nation like Great Britain could be "decisive of great issues" depended entirely on the scale on which it could be carried out. The submarine and later the airplane made it possible to carry it out on a large scale even under conditions of gross surface inferiority. See my *Sea Power in the Machine Age*, pp. 302-4, 328–32; also my *Guide to Naval Strategy*, Princeton, Princeton University Press, 3rd ed., 1944, pp. 137-40. The point remains interesting today because comparable considerations apply to the current controversy on the decisiveness of strategic bombing, especially with the atomic bomb.

[17] See William E. Livezey, *Mahan on Sea Power*, Norman, University of Oklahoma Press, 1947, chap. 1. Mahan's elevation after retirement to Rear-Admiral had, it should be noticed, nothing to do with his services to his country and his profession as a thinker and writer. He was promoted along with every other captain on the retired list who had lived long enough to be a veteran of the Civil War.

has had its effects in the realm of strategic and policy decision on naval matters.

Nor is the Navy alone in this regard. Air power is still young, but it is certainly not new. Yet it is not possible to find in any language a treatise which explores in discerning and relatively objective fashion the role of air power in war, the factors governing its potentialities and limitations, its relation to other arms, and the chief considerations affecting its mode of operation. Sea power has at least had its Mahan; the literature of air power is all fragments and polemics. That the fact is reflected in the decision-making process can no doubt be demonstrated. It would indeed be amazing if it were not so reflected.

Having said thus much, I am now obliged to point to available remedies. The term "available" must perhaps be stretched a bit, because we are dealing fundamentally with a conflict in value systems. The profession of arms requires inevitably a subordination of rational to romantic values. Loyalty and devotion to heroism are necessarily the hallmark of the calling. Action, decisiveness, and boldness are idealized, though few professions have succeeded so well in building up bureaucratic inhibitions to their realization. The qualities bred into the senior military officer by his institutional environment thus include real and relatively rare virtues, but they also include an anti-theoretical bias which is in fact anti-intellectual. His talents, often real and pronounced, are undeveloped on the side of dialectics. The emphasis is on the so-called "practical," and on command, which is to say administration. "One learns by doing" is one of his favorite axioms; whatever requires a different approach to the learning process—reflection, for example—is suspect.[18] And in his eagerness to be doing, he does throughout his career a fantastically large amount of work of a sort which contributes nothing to his greater understanding of his art even on the technical level.

His training at one of the various war colleges—which he reaches at about the age of thirty-five to forty—is looked upon as an interlude in the more active phases of his career. The courses there are of survey type and of relatively short duration.

[18] Shakespeare, in introducing the dramatic contrast to Hamlet, uses the soldier, Fortinbras.

The pressure upon the student is intense, but, partly for that reason, there is little encouragement to what one might call rumination, certainly not of a type which might carry over into the subsequent phases of his active duty.

At present the Military Establishment operates three war colleges: the Naval War College at Newport, Rhode Island, the Air War College at Maxwell Field, Alabama, and the National War College at Washington, D. C. The Army has no war college today (the National War College having taken over the plant formerly used for that purpose), but some attention is given to strategic problems at the Command and General Staff School at Fort Leavenworth, Kansas. At none of these institutions is the course which incorporates strategy of longer than eight to ten months duration, and the portion of the course actually devoted to strategy may be relatively small. It must be observed that the National War College provides a type of training which is somewhat different from that of the other two colleges. It devotes more attention to politics and international relations, and the half of the course given over to military studies surveys the problems of all three services rather than of only one.

These facts in themselves suggest an avenue of approach if reform is seriously to be furthered. We need to make of our war colleges genuine graduate schools in method and duration of training. The military staffs should be chosen for the special attainments of their members in the several fields of strategic analysis (a process which must await development of a corps of officers possessing the requisite competences), and at least for the more advanced courses (i.e., the second and third years of a system which does not yet exist), the students should be selected according to standards which give due weight to the intellectual purpose of the institution. It would also be desirable to reach down into younger age levels than are presently to be found at the war colleges. Such reform in itself would really not be enough—some consideration would have to be given the whole basis of promotion, the system of duty assignments, and perhaps also methods of training at the military and naval academies—but it would be an important start.

The military will object that it is not their purpose to train

scholars, that there are other besides intellectual qualities necessary in a military leader, and that their needs in strategic
planners are after all very limited. They are of course right.
The successful military leader must have something besides a
good mind and a good education in strategy. But that is only
to say that the military calling is more exacting than others.
In what other profession does the individual affect or control
directly not only the lives of thousands of his fellow citizens
but also the destiny of the national community and perhaps
also of western civilization as we know it? Analytical acumen
need not be emphasized to the exclusion of those other qualities
(*i.e.*, "leadership," *et al.*), but it has a long way to go to gain
consideration even comparable to the latter.

So far as concerns the limited needs of the Military Establishment for strategic planners, those needs may not be as
limited as appears on the surface. If some of those problems
were seriously thought through which are now handled by a
process often called "mature judgment," there might quickly
develop a marked shortage of thinkers. In any case, we probably
have here as in other branches of the military art a field for
specialists who are selected and trained for the specialty. Thus
far we have had specialization in everything else. And regardless of how limited was the actual need in such special skills
as strategic analysis, we should have to have a respectably broad
base for selecting those called to the task and an adequate
means of training them.

Strategic Bombing:
What It Can Do

F-51 Mustang fighter

The conflict in Korea has emphasized once again the indispensability of infantry. An enemy army in motion has to be stopped, and while there may be other ways of slowing it down and making its progress costly, an opposing army is the only thing that can halt it and push it back. The circumstances in Korea have likewise dramatized the peculiar utility and versatility of carrier forces, even in the absence of opposing naval forces. And what is most distinctive about Korea is that there are practically no targets outside the transportation system for strategic bombing forces. B-29's are not useless in Korea, but they would seem to be among the weapons we need least.

These are salutary reminders of what we should never have forgotten. Americans, who are not a phlegmatic people, will be much affected by them. The detractors of strategic bombing are certainly going to have a field day—but even so our nation as a whole is not likely to fall into the delusion that perimeter war is the only kind we ought to be worrying about. It is worth repeating that in a war *directly* with the Soviet Union, strategic bombing would be our chief offensive weapon.

The U.S.S.R. is as immune as we are to naval blockade, and has on two historic occasions shown that it can absorb great enemy armies and destroy them. A strong, well-equipped army supported by a powerful tactical air force is obviously indispensable for the containment of the Soviet armies. But while western Europe and other key areas can be defended, defense alone will not win the war. Soviet power must be shattered by an offensive, and it is obvious that a strategic bombing offensive presents fewer technological and logistic difficulties than any other kind.

Of course, the strategic bombing lessons of the last war would not automatically apply to another one; the technological circumstances and the character of the target would be very different. But it is nevertheless important to know whether our bombing of Germany was a success or, as the dissenters cry, a failure.

The Allied strategic bombing of Germany is no doubt the most brilliantly illuminated campaign in history. The facts are available, and anyone who troubles to get at them must reach four startling conclusions: First, our strategic bombing knocked the German war economy flat on its back. Second, this great result came too late to have anything like its full effect on the battlefields. Third, given only the air power actually in Allied hands, the decisive results achieved by bombing could have come much sooner. Fourth, the biggest single factor in delaying useful results was the effort devoted to "area" or urban bombing—which simply did not pay off militarily.

Let us examine the first point, which is so frequently denied. The often repeated argument, based on United States Strategic Bombing Survey statistics, that German war production in almost all categories increased drastically between the middle of 1942 and the middle of 1944, is quite beside the point, because the decisive bombing results we are talking about had barely begun by mid-1944.

In any case, it wouldn't matter

whether or not production as a whole diminished at all if the Germans were denied even one indispensable war commodity—such as oil or liquid fuel. This, in the final stages of the war, is just what happened.

In the Second World War Allied bombers knocked out two essential German industries—liquid fuels and chemicals. In an overlapping and partly competing campaign, they knocked out the German transportation serv-

B-36 heavy bomber

ices, upon which everything else depended.

German oil-production facilities were chosen as a top-priority target early in May, 1944. Immediately German oil production dropped precipitously. From an average of 662,000 tons per month, it went down to 422,000 tons in June, 260,000 tons in December, and 80,000 tons—or twelve per cent of the pre-attack level—in March, 1945. As for aviation and motor gasoline, our results were even better. Practically all German aviation gasoline was made in synthetic-oil plants by the hydrogenation process, and these plants were the first to be hit. Aviation-gasoline production declined from 170,000 tons per month to 52,000 tons the month after the oil bombing offensive began, and by the following March was eliminated.

The effect on Luftwaffe operations was tremendous. German gasoline stocks had been tight to begin with, and production losses meant immediate curtailment of consumption. Flying training was steadily shortened, and toward the end of the war, pilots were sent into action with only forty to forty-five hours of flight training. Their inexperience made them sitting ducks for our highly trained air crews. Germany's large reserve of military aircraft was grounded with empty tanks. Only fighter missions against our bomb-

ers were permitted, and these became few and ineffective.

Effects on ground combat were somewhat slower. Gasoline was restricted first for motor transport, but before the end of the war huge numbers of intact tanks were unable to reach the fighting areas or were abandoned on the battlefields for lack of fuel. Before the end, wood- or coal-burning gas generators—such as had been only moderately successful on busses and trucks —had been put on some fifty tanks.

Chemicals were never singled out as a target, but since most of the chemical industry was closely integrated with synthetic-oil production, attacks on the latter served to dispatch the former as well. When two plants (Leuna and Ludwigshafen) were shut down as a result of air attacks, Germany lost sixty-three per cent of its synthetic-nitrogen production and forty per cent of its synthetic-rubber production. Damage to five additional oil plants brought the loss in synthetic nitrogen to ninety-one per cent. Nitrogen is essential for all explosives and powder propellants. As early as August, 1944, Speer was reporting to Hitler that the attacks on chemicals were threatening Germany's ability to carry on the war. Before V-E Day the Germans were filling their artillery shells with as much as seventy per cent of inert rock salt.

German transportation became a strategic target system in March, 1944, though heavy attacks did not start until September, 1944. By the end of October, carloadings were declining rapidly and showing immediate effects in over-all production. By late November and early December all munitions production had been severely affected by the failure to move critical materials.

In late August, 1944, the Germans could no longer supply coal to the steel plants of Lorraine and Luxembourg. By February, 1945, the Ruhr was just about completely isolated. Such coal as was loaded was often confiscated by the railroads for locomotive fuel; even so, by March, locomotives were standing idle for lack of coal in districts where some traffic could otherwise have moved. On March 15, when almost the whole of the Allied armies were still west of the Rhine, Speer reported to Hitler: "The German economy is heading for an inevitable

collapse within four to eight weeks." At that time over-all carloadings were fifteen per cent of normal and moving toward zero.

As the Strategic Bombing Survey put it: "Even if the final military victories that carried the Allied armies across the Rhine and the Oder had not taken place, armaments production would have come to a virtual standstill by May; the German armies, completely bereft of ammunition and of motive

F-81 twin Mustang fighter

power, would almost certainly have had to cease fighting by June or July."

But these results of the bombing of Germany came late. The term "decisive" is ambiguous, and one could make out a strong case that our strategic bombing was decisive anyway. Certainly the fact that from the time of our Normandy landing onward our ground forces did not have to contend with any significant enemy air opposition, while our own planes were making things very rough for the German armies, owes a great deal to our strategic bombing. And undeniably the shortage of materials, especially oil, which our bombing did was 'imposing on the Germans did in fact hasten the final collapse of their armies. Nevertheless, the fact remains that the ultimate destruction of the German armies was practically assured at the successful conclusion of the break-out west of St. Lô late in July, 1944, at which time the tangible battlefield results of our strategic bombing, apart from its contribution to suppressing enemy air activities, added up to precious little. By the time those results were making themselves felt in a really big way, the Battle of the Bulge was a thing of the past and the Allied armies were well into Germany.

If the bombing results actually achieved by February and March of 1945 had come six months or so earlier, no one could say that our strategic bombing of Germany had no significant effect upon the outcome of the war. How could that have been done?

If in mid-1943 we had put into our air force some of the resources used in building up a great army and invasion armada, we would no doubt have got our air results faster; but we were committed to an invasion of France by May of 1944, and there were at the time few grounds for calling that a

B-29 medium bomber

bad commitment. There are even fewer grounds now.

We might have suffered fewer casualties by limiting ourselves to an air and naval effort, but the Russians might have made a separate peace. If they had gone on fighting, it would have been their armies and not ours which would have liberated western Europe. Whether or not the Normandy invasion was necessary militarily, it certainly paid off politically. Besides, we must not forget that the effort we did put into strategic bombing was really colossal.

The strategic bombing of Germany was almost totally a new experiment, in which a great deal had to be learned the hard way. But some of the problems could have been better anticipated. One is especially worth mentioning, because it is doubtful whether the Air Force, despite certain moves in the right direction, is paying sufficient attention to it even now. It is remarkable indeed that the U.S.A.A.F. prior to late 1942 had given very little systematic thought to the problem of target selection. Douhet, the prophet of air power, had insisted twenty years earlier that "the selection of objectives, the grouping of zones and determining the order in which they are to be destroyed, is the most difficult and delicate task in aerial warfare." Whatever its equipment, however skillful and

valorous its crews, an air force can be no more effective than the logic that governs its choice of targets.

A directive of June 10, 1943, gave both Allied air forces the primary objective of preparing the way for the invasion of France. That was an entirely proper objective, and so was the derivative conclusion that the first priority was the elimination of the Luftwaffe as an effective force.

However, the selection of the proper objective does not guarantee the choice of the proper target system. We now know that the attack upon the German aircraft industry was a failure. The attacks upon aircraft-assembly plants simply induced the Germans to disperse their facilities, which proved relatively easy to do, and the temporary loss of production resulting from the movement of equipment was about all that could be chalked up to the credit of the attacks. At any rate, front-line German fighter strength increased.

That increase was no doubt less than it would have been if we had not conducted our attacks upon the industry. But the essential fact is that *from the moment we began our attacks upon oil in May, 1944, German planes began to be rendered surplus.*

The oil industry could not, like the aircraft industry, be easily dispersed. An additional great advantage of directing the attack first at the oil industry was that the resulting shortages would have been almost immediately felt on the ground as well as in the air.

To be sure, if we had gone to work on the enemy oil industry in June, 1943, we could not have hit it anywhere near as effectively as we did a year later. But the same holds true for the aircraft industry. Only 1.1 per cent of the half million tons of bombs dropped on Germany before the inauguration of the oil offensive in May, 1944, had been aimed at the oil industry. The tonnage of bombs ultimately aimed at oil, which destroyed the industry almost completely, was about 240,000—or half the total tonnage dropped on Germany prior to May, 1944.

Another great failure in the selection of target systems was that we never made a direct and comprehensive attack upon the German chemical industry, including the synthetic-rubber plants. The fact that that industry collapsed as a wholly unexpected bonus

from our attack on oil reveals how vulnerable it was. Had we elevated it to the status of a target system in itself, we could have demolished it much earlier in the war than we did and with only a small percentage of the bombs ultimately aimed at oil.

The bombing of cities turns out to have been an inordinate waste of bombs and of bombing effort. Cities are, of course, easier to find and hit

B-45 four-turbojet bomber

than particular industrial plants, and the kind of weather encountered over Germany often left no choice. Also, in so far as plants belonging to a rational target system are to be found within cities, the latter are bound to suffer. But a good part of the "area" bombing of cities was planned as such, especially on the part of the R.A.F. The tonnages expended on that kind of bombing were enormous. Prior to our oil offensive fifty-three per cent of the bombs dropped on Germany were aimed at "area" targets, and only thirteen per cent at industry. Even during the oil offensive, 27.5 per cent of the million and a half tons dropped were aimed at cities and only twenty-two per cent at industries, the latter including the 15.9 per cent assigned to oil targets.

No doubt the chief objective of the deliberate attacks on urban areas was enemy civilian morale. Enemy morale of course suffered—the arguments that bombing heightened the enemy's will to resist are simply not supported by the evidence—but the effect of that diminished morale on production was spread out over all industrial enterprises, including nonessential ones, and in the end was trivial compared to the results of knocking out vital industrial complexes.

These conclusions about city bombing and the morale factor may have no relevance for the future. The atomic (or hydrogen) bomb may give a wholly new and horrible meaning to city bombing. But we cannot accept the conclusion that because atomic bombs are a convenient way of destroying cities, it is sound strategy to use them for that purpose. Even narrow military considerations might dictate other targets, and strategy cannot be guided exclusively by narrow military considerations.

The errors of our bombing campaign against Germany were not all

B-50 heavy bomber

errors of strategy, like those we made in our selection of target systems. Some were tactical, and others fall somewhere in between the strategic and the tactical. All of them added up to waste—and delay in securing results.

One trouble was in the selection of specific targets within the various target systems. In our bombing of railroad transportation, for example, a very large proportion of the effort was expended against freight-car marshaling yards, and usually we aimed at the center of the yards in order to hit the greatest amount of trackage. That usually left, near the entrance of the yards, stump yards which the Germans could use for high-priority traffic. The entrance, or throat, would have been a far better aiming point, but was rarely so designated. Equally important, the Germans not only had a large surplus capacity in yards, but some of the most important traffic, including troop movements, used complete trains which did not require the use of such yards at all. By far the most effective way of interdicting railroad transportation proved to be by way of line cuts —at bridges, underpasses, viaducts, tunnels, and the like.

In the offensive against the oil industry, too, there was a persistently poor selection of aiming points within the plants selected for attack. Although

accuracy in general was far below the "pickle-barrel" variety advertised before the war, *vulnerable areas chosen consistently as aiming points were invariably destroyed.* In only a small minority of the cases, however, were the most vulnerable sections of the target plant chosen as aiming points.

Strategic bombing has sometimes been jeered at on the grounds that plants usually had to be struck at again and again in order to keep them out of production. It is true that some targets recuperate fast. But repeat raids were often necessary where the right kind of raid would have put the plant out once and for all. Apart from the poor selection of aiming points within plant areas, bombs were used which were much too light for the job. The U.S.A.A.F.'s attacks were "based on the observation that it is easier to hit an elephant with a shotgun than with a rifle." The average weight per bomb of the tonnage we dropped on oil and chemical targets was 388 pounds, as against 660 pounds for the R.A.F. But it was the heavy bombs—of two thousand to four thousand pounds each —which were able to do really permanent industrial damage on targets in Germany.

One could go on through the catalogue and discourse at length about such things as the large number of bombs which failed to explode, but the most important shortcomings of our bombing campaign against Germany have been described. One does not have to think in terms of perfect planning, perfect intelligence, or perfect anything else to admit that a modest amount of improvement in prior planning, testing, and flexibility of doctrine would have brought vastly better results.

But let no one say that strategic bombing was a failure against Germany. The facts disprove it.

We know for a fact that *the destruction of the German economy was achieved with a minute percentage of the bombs actually dropped on Germany.* We may therefore conclude that given only a moderate improvement in our use of the means at our disposal, the decisive effects of strategic bombing could have come soon enough to make a great, rather than only a marginal, difference in the outcome.

What about the future? And sup-

posing we substitute the Soviet Union for Germany? The Soviet economy is far less resilient and more thinly stretched, especially in terms of transportation, than Germany's ever was. But it is also much farther away, and much greater penetrations would be necessary to hit at vital targets. On the offensive side there is the atomic bomb, with its hydrogen-filled cousin apparently in the offing. There is also a promise of a fairly long-range jet

F-86 turbojet fighter

bomber, of perfected instrument bombing, and of guided bombs. On the defensive side there are warning radar, the jet interceptor, air-to-air rockets fitted with proximity fuzes, and ground-to-air guided missiles, also with proximity fuzes.

There is no guarantee that a strategic bombing campaign would not quickly degenerate into pure terroristic destruction. The atomic bomb in its various forms may well weaken our incentive to choose targets shrewdly and carefully, at least so far as use of those bombs is concerned. But such an event would argue a military failure as well as a moral one, and it is against the possibility of such failure on the part of our military that public attention should be directed.

What we have learned from the German experience is this: If we had to do the business all over again with the same weapons, we could do in a few months what in fact took us two years, and we would do it with far less destruction of urban areas and of civilian lives than occurred in Germany in the Second World War.

And this too should be noted:

We would lose far fewer lives among our own combat men, both in the air and on the ground. Strategic bombing can be a way of saving life in war as well as of destroying it.

—BERNARD BRODIE

MUST WE SHOOT FROM THE HIP?

Bernard Brodie

4 September 1951

THE RAND
CORPORATION

STATEMENT OF THE PROBLEM

The spacing or scheduling of atomic air strikes in the event of war has thus far been considered by the Air Force as strictly an operational problem to be left to Strategic Air Command for resolution according to its maximum delivery capabilities. Those delivery capabilities are of course fixed only for the short term; but in both short term and longer term planning, the prevailing attitude is that the more rapid the delivery of our atomic stockpile (or at least that major portion of it allocated to Phase I operations), the better. The reasons for this conviction primarily involve fears of extreme hazard deemed to attend any delay or slowness in executing our strike program; but "objective" considerations are also presumed to demand -- for quite independent reasons -- utmost speed in completing the attack campaign. In other words, compressing and pushing forward in time a campaign disposing of a given number of bombs will mean, according to this conception, more bombs on target and also more effectiveness per bomb.

Before we go into the specifics of this conviction, it is important to notice that unlike most other biases with which RAND has had to contend, this one is practically universal within the Air Force and for that matter within the Military Establishment. Undoubtedly there are differences in fervor of attachment to the principle of shooting the mostest bombs the fastest, but there appears to be no important officer or party within the Military Establishment who seriously questions that principle. An interesting reflection of this universality is contained in the SECRET staff memorandum on air bases prepared by Col. H. R. Maddux for Lt. Gen. Edwards and circulated within RAND as D(L)-985.

Section 9 (p. 9 of the RAND copy) of Col. Maddux's paper begins as follows: "Explicit in Air Staff thinking has long been a philosophy of strategic bombing which firmly believes the effectiveness of the strategic bombing offensive will be greatly increased, provided a saturating number of atomic bombs are released simultaneously over all important targets. This destruction time over target should be as early in the conflict as is practicable with achieving maximum effects." Later in the same section Col. Maddux goes on to imply that even a 5 per cent increase (i.e., from 85% to 90%) in effectiveness -- presumably as measured by number of bombs reaching target -- would justify a ten-fold increase (i.e., from 100 to 1,000) in concentration of bombing attack, and then adds: "Air Staff thinking should be in the direction of achieving this goal of dropping 1,000 atomic bombs simultaneously over the Soviet Union if possible on the day -- or the day after -- the Soviet Union launches World War III." This leads him inevitably to the argument that enough bases as well as aircraft must be provided to make such an attack possible.

Against this apparently universal conviction with the Air Force, some of us at RAND have developed the hunch that bombs may be delivered too fast -- that the goal to which Col. Maddux refers

in the last quoted sentence above is the wrong thing to do even
if we had, or could develop without concern for expense, the capability of realizing it. Those of us who share that hunch feel,
first, that pouring on the bombs as fast as we can is very likely
the wrong technique for _any_ objective; secondly, that pursuit of
psychological or direct political objectives calls for techniques
which inevitably require a certain deliberate prolongation of the
attack; and thirdly, that in view of a number of circumstances
which we believe to exist, psychological or political results may
be at least as much worth pursuing as strictly material or economic
ones.

It is the second of these points that the Social Science members of RAND have done the most thinking about and are surest of,
though even here our sureness is tempered by uncertainties concerning target selection, precise distribution of attacks through time,
appropriate methods for exploiting the attacks politically, and the
like. On the other hand, while we are modest in our claims for our
own point of view, we are convinced that a similar modesty, on the
other side would be most becoming and would expose a number of demonstrably false notions as well as a variety of beliefs or premises
which are accepted as fact without ever having been thought through,
We are convinced above all that the problem is an exceedingly important one. The proper timing or scheduling of our strikes is no
doubt as important as the selection of targets to be struck, and
it appears clear to us that the two problems are intimately related
and must be considered jointly. Thus far we have had within the

Air Staff quite independent consideration of the target selection problem, and practically no consideration (in terms of a payoff function) of the strike-timing problem.

Air Force expectations of gain from an early and concentrated attack, and corollary fears of catastrophe resulting from prolongation, are primarily as follows:

A. Expected gains from Concentrating the Attack in Time

    1. The "paralyzing" or "devastating" blow idea. This thought, which is quite strongly held, implicitly places very heavy reliance on psychological effects, but assumes -- wrongly, in our opinion -- that these effects are maximized by concentrating on one big crack of doom. There is little doubt that the more ardent supporters of this idea really expect the enemy to fold up immediately upon receiving this "Sunday Punch" of A-bombs, though they will not readily own to such expectations.

    2. The "recuperability" factor. This idea is the obverse on the material side of the previous point, which implicitly stresses non-material results. It is simply the well-known (and to a degree clearly valid) point that if an industry is destroyed slowly and piecemeal, the first portions destroyed can be restored before over-all destruction has proceeded very far, but if

80 or 90 per cent of a key industry is destroyed, the whole industrial basis for recuperation tends toward "collapse".

3. The "depth" factor. Destroying the enemy's
   production facilities early rather than later
   means so much less total production for his
   war machine.

4. The "retardation" factor. This point is handled
   rather gingerly, and generally is discussed
   within the Air Force only under Army duress;
   but it is intuitively felt that if strategic
   bombing can do anything to keep the Russian
   armies from moving across Europe, it will only
   be by the kind of crushing blow which causes
   the quick and complete collapse of the whole
   enemy nation.

B. Risks from Prolongation of the Offensive Campaign

1. Grave risk of diminution or elimination of Strategic Air Command capabilities, through losses
   of our bases (enemy attack or allied defection),
   the destruction of our aircraft on the ground, or
   both.

2. Disproportionate losses because of the small scale
   individually of attacks spaced through time.

3. The increasing attrition rates we will suffer because of our "training the enemy defenses." The

most successful penetration is presumably the first one: subsequent attacks become increasingly costly and thus less effective.

4. Enemy strategic bombing of the United States may cause this country to "collapse" politically and militarily before we have progressed very far in any leisurely ordered Strategic Air Command campaign.

It will appear in the commentary to follow that Air Force expectations of positive advantage from concentrating the attack in time are in the main either dubious or demonstrably wrong. Much more difficult to deal with, however, are Air Force fears of the hazards encountered in deliberately prolonging the campaign, especially the fear that if we take our time about delivering bombs the enemy may deprive us of our capabilities for delivery. On a lower order of urgency (from the point of view of logic,

---

I put the word "collapse" in quotes here and elsewhere because it is normally used without any specific content of meaning. If we are to use such a word meaningfully, we must be able to visualize the mechanics of the situation so described. We can scarcely learn how to produce collapse unless we know what collapse is. No doubt there are different kinds of situations which can legitimately be called collapse, but it is these very differences which oblige us to spell out what we mean by the word in any given context. The requirement that this and comparable words be spelled out would expose within the Air Force, and possibly elsewhere, the prevalence of some pretty bizarre fantasies.

though not necessarily of persuasion) is the argument (B-4) that unless we hurry up our attacks we may suffer national collapse from enemy attacks before our own offensive is completed. This is of course the usual deference, in reverse, to the Sunday Punch idea. A superficial but possibly adequate answer is that the argument is largely irrelevant, for unless there is a very high probability that our concentrated attack can be immediately decisive, we will have to prove capable of absorbing the enemy's blows anyway or acknowledge defeat. Also, the enemy's capacity to destroy the facilities upon which maintenance of our strategic bombing capabilities depends would seem to provide all the more reason for husbanding those capabilities rather than expending them at the outset. There may be more to the problem than that, but certainly no one is urging any delay whatsoever in going after enemy strategic air capabilities if we know how to reach them. Any accessible target directly connected with those immediate capabilities and promising a <u>reasonable payoff sho</u>uld be attacked at once. But this is a

---

It is not too fanciful to suggest that in one way the existing Air Force bias tends to compromise whatever chances we may have to get at enemy strategic air capabilities. The slogan "finish the campaign quickly" reflects only one side of the bias, the other being "keep the first strike big" -- i.e., keep the campaign concentrated, <u>if necessary by delaying the first attacks</u>. Some lightening of this emphasis on concentration might very well permit us to get some bombs delivered a few days earlier than we otherwise might. Incidentally, one hears this emphasis on concentration justified in important places on the grounds that it conforms with the "principles of war," which notion is to be remembered whatever we may think of its intellectual content.

---

specialized target system rather than a general one, and presumably will account for a minor portion of our indicated targets.
What we are concerned with is the ordering of our general strategic bombing program _after_ the topmost priorities are accounted
for.

It is easy enough to say that these fears have not really been
thought through, as indeed they have not been, and that one should
calculate the risks before deciding not to take them. It is up to
us to calculate those risks to the best of our ability. Whatever
ideas we finally come up with, their effectiveness within the Air
Force will depend not only on our manifesting awareness of the
risk problem but also on our demonstrating a concerted effort to
get at the answers to that problem. In other words, we have to
prove first of all to ourselves and to others that such spacing
of attacks as will result from deliberate prolonging of the campaign need not unduly hazard or excessively reduce our overall delivery capabilities. This will require answers to some specific
questions such as will be presented in the ensuing commentary.
And if these answers are forthcoming at all, they will have to
stem from divisions in RAND other than the Social Science and
Economics divisions.

We may admit that from the point of view of non-material effects, throwing all our bombs as rapidly as possible has a certain
loose rationale not to be found in any deliberate extension of the
time over which the campaign is to endure. The latter argues a
specific objective in time which the former need not pretend to.

Exhaustion of the stockpile (or of our delivery capabilities) may be reached with the objective not yet attained, in which case the deliberate spacing of attacks may prove to have been pointless and possibly disastrous, <u>unless</u> it can be shown that the spacing also permitted greater net material effects (especially strategic as opposed to purely physical effects) per bomb available in the original stockpile. At least one RAND consultant, Mr. H. J. Barnett, has argued for a concentrated A-bomb attack early in the war, but whatever the logic of his individual points it is clear that his position was based fundamentally on the assumption of large continuing American A-bomb production throughout the course of a long war.[3] In view of the facts that the enemy strategic air force will almost certainly place a high priority on elimination of our atomic bomb production, that they know exactly where our key facilities are and will be, and that the RGZ's necessary for the elimination of such production are not numerous or likely to become so soon, that assumption deserves some special scrutiny. Mr. Barnett also dismissed as unknown, unknowable, and therefore presumably unimportant the non-material or psychological effects which the Social Science Division feels may be the cardinal issue of the debate. Also, both he and his

---

[3] See D(L)-742: H. J. Barnett and R. T. Nichols, "Time Distribution of Bombing", April 17, 1950.

---

collaborator-opponent in the paper I am alluding to, Mr. R. T. Nichols, were arguing the cause of concentration _versus_ more or less equal distribution of the original stockpile over a five-year war, and it is clear that there are many other alternatives to consider. We might all agree that some kind of concentration is necessary, but that it make a great deal of difference whether the concentration extends over two weeks or three months. Similarly, there are all sorts of different patterns of attack that might be fitted into a period of as long as three months.

At any rate, none of these questions should be prejudged. The Barnett-Nichols paper appears to have been an isolated exercise dealing with a few facets of the problem of proper time distribution of an atomic bombing campaign, and so far as I know the work on this problem has not been carried further in any serious and systematic way. I submit that because the issue _is_ prejudged by the Air Force, which has settled upon utmost concentration of attack as the obviously correct answer, a comprehensive and systematic examination of the problem should become a major RAND project. The character of the Air Force bias clearly works in the direction of producing the most expensive kind of strategic bombing force, and if the judgment is in error it is very likely also to compromise our entire war strategy by causing the rapid and wasteful expenditure of our greatest single strategic asset -- some might say our only great strategic asset. I can think of few if any problems of comparable importance confronting RAND today.

The problem, as I see it, is: How can we maximize the overall strategic results of our strategic bombing campaign through manipulating the rate of expenditure of an A-bomb stockpile which has the characteristic of being absolutely limited in size, that is, where a bomb used means one less in the remaining capability.↓ This problem seems to me divisible into four main components: (1) effect of such manipulation on material results, (2) ditto on non-material results, (3) ditto on operational hazards, and (4) cost comparisons between an air force designed for utmost speed of delivery and one designed for more leisurely delivery. We must consider all these aspects in a mutually connected fashion, but we should not betray ourselves into devising a specific schedule of delivery. The latter enterprise we can leave to the Air Force. We will be making a sufficient but necessary contribution if we simply jar the prevalent complacency on the

---

↓ I emphasize this point not only because of my assumption that our A-bomb production is vulnerable but especially because it highlights the error in the thesis that concentration of attack is in conformity with the "principles of war," presumably the principle of concentration of force. (See last sentence in my footnote No.2 above). The principle of concentration of force has of course always applied to those kinds of forces which are not expended simply by virtue of being used, and which are therefore more likely to be preserved through concentration than the reverse. The principle which may on occasion dictate the concentration of men and their guns, or tanks, or other weapons is by no means likely to suggest the swift expenditure of a limited fund of missiles. Of course where the missiles are in practically unlimited supply, or at least no serious bottleneck, the necessity for the distinction does not exist.

---

doctrine of shoot-from-the-hip-and-empty-the-magazine.

Since there has already been done on other projects within
RAND a good deal of work which is applicable to this problem,
and since we must frankly recognize and designate those areas
where relevant data are not only unknown but also essentially
unknowable, the project I have in mind should not take a great
deal of time. A report which took us four to six months to produce might be not merely as good as but a great deal better than
one which took us a year.   During that time the Air Staff and
Strategic Air Command will be blithely doing their planning, and
doing it on a basis where those questions to which we could essay
only tentative and contingent answers had not even been asked.

It is of course obvious that the question I am posing here,
like most others pertaining to the strategic air campaign, cannot
legitimately be considered apart from the overall strategy of the
war. In fact, the possibility that the war may last five years
instead of five weeks is one of the major weaknesses of the Sunday
Punch idea. However, I plan to take up the issue of the objectives
of strategic bombing in relation to our overall strategy in a separate paper -- as do others within RAND -- and for the time being
it might be useful, especially for political reasons, to consider
the problem I have outlined above as a separate one.

And to narrow the issue further, I should suggest distinguishing between the problem outlined above and another which is closely
related to it, namely, what proportion of our atomic stockpile

allocated for strategic bombing should be kept out of Phase I
operations as a reserve? The same prevalent bias which makes
for attachment to the Sunday Punch idea obviously makes for a
relatively small reserve, and for the moment it is sufficient
that we be cognizant of this in our assumptions. Thus we could
set up a problem somewhat as follows: Assuming a fund of 500
/purely arbitrary figure7 bombs of 40 KT yield /or other stated
standard7 allocated for Phase I of SAC operations, and assuming
further that not over 150 such bombs are withheld as a reserve
for strategic air operations after Phase I is completed, what
is the optimum time and amplitude distribution of the attacks
comprising Phase I?

COMMENTARY

The methods of use which have brought the atomic weapon its greatest triumphs to date are the methods which, under existing biases, we would abandon in the event of war. Insofar as the explosions at Hiroshima and Nagasaki hastened the end of World War II, as they undoubtedly did by some unknown margin, it was not the two expended but the threat of more to come which tipped the balance. The damage done by those two explosions was, in terms of remaining overall enemy capabilities, literally nothing; the demonstration value was everything. Similarly, in the post war period we have kept the Soviet Union in check almost exclusively through the threat of our growing and much publicized atomic stockpile -- at least through nothing else that is visible to us.

But the existing mood is, in the event of war, to seek to expend almost all we have as quickly as we can. So heavy a reliance upon an initial blow can be justified only by the expectation that the results will be absolutely decisive. What grounds we have for expecting such decisive results is not clear. In fact, the process of thinking out this question has hardly begun, nor does the necessity of doing so appear to be realized. One hears in the Pentagon assertions that so powerful and early an attack as that now planned by SAC would "break the back" of the Russian economy, which, whether true or not (and I think not), still leaves open the question whether such physical and economic results will cause political changes within the S oviet Union which will induce their leadership to surrender or seek a negotiated peace on terms favorable to us, or whether they will not be offset and possibly even nullified by the Soviet conquest of the economy of Western Europe.

One encounters references to the psychological and political results which will follow from the crushing impact of the initial blow, but these references are always extremely vague and often naive in terms both of realities of the Soviet governmental structure and of existing knowledge, however meager, about human psychological and political behavior in disaster situations. To be sure, political and psychological conditions highly favorable to us _may_ follow, but we have no right to expect it -- and our techniques of bombing have scarcely been chosen to exploit such effects, let alone maximize them.

One would think that the aim of producing important psychological and political results would demand above all the capacity to continue exerting pressure in some way comparable to that exploited in an initial blow. The kind of mass attack envisioned for the opening period of the war will leave an urban population completely unnerved, distraught, and for the most part benumbed. It will be preoccupied with personal loss and with bare problems of existence. If comparable World War II experience is any guide, such a population is politically apathetic. Any attack of the intensity and duration now envisioned would undoubtedly be a terrible period for the Russian people. But we have no valid grounds for supposing that the governmental structure, with all its coercive apparatus, will be critically impaired. Thereafter the situation for the Russians will improve, however gradually -- at least there will be no heavy bombing.

Under present conceptions, it is not too much to say that we shoot our bolt and then wait for something to happen, being then quite unable to affect what will happen. We permit ourselves little or no opportunity for coordinating bombing attacks with political warfare. We permit ourselves no means of tying our attacks, especially on cities, to specific war acts of the Russian government and armed forces in a manner calculated to impress the Russians, first, that the sole responsibility lies with their government and, secondly, that they have an alternative to being destroyed.

Also, the compressing of the campaign in time leaves no opportunity for gauging the strategic as opposed to the physical effects of our earlier strikes. We have made provision for post-strike reconnaissance, most of which will be done by radar. The radar scope will show holes where we previously received "blips". From that we will deduce that the target was "destroyed". That is hardly satisfactory even for determining physical damage, but it leaves untouched the question of what effect the actual destruction is having upon the enemy's economy and political structure, and upon his capacity to survive and to wage war.

These considerations suggest that one cannot wisely select targets or target systems on a comprehensive basis without some knowledge (or control) of the sequence in which they will hit and of the collateral pressures to be exerted. Certain basic systems, yes, (e.g. atomic energy, petroleum, and enemy air capabilities if

accessible), but not a comprehensive program which commits by far
the major portion of our stockpile. In other words, the relationship between the target on the one side and a time and method of
attack on the other is properly a reciprocal and not a one-sided
one. One must leave some room for playing by ear according to
previously-prepared but flexibly-held concepts. That is the way
we would fight a war if we did not previously bind ourselves to
another way, which is what we are in danger of doing.

Among the objections mentioned in the preceding section to
extending the strategic bombing program over time is the one which
concerns enemy industrial recuperation, Granted that the telescoping in time of a strategic bombing offensive will greatly reduce
the enemy's capacity for recuperation, that leaves untouched the
question of how much telescoping is necessary to accomplish this
end, with what target systems, and with how many bombs? From the
recuperability standpoint, the delivery of any given number of
atomic bombs over six months to a year may be about as good as
six weeks or less. Moreover, recuperation is affected by ability
to re-attack at least as much as by initial destruction. One must
also refer to that relatively intact economy beyond the Soviet borders cavalierly dismissed as unimportant in certain Air Force cir-
cles.

On the operational side, there is no doubt much to be said
for the importance of hitting while the hitting is good. What
I question is the assumption that that pertains only to the opening stages of the war. I lay no claims to expertness in these

matters, but I can think of certain questions concerning this proposition which seem not to have been considered.

First, if we remember our constant (though possibly unreal-
istic) assumption that the enemy will initiate the war, will his
defenses not be well mobilized from the beginning?

Second, may not our early attacks weaken his defensive capabilities, especially if they are directed toward that end?

Third, will we not also learn a few things from the results
of our strikes? Is the learning which results from the early combat so one-sidedly in favor of the defensive?

Fourth, is there not a great difference between the learning
accorded the defense by continuous raids (which are what is usually
envisioned) and that which results from individual strikes widely
spaced in time and using different methods of approach? The lessons which the defense derived from the 90-day German V-1 attack
on England (to mention the classic example) would have come much
more slowly from a series of individually concentrated but widely
spaced attacks.

Fifth, insofar as our urgency stems from a fear of losing advance bases, such concern might suggest other sources of action besides that of dropping all our bombs simply for the sake of getting
them dropped. What can be done to make those bases more secure?
How can we organize our forces and plan our strikes to reduce the
penalty suffered by loss of advance bases? In any case, let us
by all means calculate the risks before deciding not to take them.
We need to know, among other things, the minimum size cell for any

attacking force if disproportionate losses are to be avoided, the
utility of isolating geographical areas within the target region
and taking them one at a time, and the ways in which techniques
of approach can be varied through a campaign to give the defender
a maximum of confusion.

But we should also remember that the operational factor is
after all not the only one that matters. It gives us the limits
of the possible. Within those limits, the operational factor becomes one input among several -- a vitally important one to be
sure, but nevertheless subject to other considerations. If we
have to pay a somewhat higher price for one kind of campaign rather
than another, we should not only seek to determine the price disparity between the two but we should also leave the planner free
to gauge the payoff in each case against the cost. The ultimate
payoff is the only thing that counts, the forces involved being
a means to that end (and an expendable one at that).

The doctrine of "Don't divide the attack" is reminiscent of
the similar doctrine of "Don't divide the fleet" which betrayed
Admiral Halsey at Leyte Gulf and committed him to the absurdity
of hurling ninety ships at sixteen inferior ones while leaving
the essential area unguarded. But Halsey lost only a gambit and
not a war; in one sense he did not even lose the battle, and he
was able at the end of his service to retire with honors. We are
dealing here with far greater risks, and also with a situation in
which the strategic bombing campaign must perforce play a far
greater role in our overall strategy than Halsey's isolated action

could possibly have done.

One might also point out that the predictions concerning the two World Wars which proved almost universally wrong were the predictions concerning their duration. Also, in each of those wars, the side which made the most telling early blows and the farthest advances was the side which ultimately lost. There was certainly no necessary connection in those events, but they should suggest some qualification to the doctrine of always "getting thar fustest with the mostest". Incidentally, it was a Confederate general (Forrest) who originally made that crack, and the Confederates also lost.

Material and Non-material Results

I turn now to the question of psychological or non-material results of a strategic bombing campaign as against the purely material ones, although, as will presently be made clear, I do not feel that in practice there is any essential conflict between them.

Whether we can win a war by relying upon strategic bombing almost alone, as we would have to do if war broke out within the next two years, is a question to which there can be no single, conclusive answer. We should first have to be clearer on many things besides our own physical capabilities. It may be that we cannot achieve our objectives unless we rise above the purely hardware conception of strategic bombing. The question of whether steel or electric power is the better system to attack becomes relevant only after a number of other questions have been answered, questions pertaining to what it is we are really trying to do.

Consider the Soviet economic losses during the first five
months of the German-Soviet war in 1941. During that period,
the USSR lost to the enemy territory which had contained:

                40 per cent of the country's population
                63 per cent of the coal output
                58 per cent of the steel output
                68 per cent of the pig-iron output
                60 per cent of the aluminum output
                38 per cent of the grain crops
                95 per cent of ball bearing production
                99+ per cent of rolled non-ferrous metals, etc.

The achievement of such results by strategic bombing would no
doubt be considered very good. And if horror be a necessary ingredient, the Germans provided that in plenty. Some hold that it
was that which cost them the war. Yet despite these great losses,
and despite the fact that great attritional land battles were going on concurrently -- battles in which the Soviet armies lost
some four million of their effectives in the first six months of
the war and some two-thirds to three-quarters of their available
tanks and aircraft -- the Russians managed to stop the huge German armies and subsequently to launch an offensive which contributed enormously to the common victory. There was Lend-Lease help,
to be sure, but that was hardly as great as what the Russians could
extract from the economy of Western Europe.

And we are assuming that the raising of some of the above-men-
tioned percentages marginally and of others substantially will be
enough to make all the difference, even if there are no great land
battles (or only very brief ones) and the Soviet Union has taken

over all of Eurasia. This is a vast assumption.

One might well wonder whether the A-bomb destruction we are
presently capable of inflicting in the Soviet Union would actually
overshadow the horrors which that country has already experienced
under its present regime and which that regime easily survived.
I am thinking of the civil war (following hard upon World War I),
the collapse of the economy in the period preceding the NEP, the
great famines of the 20's and 30's, and the devastation of World
War II. Certainly an A-bomb attack could not match these horrors
in duration of effects, even if it could overshadow them in short
run intensity.

There is one defense against strategic bombing of the conventional economic variety which is nearly absolute and which we seem
to be considering scarcely at all. I mean the stockpiling of finished commodities of war, which in the Soviet Union is going on
apace. Some materials can be stockpiled only indifferently well,
and the effectiveness of the others is being constantly corroded
by obsolescence. But in the absence of heavy attrition these factors may be far less important than we generally assume. At any
rate, we need some new approaches to the questions of "depth" of
various systems and of enemy "minimum requirements" on both the
combat and production side. Such new approaches might well suggest not only radically different target systems and different
programing of attacks, but also basically different objectives
from those the Air Force seems currently wedded to.

Among Air Force officers, interest in psychological or political effects has the characteristic of being much more often implied than mentioned. Often too it clearly plays a far greater role in ju judgment on target systems than the officers making the judgment are ready to admit to themselves or others. And indeed such effects deserve important consideration. Capacity to fight effects willingness to fight and visa versa, and faith or lack of faith in ultimate victory certainly affects the efforts which will be directed towards restoration of damaged industries; but that is by no means the whole story.

More important is the fact that psycho-political results cannot be divorced from economic ones, so that it is impossible to rule them out in effect even when we are indifferent to them in theory. And the results we achieve on the political front may be the opposite to those we desire and may tend to offset to some extent the favorable economic results. Both categories are after all only means to an end, that end being the early and favorable conclusion of the war, and on a basis that will make the peace at least livable.

The goal of securing a final and favorable conclusion to a war usually argues a basic change in the psycho-political climate in the enemy country. In a full-scale war with the Soviet Union, it would be almost axiomatic that there could be no surrender by the enemy, or readiness to negotiate on our terms, without a revolution in his government -- that is, without collapse in the control of the present regime such as would permit some other group to take over.

Psychological objectives can no doubt be to some degree independently targeted from economic ones. The former, for example, might concentrate on cities, while the latter would concern itself with vertical systems with small regard to the urban or non-urban location of individual targets. However, choice of targets may be much less important than methods of attack. For example, the question of whether or not we go after cities would be quite secondary to the question of whether or not we introduce some system of warning (for example as outlined in the RAND study "WARBO") to the resident population. Also, the spacing of attacks, and the propaganda exploitation of those already made and those to come, will make more difference in psychological impact than whether the RGZ is an electric power plant or a steel mill. It cannot be too much stressed that there is no essential conflict between economic objectives and psychological ones. Bombs must in any case destroy structures, and whether the structures chosen reflect primarily a PW objective or an economic one is a matter of degree rather than of kind.

Are Human Casualties a Bonus?

Among the basic questions which appear not to have been clearly resolved either in Air Force doctrine or in RAND studies concerning strategic bombing is the following: in the selection

and execution of a strategic bombing plan for enemy
countries, is it desirable to maximize human casualties or
to minimize them, or is it a matter of relative indifference how many casualties result from the destruction of
targets selected on other grounds?

The answer adopted by the Air Staff, and I believe
by most of RAND for that matter, is the one which embraces
indifference but which regards slaughter of people attending
destruction of an economic target as a "bonus."

Let us be clear that for the purpose of the present
discussion we are not concerned with moral considerations
per se. Agreed that no one wants to kill people uselessly,
and that the war we are talking about would be one in which
the stake is nothing less than sheer survial, the question
whether we should maximize, minimize, or disregard human
casualties in our strategic bombing campaign can be put on
a plane where the sole criterion is whether we thereby help
or hinder our program towards victory and the achievement of
our national objectives. Certainly it is intrinsically an
important enough question to be considered in itself.

The question of whether it is or is not a good thing
to target people rather than industrial facilities has been
studied within RAND (I have in mind especially an incisive
paper by Jack Hirshleifer less than a year ago on the subject),
but usually from the point of view of economic consequences
alone. The idea is that people, especially in cities,

represent certain skills, and that to deprive the enemy
of those skills may be a very good supplement to or even
substitute for depriving him of his industry. While there
is no unanimous agreement on the matter among RAND staff
members in both the Social Science and Economics Divisions,
there does seem to be some consensus on the view that highly
developed war essential skills are rather thinly distributed
in a population even within a city; that people, unlike
buildings, can hide or flee; and that some measure of
warning is likely even if the attacker does not offer it.

The fact that these questions are considered almost
exclusively in terms of economic results is only another
example of the heavy economics bias which has prevailed in
this area of thought since World War II. This bias was
confirmed by the fact that under the conditions and methods
of World War II, morale attacks on cities were or appeared
to be a complete bust. The question now is whether we
should not be ready to revise our thinking in view of the
radically new conditions created by atomic and other weapons
of the availability of new methods of attack, and of the
great difference in political climate between Nazi Germany
and the Soviet Union.

There was very little basis for distinguishing between
the people and government in Nazi Germany because of our
knowledge that Hitler had the fervent support of the
overwhelming mass of the German people. Our intelligence

about the Soviet Union indicates a very different state
of affairs, and it would seem the better part of wisdom
to consider most earnestly whether and how we could exploit
that situation in our strategic bombing.

Almost all references to psychological results of a
bombing campaign reflect the quite unexamined assumption
that such results are increased only through killing more
people. Among the considerations which would seem to suggest
the opposite, that is, the desirability of minimizing
casualties -- or at least of appearing to wish to do so --
are the following:

a. A corpse presents no problems other than
disposal. All his anxieties are liquidated
as are those of his family concerning him.
Liquidated too are all his potential
hostilities to the regime which governs him.
A corpse makes no demand for food or shelter.

b. Fear and flight of survivors are the maximum
dissolving agent, especially if the regime
proves powerless to provide for fugitives and
if we provide incentives to the population to
bring pressure to bear upon the regime. To
do so requires some connection between our
bombing and our stated war aims, and presenta-
tion of that connection in a form which can be

translated into operational demands. Of
course, a split from the top is more meaningful
than pressures from below, but in either case
we must provide and develop incentives to
surrender. Incidentally, it would probably
require far fewer bombs per thousand head to
create fugitives than to create an equal
number of corpses.

c. An indiscriminate bombing of populations will
very likely have a disproportionate affect
upon the ruled as against the rulers, since
the latter will enjoy the prompted internal
warnings and the deepest air raid shelters.

d. Our intelligence indicates overwhelmingly that
the Russian people do not love their regime.
If they become convinced that we want to kill
Russians rather than destroy Communism, all
the value of that potential disaffection is
destroyed. We should then be repeating the
great blunder which the Germans committed in
the Ukraine where the population was in the
beginning favorably disposed towards them.

e. There are in any case far too many Russians for
us to kill. It is not too much to say that we
need Russians in order to defeat Russians.

The above comments are intended only to be suggestive
of points which deserve further study. It would be wrong
to suppose that the relevant studies could prove anything
in the sense of giving us final and conclusive answers to
our questions. But they could no doubt suggest things we
could do (or avoid doing) without serious cost and with the
possibility of great profit. They would pay off sufficiently
if they only disclosed methods of avoiding egregious blunders.

In any case, we have no justification for regarding
whatever large scale slaughter results from our bombings as
a "bonus." It may be a negative bonus, harmful to our
strategic and political goals. If we do not know that it is
a bad thing to kill Russians indiscriminately, that is not
the same as saying that we know it to be a good thing.

The special relevance of the above observations on
casualties to the problem discussed in the present paper is
this: If we find ourselves obliged for a variety of reasons
to bomb targets situated within cities -- as seems almost
inevitable -- it may becomes a matter of great urgency so to
space our attacks and to attend them with such warning that
the Russian population will not inexorably conclude that we
are solely bent upon their destruction, denying them all
opportunity of reprieve or escape. Also, it might be a very
important factor in helping us to decide such problems as
whether the centers of cities or industrial concentrations

within cities should be the RGZs selected.

We should remember that the spectacle which Germany
provided in World War II of fighting to the very end of
her capacity is the rare exception in modern times -- an
exception for which we have no reason to be proud. The
surrender of Italy and Japan in the same war, and of Germany
and especially of Russia in the previous war, show that the
will to resist may collapse long before the physical capacity
to do so -- provided that that will is properly conditioned
by the conqueror and that the seeds of disaffection already
exist in the target population. The Soviet Union looks like
a perfect setup for the attack which exploits psychological
weapons, and the atomic bomb looks like the perfect weapon
for psychological exploitation. Why not bring these two
things together?

The Goldhamer Paper

Before leaving for Korea, Herbert Goldhamer, upon
request from the Missiles-Aircraft Project Committee, drafted
a paper on the importance of strike spacing for the achievement of psychological results in a strategic bombing
campaign. His paper was commented upon by several other
members of the Social Science Division. Inasmuch as Herb
was obliged to do this paper in great haste, and since he
will no doubt want to revise and expand it upon his return,

I have chosen in the following not to reproduce it but
simply to outline its salient features. Where I or others
take exception to or wish to qualify his observations, I
have added the relevant comment in brackets.

Goldhamer lists the non-material results of strategic
bombing as follows:

  a. Dispersion of industrial and non-industrial
     population outside the threatened city.

  b. Diversion of effort towards passive defense.

  c. Refusal to work, sabotage, slow down if workers
     are not permitted to leave cities or are not
     given adequate passive defenses.

  d. Rioting, political demonstrations.

  e. Lowered productivity, disorders in countryside
     and small towns resulting from influx of urban
     population.

  f. Weakening of Politburo will to continue the war
     either as a result of population pressure or
     directly from physical damage.
     /Goldhamer for some reason stopped short of
     the ultimate objective, namely, the overthrow
     of the war party by one seeking or ready to
     seek peace./

The magnitude of effects will depend primarily on the
following:

  a. Magnitude of destruction and death.

b. Diffusion of knowledge on a, or of warning
in advance of a.

c. Circumstances under which war starts /some of
us think that this point will be of purely
academic signifigance following the first
A-bomb attack7.

d. Capabilities and policies of the Soviet Union
in alleviating misery.

e. /Not included by Goldhamer7 Soviet Union
military successes, especially in Western
Europe.

Goldhamer stresses that the threat of calamity, of
impending disaster, rather than past attacks and present
misery, is most conducive to political behavior. Moreover
the threat must continue for a long enough time to produce
the desired effect. More precisely, the time must be long
enough to

a. Permit full diffusion of knowledge of completed
attacks.

b. Permit anxiety to "rise to its highest pitch."

c. Permit assaults and pressures on Soviet Union
authorities.

d. Permit Soviet Union authorities to consider
and accept conditions under which hostilities
will cease.

The estimate of the time required for diffusion of

knowledge of "the full extent of past devastation", even
in the face of communicational obstructionism of authorities,
is reckoned by Goldhamer as being two weeks for a three
hundred mile radius around each city attacked, i.e., about
twenty miles a day. This time also allows for full
diffusion of United States warnings. /Some of us would
question the grounds upon which these estimates are based,
but at least we have a figure for consideration._/

Additional time will be necessary (after diffusion of
full knowledge) for the mass of the population to become
engaged in acts of other than "largely personal significance."

Goldhamer then considers two cases: A. The authorities
countenance evacuation and B. The authorities resist
evacuation. Under A, "the authorities could more readily
permit evacuation of essential industrial workers in the
case of an intense, short campaign." /This assumes that the
Soviet Union authorities will know from the character of the
first blows that the campaign will in fact be short._/ Under
case B, developing tension and "potential drive toward
dissident action will be cut short by the rapid termination
of the campaign."

The threat must endure over a time "long enough to
permit anxiety to generate its own intrinsic accumulation."
(This stresses the "self-generating" quality of anxiety).
"Invariance of the threat may still produce an increase of
anxiety over time."

Additional time is needed to permit civil disturbances generated by personal anxiety to develop into mass assaults or pressures upon the regime.

The longer the campaign, the greater the period over which there still remains resources worth preserving by peace. Goldhamer introduces six weeks as the boundry of the "relatively short period" and twelve weeks as a "relatively long period" /there is all sorts of room for argument about this one7. It is desirable that "the threat should increase over time in certainty and temporal proximity". This could be secured by applying some number of bombs each week throughout the twelve-week period. But to get the desirable effect the threat should increase at an increasing rate. Thus, the number of target cities specified for a campaign should not be picked independently of the campaign.

It is desirable that attacks be fairly continuous. "Periods of non-attack should probably not last more than a week . . . . in any case, interludes should not grow longer over time," /several of us disagree with this point, for reasons which will be explained elsewhere7.

Twelve to sixteen weeks is posited by Goldhamer as the ideal time duration of the campaign. The additional produc-tion permitted by this spacing is unimportant. This amount of time would also permit intelligence on the effect of completed strikes, e.g., on the evacuation of people and equipment. Such intelligence might indicate a need to speed the pace of attack /or visa versa7. /I do not specifically disagree with the Goldhamer time period, but I do feel that we are at the present in no position to venture any kind of estimate at all. A large amount of work needs to be done first7.

If the evacuation of industrial workers is not allowed, anxieties of evacuated non-essential population into the countryside is increased. If such evacuation does occur "the aim of destroying industrial production will have been achieved with smaller cost in human lives, while preserving incentives for the Soviet Union authorities to negotiate peace terms (and maximizing opportunities for antigovern- mental action). It is possible in the early stages of a campaign to secure simultaneously the benefits of both population and industrial bombing by concentrating this phase of the campaign on smaller cities. It would have the additional advantage of putting the first attack where least expected, while maintaining assurance to the larger cities that their turn was coming. Such a policy would tend to concentrate impending doom on the larger cities where dissident political action would be of greatest significance, /most of us agree with the general idea, but would qualify or refine it in various ways7.

"The more dubious one is of the possibility of achieving

victory with the resources one has at the beginning of a war, the more necessary it will be to spread these resources over a longer rather than a short period." One cannot be indifferent to Soviet Union attacks, but the worst possibility is that of the Soviet Union having the last bomb.

We need to have clear and satisfactory political objectives to be communicated to the people of the Soviet Union if the political bombing of the campaign is to be maximized.

Finally, Goldhamer allows the relevance of other considerations, for example attrition rates, but obviously feels himself in no position to pass judgment upon them /this emphasizes the importance of an All-RAND attack upon the problem7.

Acknowledgments

"The Implications of the Atomic Bomb for International Relations," by Jacob Viner. From *Proceedings of the American Philosophical Society* (January 29, 1946). © 1946. Reprinted by permission of the publisher.

"War in the Atomic Age," and "Implications for Military Policy," by Bernard Brodie. From *The Absolute Weapon*, edited by Bernard Brodie, copyright 1946 by Yale Institute of International Studies; renewed 1974 by Yale Concilium on International and Area Studies. Reprinted by permission of Harcourt Brace Jovanovich, Inc.

"The Security Problem in the Light of Atomic Energy," by Bernard Brodie. From *A Foreign Policy for the United States*, edited by Quincy Wright (Chicago: University of Chicago Press, 1947). Copyright 1947 by University of Chicago Press. Reprinted by permission of University of Chicago Press.